The Old Poetries and the New

Poets on Poetry

Donald Hall, General Editor

The Old Poetries and the New

RICHARD KOSTELANETZ

Ann Arbor　　　The University of Michigan Press

Copyright © by Richard Kostelanetz 1981
All rights reserved
Published in the United States of America by
The University of Michigan Press and simultaneously
in Rexdale, Canada, by John Wiley & Sons Canada, Limited
Manufactured in the United States of America

Library of Congress Cataloging in Publication Data

Kostelanetz, Richard.
    The old poetries and the new.

    (Poets on poetry)
    Includes bibliographies.
    1. American poetry—20th century—History and
criticism—Collected works. I. Title. II. Series.
PS323.5.K6 1980   821'.52'09   80—16318
ISBN 0—472—06319—7

Acknowledgments

Interviews and essays contained in *The Old Poetries and the New* first appeared in the following journals, newspapers, magazines, catalogs, and books:

American Book Review, "A Magazine of Worse" and "Field's Faceless Fusiliers."

Blank Tape, "A Conversation on Visual Poetry."

Commonweal, "Sabotaging the New Poetry."

Contemporary Artists, "Dick Higgins."

Contemporary Poets, "Emmett Williams."

Dell Publishing Co., Inc., "Reactions and Alternatives."

The End of Intelligent Writing, by the author, "The New Poetries," permission granted courtesy of Andrews and McMeel, Inc.

Margins, "The New Class."

New Republic, "Allen Ginsberg."

New York Arts Journal, "John Cage" and "Jerome Rothenberg."

New York Times, "John Ashbery," originally appeared in *New York Times Magazine* as "How to Be a Difficult Poet."

New York Times, "Polyartist's Poetry," which originally appeared in *New York Times Book Review* as "Master of Several Arts." Copyright © 1979 by the New York Times Company. Reprinted by permission.

Outerbridge & Dienstfrey, "Imaged Words & Worded Images."

Performing Arts Journal, "Text-Sound Art in North America," originally published as "Text-Sound Art: A Critical Survey," in two parts, in *Performing Arts Journal,* Fall 1977 and Winter 1978. The research informing this essay was done with the aid of a 1976 grant from the Visual Arts Program of the National Endowment for the Arts.

Twenties in the Sixties, by the author, "Poetry Readings."

Visual Language, "Manifestos."

Wordsand, "Art Autobiography."

Writer's Digest, "Poetry in America."

For Aviva Ebstein

Preface

Not until I read Donald Hall's *Goatfoot Milktongue Twinbird* (1978), the first of the books in this series, did I realize that, nuts, I too had written a book's worth of critical and theoretical essays about poetry. I duly listed them and sent a proposal to Hall, who generously asked to see a manuscript. I say "generously," since our previous exchanges of letters had been contentious and each of us had slighted the other in print. After a cordial correspondence, he took the manuscript for his series and made some useful editorial suggestions as well. Professional life should always be so easy, and publication such a pleasure. Hall and I have never met, but this experience suggests he must be a good guy—full of ironic generosity. The dedicatee, a lovely lady, supervised both the author and the preparation of the manuscript from the beginning; Charles Doria and Meg Sullivan contributed editorial help. Thanks to all of them.

The following essays were written for a variety of publications, for a variety of reasons (as well as rates of pay), and this circumstance perhaps accounts for variations in diction and cultural pitch. Were I to write *The Old Poetries and the New* from scratch, it might be a more unified book, but I doubt if it would be a livelier one. My title introduces a distinction that becomes the book's theme, separating one section of essays from the other and, more important, my discussions of certain kinds of poetry from discussions of other kinds.

I would be remiss if I did not note here that the moniker of this series, "Poets on Poetry," bothers me. For reasons mentioned in my "Art Autobiography," identification as "a poet" scarcely makes me smile. Indeed, I consider myself less "a poet" than someone who has at times written poems that have, thankfully, been published and anthologized around the world. Categories function best when they describe work, not people. Thus, with the third word of the series title I am prepared to live. All of these essays deal with *poetry*, or language works which I take to be poetry, and had I not begun to make my own poetry, in 1967, none of these essays, all of them written since then, would be as they are now.

Some readers might like these essays better than my poetry, or vice versa. Such opinions are neither unexpected nor objectionable. However, the piety that poetry is intrinsically superior to criticism (or vice versa) is one that I find profoundly offensive. One does Literature's work in different ways; no activity is necessarily more important than another. It is my hope that my essays about poetry might survive with my poems; that is one reason why I collected them into a book.

I repaired some stylistic clumsiness and thought often about expunging repetitions before deciding that, since some of my ideas were unfashionable and, alas, easily misunderstood, especially in the world of American poetry, perhaps they are worth repeating. Every effort has been made to identify the sources of original publication of the following essays and to make full acknowledgment of their use. If any error or omission has occurred, it will be corrected in subsequent editions, provided that appropriate notification is submitted in writing to the University of Michigan Press. May I ask publishers and foundations to note that four more books appear to lie behind these essays—one, a critical study of experimental literature in America since 1959; two, an anthology of "The New Poetries in North America"; three, a critical book on the experimental tradition in poetry, not only in America but elsewhere; four, an anthology of the innovative tradition in American poetry.

Richard Kostelanetz

Contents

A few characteristics of the will to a new style and their counterparts in the old art expression are:

definiteness instead of indefiniteness
openness instead of closedness
clarity instead of vagueness
religious energy instead of belief and religious authority
truth instead of beauty
simplicity instead of complexity
relation instead of form
synthesis instead of analysis
logical construction instead of lyrical representation
mechanical form instead of handiwork
creative expression instead of mimeticism and decorative
    ornament
collectivity instead of individualism, and so forth.

The will toward a new style expresses itself in many ways. [Theo van Doesburg, "The Will to Style," 1922]

The new poetry has truly been completely liberated from these logical classifying elements of human consciousness. It knows neither a next-to-each other nor an after-each-other. Its dimensions are in the spaceless and the timeless. This applies however only to the new poetry. It is *a priori* super-dimensional, super-real and counter-morphic. [I. K. Bonset, "About the Sense of Literature," 1926]

There has been a shift in emphasis in the practice of the arts of painting, music and dancing during the last few years. There are no labels yet but there are ideas. These ideas seem primarily concerned with something being exactly what it is in its time and place, and not in its having actual or symbolic reference to other things. A thing is just that thing. It is good that each thing be accorded this recognition and this love. [Merce Cunningham, "The Impermanent Art," 1957]

The existing monuments form an ideal order among themselves, which is modified by the introduction of the new (the really new) work of art among them. The existing order is complete before the new work arrives; for order to persist after the supervention of novelty, the *whole* existing order must be, if even so slightly altered; and so the relations, proportions, values of each work of art toward the whole are readjusted; and this is conformity between the old and the new. [T. S. Eliot, "Tradition and the Individual Talent," 1919]

I

The Old Poetries

Poetry in America

(1975)

Poetry has become the principal American literary form, supplanting fiction in the chariot of artistic leadership. Especially among the young, bad poetry has not only become more popular than bad fiction—witness the sales of Rod McKuen's books—but good poetry has also become more prestigious and perhaps more glamorous too. It is indicative, after all, that a Minnesota-born folksinger initially named Robert Zimmerman took his stage name from the great Welsh poet Dylan Thomas, or that John F. Kennedy invited Robert Frost to participate in the presidential inaugural, or that early leaders of the antiwar movement included several prominent poets. More young people want to write poetry, nowadays, than fiction, plays, or criticism (and perhaps *all* of these other genres combined), and these aspiring poets provide, incidentally, the best American audience for poetry. Poets are generally considered more "interesting" than other kinds of writers, for most of us would rather meet Robert Lowell or Allen Ginsberg or even McKuen than William Styron, Arthur Miller, or Herman Wouk.

The ascendancy of poetry is perhaps the key development in literature of the past decade. One of the most attractive recent presidential candidates, Eugene McCarthy, writes poetry, as did Ho Chi Minh and Mao Tse-tung before him, and McCarthy recently taught a course in poetry at a respectable university. Professional basketball players have published whole books of their poems, as have such rock superstars as Janis Ian and the late James Morrison. Buckminster Fuller is a part-time poet; so is the composer John Cage. Steve Tannen, defensive cornerback on the New York Jets, publishes his poems in periodicals, and Muhammad Ali, back when he was customarily known as Cassius Clay, was usually good for a ditty or two. One would, by now, scarcely be surprised to learn that Henry Kissinger, or Thomas Eagleton, or even George Wallace have been scribbling poems on the sly, and such revelations would surely enhance, rather than lessen, their respective images, at least among the young.

One symptom of poetry's success is the sheer increase in the number of publishing poets. Although statistics of avocational work are always imprecise, there are now probably twice as many practicing serious poets in the United States than there were a decade ago. A registry recently compiled by Poets and Writers, Inc., a New York cultural foundation, contains over 1,500 names, with at least one serious poet resident in every state. (Fewer than a handful are currently expatriate, though one suspects that this number is likely to increase in the next few years.) American publishers have recently issued collections of black poetry, feminist poetry, Puerto Rican poetry, American Indian poetry, Chicano poetry, Oriental-American poets, etc., and American residents reportedly create distinguished poetry in nearly all of the world's major languages.

Although U. S. poets write in an incredible diversity of styles, and live all over the place, their art unites them into a single implicit community, whose members know each other largely by mail or print. Rare is the poet who has actually shaken hands with more than fifty of his colleagues; yet most have a fairly good awareness of what their peers are currently writing, as well as a certain professional loyalty. It is not surprising, for instance, that the poet Harvey Shapiro, who works as a senior editor of the *New York Times Magazine,* should like to commission other poets to write prose articles for its pages.

American poets come in as many shapes and sizes as the rest of us. Some are small, others slender, while the late Charles Olson, the acknowledged dean of the Black Mountain school, packed nearly three hundred pounds into his six-foot nine-inch frame (partially contributing, no doubt, to his immense personal charisma). Some poets are good-looking—Mark Strand and W. S. Merwin, among the men—while others exemplify the kind of studious homeliness that is currently thought to be attractively "interesting." Diane Wakoski, who now cuts a rather compelling figure, once wrote whole poems about her supposed ugliness. Female poets of all ages usually have straight and/or long hair, but no other superficial generalization, in my observation, can be made.

Male poets under forty tend to have longish hair and beards, though that scarcely means that all young, bearded long hairs are poets or even aspiring poets. (What it does mean, however, is that many young regard a typically poetic appearance as worth imitating. That is also one reason why poets aged forty, say, tend to look much younger than executives of the same age.) The profession of poetry once afforded a license for eccentric dress, but by now many people under forty-five living in a sophisticated city or around a campus look bohemian.

Poets often appear quite nervous, not just when they are reading their poems to audiences, but in everyday activities, too. However, so do other people who are deeply committed to work where performance can vary so enormously—actors, inventors, athletes, trial lawyers. One reason for this nervousness is that their professional capacities are tested each work day, and the tragic fact is that the work they produce nearly always falls short of their ideal. That is, just as baseball's greatest pitcher cannot throw a no-hitter every time, so not even Shakespeare could write a perfect poem every day. Many poets die prematurely—of suicide or of such self-inflicted vehicles as alcohol or drugs—while those who survive into their eighties tend (except, of course, for Ezra Pound) to be irremediably square.

The stylistic diversity of U. S. poetry today is unprecedented, as the past decade witnessed a series of stylistic reactions to the T. S. Eliot-kind of poetry that was dominant at the end of World War II. Scarcely any prominent poets today write in rhymed meter that would echo the English tradition that runs from Shakespeare through William Butler Yeats, for nearly all native poets prefer looser forms of structuring. Other poets have followed Charles Olson's advice to lay grammatically unconnected phrases all over the space of the page; sometimes this is called "composition by field." Many poems articulate personal feelings, for the unrhymed lyric is a particularly popular form. Lines of words in contemporary poetry are often very short, or sometimes quite long. The language can be formal or earthy, while rhythm can be pronounced, or muted, or even nonexistent. A few more "experimental" poets are exploring forms of organization unlike anything read in poetry before.

Gone by now are the very restrictive definitions of poetry that were dominant at the end of World War II, for all of these reactions to the post-Eliot establishment —all of these stylistic alternatives—have made a liberal definition of the art more useful: merely and simply, poetry is language that is heightened in an artistic way. This definition thus encompasses such extremes as visual poetry, in which language is visually enhanced, or sound poetry, which scrupulously avoids conventional syntax to emphasize the sound of pure language. By rejecting Eliot's famous doctrine of poetic impersonality, much recent poetry is very intimately personal, as poets speak freely of their own madnesses, abortions, homosexuality, and extramarital affairs. Among some "confessional" poets, it is ideal that "nothing is withheld."

Most poets write at desks or tables, in isolated spaces, for distractions are usually more disturbing than inspiring. Rare is the American poet who feels he has enough "time to write." Poets with families often complain about how "the kids keep me from my work," and Laurence Lieberman, for one, customarily naps in the early evening so that he can write into the night, after the kids have gone to sleep. One bachelor I know turns off his telephone. "It's not likely to be," he muses, "someone who wants to do me a favor." It was Allen Ginsberg, primarily, who initiated the alternate custom of continually carrying a large notebook into which he immediately pours his thoughts and perceptions, later examining the results for their poetic quality. Since Ginsberg has sometimes explored unusual states of mind (that mostly come from taking hallucinogenic drugs), his poetry often records hyperconscious impressions that would not be remembered afterward. That explains why even his greatest poems were written in amazingly short periods of time—"Howl," for instance, reportedly took a weekend—but only rarely in his unending creative life has Ginsberg pitched no-hitters.

Most poets think about poetry much of the time,

even if they are engaged in other activities, often making notes of perceptions, creative ideas and even choice phrases that come to them in the course of the nonwriting day; that's one part of the discipline that every serious poet patiently acquires. "I get good ideas while driving the car, or eating alone, or making love," one explained over lunch, "but the trouble is that unless I write them down at once, I'm liable to forget something useful, and then kick myself for forgetting. This obsession with putting it down can be embarrassing, of course, especially if my note-taking reveals that my mind isn't concentrating where everyone around me thinks it should be. That's a price of writing poetry." He paused, perhaps still ashamed of his self-centeredness. "Besides, isn't everyone better off if I put the idea down on paper than letting it fill up my distracted head?" And he whipped a 2-by-4-inch notebook out of his jeans, and asked to borrow my pen.

Very little money can be made from poetry alone, as most magazines publishing it pay nothing, and few published books of poetry earn more than a few thousand dollars royalties. Indeed, rare is the American poet whose annual receipts exceed the cost of paper, pencils, typing, xerox, and postage, even assuming, as the poet must, that his creative time is free. Thus, nearly all American poets do other things to subsidize their art, spending time and energy that might otherwise be devoted to creative work. Indeed, even Rod McKuen, whose royalties provide a regal income, nonetheless supplements it with records and personal appearances. Some live off their inheritances—the poet James Merrill's father having established America's most successful stockbrokerage firm, while James Laughlin's family owned part of a major steel company. Other beneficiaries include wives supported by their working husbands: Anne Sexton,

Ann Darr, Siv Cedering Fox. Some leisured males are financed by their dutiful wives or girl friends, and I know of one very attractive homosexual poet who has had a succession of well-to-do boy friends. William Everson was a lay brother in a Franciscan monastery until he remarried, and the late Thomas Merton was a Trappist monk in Kentucky. The late Hyman J. Sobiloff was a successful financier whose poetic interests (and ambitions) led him to support selected poets, but private patronage, from nonrelatives, is nowadays very hard for a poet to come by. Robert Graves once joked that poets should write prose only for money, but no American poet of note has followed Graves's example of earning most of his living from free-lance prose.

The fact is that most American poets are employed as teachers—in high schools, colleges, private preps, and even elementary schools—partly because the subject they teach, usually English, relates to their creative work. These professing poets can be divided into two groups: those holding permanent teaching positions, who are the real "academics," and those transients who migrate from place to place for various stretches of time. The "poet-in-residence," as he is generally called, customarily teaches a workshop or two in creative writing and perhaps a survey course in modern poetry. (A few ambitious souls, however, make a principled point in not teaching poetry but something else—history or prose classics, for example.) Most find that their job drains them of the time and energy they should like to save for their art, and so they continually fight not for higher salaries (which epitomize philistine ambition) but for more free time. Few "poets-in-residence" teach more than two days a week, while Robert Fitzgerald, who holds the Boylston Chair at Harvard, spends only one semester of every two in Cambridge. The poet Kenneth

Koch founded a poetry workshop in a New York elementary school, and his success with children brought other poets, along with government money, to the lower grade levels.

Another source of income is poetry readings, whose fees can range from $1,500 to nothing—the polite minimum being $150 plus expenses—and among the typical sponsoring organizations are churches, women's clubs, cultural societies, museums, and, of course, universities. Rare, and culturally impoverished, is the college that does not have a few poetry readings every year, and some have as many as one or even two a month. Sometimes, the visiting poet will be asked to stay overnight and conduct a few classes, or meet students and examine their creative work. Poetry readings have also become more plentiful in metropolitan centers. During a typical New York week, over a dozen were open to the public at universities, coffee houses, bars, churches, and private lofts.

These performances also attract the poetry groupies, both male and female, who also come in all shapes, sizes, and ages, the most ambitious of whom boast of having scored a succession of stars. (Indeed, when several older poets publicly puff the work of someone under thirty, it is not unreasonable to suspect that the young poet's talents include selective promiscuity.) The after-performance festivities usually reveal, however, that the most popular pleasure for American poets is not sex or drugs, but drink, which is customarily consumed to excess. Nearly as rare as the teetotaler is the constantly sober U. S. poet. One academic hostess once told me that "most poets are as self-consciously charming as other junior-grade celebrities: only the really famous ones are ever offensive."

Though few poets can resist an invitation to declaim,

the best way to communicate beyond the sound of one's voice still is print. Scores of magazines publish poetry, ranging from the *New Yorker* (which pays the highest rates), *Esquire* and the daily *New York Times*—all of which have circulations approaching one million—down to mimeographed journals that poets print by themselves and circulate largely to their friends and, perhaps, relatives. "Underground" newspapers featured poetry until they succumbed to pornography or, more commonly, bankruptcy. *Poetry,* which is the oldest and most popular of the journals devoted exclusively to poetry, remains fairly cautious and conservative. Thus new poetry magazines have emerged to fill the growing gap, their spikey names reflecting anti-Eliot, antiacademic style and determination: *Unmuzzled Ox, Panache, Mother, Dragonfly, Abraxus, Mojo Navigator,* and *grOnk.* Another new periodical, *Black Box*, sets a persuasive precedent by arriving by mail, as a pair of cassettes. Poetry-publishing magazines have the power to disseminate one poem (or one poet, or one kind of poem) rather than others, and this selectivity gives their editors a certain control over their readers' tastes. It follows that the most powerful U.S. poets are those who edit poetry for the best-circulated magazines.

Publishers of poetry books include the very largest firms, such as Doubleday and Harper & Row, both of whom issue a token few collections every year, and small one-man presses whose limited editions are often printed by hand at home. Perhaps the most "prestigious" American poetry publisher is Farrar, Straus & Giroux, whose junior partner, Robert Giroux, was also T. S. Eliot's American editor. His firm features the chiefs of that generation now between fifty and sixty—Robert Lowell, John Berryman, Elizabeth Bishop and Randall Jarrell—but its neglect of younger figures is not untypical of commercial publishing. Most large firms have "poetry advisors," who are older poets customarily inclined to recommend their former students and protégés, instead of possibly superior novices or stylistically more radical poets. It is unfortunate that books of poetry are not reviewed often enough in newspapers, even in the *New York Times Book Review,* and too much poetry reviewing in smaller journals represents poets puffing their friends or, less often, blackballing their enemies.

Given the swelling influx of new poets, it is inevitable that nearly all of them should find the established outlets recalcitrant, and is just as inevitable that a determined few should set up new poetry-publishing firms: Broadside in Detroit, Kulchur in New York, Black Sparrow in Los Angeles, Jargon in North Carolina, the House of Anansi in Toronto. These are among the most prominent, each surviving for more than several years, while poets find other smaller presses that arrive and disappear with the seasons. Almost every major American city has at least one bookshop that carries nearly all the new poetry that comes its way—Gotham and Phoenix in New York, City Lights in San Francisco, Cody's in Berkeley, and Grolier in Cambridge. One contentious poet reportedly growled that, " 'Poetry Lovers' who don't buy books of poetry are sons of bitches," and most of us would agree.

Publishers also issue anthologies, which come in two distinctly different forms: retrospective selections of a past historical period (such as my own *Possibilities of Poetry,* which appeared in 1970), or taste-making introductions to new poetry and new styles (such as my own *Imaged Words & Worded Images,* which appeared in the same year). Anthologies are best used as selective introductions to poets and/or kinds of work that the reader may wish to pursue more extensively on his own. It is indicative, to repeat an earlier point, that U.S. publishers have issued several collections of "young" poets but none exclusively devoted to young fictionists.

It has never been easy for a poet, even the greatest poet, to get published; and in spite of the growth of poetry's audience, publication is no easier now. To be blunt, since poetry is not remunerative, the work is hard, and failure is both frequent and demoralizing, why should anyone be a poet? To make matters worse, the "business" is very competitive, and suicides are not infrequent. Why? Why? One reason is the promise of participation, hopefully with honor and influence, in an age-old spiritual enterprise, for every poet was at one time inspired by the desire to write something that will "take its place" along with Shakespeare, Milton, Keats, and Eliot. Another, more personal, explanation is the overwhelming pride that the poet has in discovering, initially for himself, that the collection of words he has put together is indeed magical and perhaps memorable. Although this pleasure is rare, given the difficulties of creation, the high moments can sustain the spirit through a great many dark days—and that spiritual benefit becomes not only the poet's but, at best, the reader's, too.

Reactions and Alternatives
Post–World War II American Poetry

(1970)

Free verse gave wings to lyricism; but it was only one stage of the explorations that can be made in the domain of form. [Guillaume Apollinaire, "The New Spirit and the Poets," 1917]

The history of the American arts from 1900 on is often a record of successful flank attacks made by "outsiders" upon an entrenchment of taste and technique against which straightforward frontal attack would have failed. [Louise Bogan, *Achievement in American Poetry*, 1951]

The history of literature—the record of the relatively few works that ultimately count—generally assumes the form of a succession of chronological periods, each of a distinct character, in each of which certain styles of writing became more predominant or influential than others; and the beginnings and ends of literary eras usually coincide with important public events, such as major wars or economic booms and busts. With this in mind, we can see, even in close retrospect, that for literature as well as life the years after World War II were considerably different from the twenty years that went before. For verse written in English, the period between 1920 and 1940 represents the establishment of literary modernism, as defined by the achievements and impact of two great American poets, T. S. Eliot and Ezra Pound, in addition to two complementary English figures, the young W. H. Auden and the rejuvenated William Butler Yeats. These were the poets who made the decisive and persuasive breaks with entrenched nineteenth-century practice, as well as wrote the innovative masterpieces admired by the succeeding generations. "I do not know for certain," wrote William Empson of Eliot, eighteen years his senior, "how much of my own mind he invented, let alone how much of it is a reaction against him or indeed a consequence of misreading him." However, even though Eliot, Pound, and Auden lived into the post-World War II period, continuing to publish new work, as did several secondary American masters of that earlier period—Marianne Moore and E. E. Cummings, Conrad Aiken and John Crowe Ransom, Robert Frost and Wallace Stevens—the definition of recent American poetry has been shaped by younger hands. In distinct contrast to the promising post-World War II English poets who repudiated Eliot and Pound for pre-1920 styles, the younger American successors went beyond the elder greats in various ways. For one thing, this period after 1945 has been decidedly more plural than its predecessor, as many apparently valid directions were intensively explored and no particular conception of poetic art or individual poet became pervasively influential—how different in coherence and tone and point of view are such indubitably major poets as Robert Lowell and Allen Ginsberg, Theodore Roethke and Kenneth Koch, David Ignatow and Gary Snyder, John Berryman and Galway Kinnell. Nonetheless, what perhaps unifies the variety of the period is the sense that most of the important work represents alternatives to

Eliot's and Pound's (and, to lesser extents, Auden's and Yeats's) ways of making poems.

Indeed, the impact of these masters of modernism was so powerful and pervasive that it was hard for a maturing poet, coming of age between 1922 and 1945, not at least to sound like them; even some contemporary Africans writing in English still echo Eliot. This ubiquitous influence is perhaps the primary reason why the more powerful "flank attacks" occurred not at the end of the war but about a decade later, largely from poets who came of intellectual age after 1945—not from the second generation of modern poetry, whose birthdates fall between 1900 and 1922, but from the third, poets born after 1923. (Indeed, the one older poet who became so influential his work was all but contemporary, William Carlos Williams, was a college friend of Pound, perhaps the first of his many literary pupils; for not only did Williams develop *before* Eliot's influence but Eliot reportedly kept Williams unpublished in England during his lifetime.)

Roughly and generally, the established style of poetry in 1945 was intricate in meter, approximately regular in length of line, ironic and elegant and sometimes aphoristic, controlled in texture and restricting in form, complex in thought and solemn in tone. It was rich in allusions to the history of literature and culture, distinctly formal in diction (the taste in language reflected in the choice of specific words), impersonal in ambience (as formulated by Eliot's "objective correlative"), observational in perspective, cosmic in concern, associational in poetic syntax, reverent toward both the tradition and the work of poetry, and implicit in ultimate subject, which the reader generally has to deduce. To Donald Hall, this is "a poetry of symmetry, intellect, irony and wit." These were poems, in Howard Nemerov's phrases, "which want to be read hard and which respond to closest attention." To Louise Bogan, "It was a style which tended to veer, it is true, toward verbalism on the one hand, and extreme condensation of meaning and idea, on the other. At its worst, a core of overcompressed thought was surrounded by an envelope of overinflated words." Perhaps because most of the great poems of the period between the wars exemplified this brace of approaches to the problems of poetry and the materials of human experience, the "promising" young poets in the late forties tended to appropriate most, if not all, of these strategies, perpetuating the established styles of 1920-1940 well into the fifties.

Nonetheless, the significant developments in recent verse, as well as the remarks that follow, focus upon diverse snappings of the stylistic threads woven by Eliot, his contemporaries, and his immediate artistic heirs. The history of art, it is true, sometimes portrays a certain style as a string on the stage of history running through the heads of many individual artists; yet not only is this image an analytic convenience for regarding continuities amid idiosyncrasies, but it is also a reasonably accurate metaphor for how literary ideas and artistic structures actually pass from one articulate mind to another. One reason is that the influence of immediate predecessors and particular contemporaries is generally more apparent in an artist's work than his debts to specific figures in the common tradition.

The new poets who commanded the most attention during and immediately after the war tended to echo these predominant stylistic traits of their elders, as well as their archetypal and mythological concerns. Among these prematurely mature poets were Robert Lowell, whose characteristic subjects then included Jonathan Edwards and other aspects of historical New England

and whose metrical language was audibly indebted to Gerard Manley Hopkins; John Berryman, who wrote in retrospect, "I wanted something that would be both very neat, contained and at the same time thoroughly mysterious"; and Delmore Schwartz, who favored philosophic poems inspired by Plato and Socrates, in addition to weaving elaborate Freudian symbols for psychic dramas:

> The heavy bear who goes with me,
> A manifold honey to smear his face,
> Clumsy and lumbering here and there,
> The central tone of every place,
> The hungry beating brutish one
> In love with candy, anger, and sleep.

So powerful was the post-Eliot establishment at the time that other ways of making poems went all but unnoticed.

Certain poets, such as Randall Jarrell and Karl Shapiro, who first adopted the dominant style and received critical acclaim, recognized, after their war experiences, that strictly structured forms do not allow for certain expressions of immediate concerns and they therefore explored alternative styles. Jarrell discreetly revealed his personal history in poems published just before his death in 1965, while Shapiro even excised from his canon those poems reflecting Eliot's influence and resorted, in *The Bourgeois Poet* (1964), to prose paragraphs that repudiated rhyme, versification, the line breaks, and much other nineteenth-century baggage. Indeed, the old style so dominated the blossoming poetic imaginations that no recent native poet captured the post-World War II disappointment as effectively as *The Waste Land* did for a comparable earlier postwar period, or as Paul Celan's "Todesfuge" (1952) did for German-speaking readers.

The truth is that persuasive art about unprecedented history invariably demands radically new forms.

Reactions to Eliot, even among the epigones, were perhaps inevitable, although less extreme. In 1949, Delmore Schwartz, who only four years before lauded Eliot as "the international hero," publicly questioned the benefits of his "literary dictatorship"; and within a few years, more sensitive critics could easily mock the stylistic, experiential, allusive, and tonal uniformity of the younger poets included in the expanded post-World War II editions of the major classroom anthologies of "Modern Poetry." By the sixties, poetry based upon these familiar strategies became known as "academic" verse, whose representatives and advocates included such professor-poets as Anthony Hecht, Paris Leary, Robert Pack, Donald Finkel, Donald Hall, Louis Coxe, and Daryl Hine, in addition to such British immigrants as W. H. Auden, Donald Davie, and Thom Gunn. True, not all academics wrote "academic" verse, but nearly all such poetry came from full-time professors; but too often in this work, as James Dickey judged, "Painfully contrived arguments in rhyme substitute for genuine insight." By the late sixties, many of these writers offered statements and manifestos so defensive in stance that they seemed to know as well as the avant-gardists that the time for neoclassicism had passed.

Even though a particular style in art may command primary attention, as well as inform the masterpieces of a certain moment, its widespread impact can never prevent the simultaneous development of other techniques. In America, all through the thirties, a number of talented poets, most of them scarcely recognized, if not barely published, were working in alternative ways. The critic Yvor Winters, himself a skilled poet, fathered a school of unashamedly "reactionary" poets—the best is J. V.

Cunningham—who offered declarative statements in rhyme; another tendency, represented by such otherwise different figures as Robert Penn Warren, Muriel Rukeyser, and Winfield Townley Scott, favored dramatic narratives. A third alternative direction that, unlike the other two, subsequently earned more interest and acclaim, grew from the example of the late Theodore Roethke, author of many of the greatest individual poems of the recent period, and his closest compatriot in poetry at the time, Stanley Kunitz, whose work is similar but usually more difficult, more considered, and more intellectual. As early as 1934, Roethke wrote to a friend, "I'm tired of all this Eliot-Pound worship"; and he dissented, as did Kunitz, from the canon primarily in using personal materials, particularly the stuff of dreams, in rather restricted, traditional rhythmic structures patently more indebted to Yeats than to Pound or Eliot:

> My secrets cry aloud.
> I have no need for tongue.
> My heart keeps open house,
> My doors are widely swung.
> An epic of the eyes
> My love, with no disguise.

The result was an American kind of surrealism, different from the more European hysterical surrealism of San Francisco-born Philip Lamantia, as Roethke and Kunitz dealt largely in restrained monologues, occasionally in outright songs, whose landscapes are invariably interior and whose symbols are personally revealing. Twenty years ago, unlike now, such work represented a considerable departure. Both men continued more or less in this lyrical mode, tending toward longer lines and more open structures. Roethke's last poems include titles like "Journey to the Interior," the "interior" being of course his own psyche, and Kunitz in 1963 wrote:

> What's best in me lives underground:
> Rooting, and digging, itching for wings.

By the late fifties, John Berryman staked his position on personal materials, creating elegant yet ragged, evocative yet obscure, symbolic fantasies he called "Dream Songs." At first many of these pieces seem impenetrable; but once their source is identified as psychic processes and their theme as, in Berryman's words, "the turbulence of the modern world, and memory, and wants," then the previously puzzling metaphors and symbols often all but explain themselves.

One of the earlier alternatives to Eliot was already defined by Ezra Pound, whose role in the stylistic history of modern poetry is rather dichotomous. On one hand, he supported both Frost and Eliot, even editing the latter's *The Waste Land* and receiving its dedication as *"il miglior fabbro."* On the other hand, through his later *Cantos,* as well as his post-World War II correspondence, Pound directly influenced the spatially open, idiomatic, metrically irregular, academically irreverent word-collages of William Carlos Williams, Louis Zukofsky, Charles Olson, and younger poets vehemently opposed to Eliot's ways. Williams rejected verbal ornamentation and English metric in addition to "the ash-heaps of the past," instead rooting his poetry in concrete understanding, realistic portrayal, visceral perception, immediate detail, concentrated statements, American idiom, and formal freedom ("Finally I let the form take care of itself"). The major work of his post-World War II career, *Paterson* (1946-1958), extended these principles through a long poem, as well as evoked a universe of life out of the microcosm of a New Jersey city. (Behind nearly every major contemporary long poem in Americanese, as Leslie Fiedler notes, stands the example of Ezra Pound.)

Olson, a generation younger than Williams, drew from both him and Pound to evolve, in the late forties, a theory of "projective verse." In an essay of that title, somewhat obscured by a bombastic and convoluted style, Olson's major points include preferences for American language and experience, the formal idea of the poem as an open (more precisely, unclosed) field of energy, cognizance of the expressive possibilities intrinsic in the typewriter, freedom from constraint in the shape and syntax of poetry—how words may be laid out on the page or grammatically connected to each other. (Thus, he logically opposed both the sentence's period and the closed parenthesis as encouraging the completion of expression.) Olson's theory notwithstanding, his own poetry is incorrigibly erratic, both in wholes and in parts, as words and phrases are spread asymmetrically across the page, all informed by nonmetrical prosody, generally mundane language that is sometimes incantatory and often slips into outright prose, anthropological resonances, associational coherence, and esoteric allusions (that conclusively repudiate certain claims made for its antiacademicism)—in sum, a kind of abstract poetic shorthand for discontinuously organizing a great range of concrete and universal material. Thanks in part to his personal charisma, his commandingly grandiose physical presence and several vociferous disciples, Olson became the father of the Black Mountain school of American poetry, named after the late, lamented North Carolina experimental college where all its members taught or studied—Robert Creeley, Robert Duncan, John Wieners, Jonathan Williams, Edward Dorn, among others—and nearly all these writers also emulate Olson's unusual prose style. Yet, perhaps because none of them is imaginatively as extreme and unconstrained as Olson, or intellectually as rich (except for Duncan), their work seems considerably less interesting than the master's—at worst, merely exercises in unusual line-breaking.

Instead, some of the more adventurous extensions of Olson's suggestions have come from writers outside his immediate camp. The composer John Cage, a sometime colleague at Black Mountain, has developed in several word-pieces entitled "Diary" a stylistically inventive shorthand for miscellaneous remarks, and the architect-dymaxicrat Buckminster Fuller, another Black Mountain compatriot, evolved a concretely speculative, if not visionary, poetry, while two younger writers, John Giorno and Ronald Gross, have both ingeniously made expressive poetry entirely out of sentences lifted verbatim from newspapers, advertisements, and other popular sources; and an even younger poet, Dan Graham, roots his work in immediate, unedited factual detail. In short, all these imperfect, exploratory, structurally open poetries seem inevitable responses to an open, exploratory, imperfect age.

One inevitable reaction to Auden's and Eliot's poetic impersonality was the direct exposure of personal experience, not with the symbolic shields of Roethke and Kunitz, but in declarative statements made in the first-person voice of the poet. The most compelling poems in this mode deal with the most intimate of aggravations— the state of the poet's marriage or current affair, the tensions of close relationships, major operations, sojourns in mental institutions, social and spiritual insufficiencies. To the critic-poet Jonathan Cott, this poetry represents the "projection of exacerbated sensibilities"; to other critics, this is "confessional" poetry, written partially to purge the poet's mind of haunting preoccupations. However, in the best pieces, the lines evoke not an individual's problem but a more general experience, as W. D. Snodgrass, who reportedly influenced his teacher Lowell to risk also more intimate subjects, writes in "April Inventory":

> I taught myself to name my name,
> To bark back, loosen love and crying;
> To ease my woman so she came,
> To ease an old man who was dying.

Another Lowell pupil, Sylvia Plath, declares in "Elm," written just before her suicide:

> I am terrified by the dark thing
> that sleeps in me.

A related process informs the recent work of Brother Antoninus (né William Everson), who descends stylistically not from Eliot, Williams, and Lowell but from Robinson Jeffers, to arrive at an approximately similar poetic position. His best poem, "In Savage Wastes," includes such stanzas as:

> I too, O God, as You very well know,
> Am guilty.
> For I sought and found not,
> I searched, but was not successful.
> When I failed, You drew back the veil,
> And I am in terror.

However, in contrast to Antoninus's work, most "confessional" poetry uses more formal, less mundane diction, stricter prosody (if not occasional rhymes) and forms more transparent than blatant; for these characteristics in particular distinguish it from the kind of first-person poetry developed by and from Allen Ginsberg.

The writers called "beats" are important in the history of recent poetry less for the publicity their activities accrued—publicity, like other forms of journalism, being inherently ahistorical—than for an all-but-comprehensive attack upon the post-Eliot establishment; and their claims to greater vitality inevitably capitalized on both the smug dreariness of a declining style and the diminished energies of its former masters. It was not only that Ginsberg, Lawrence Ferlinghetti, Gregory Corso, and poets trailing in their wake created rather persuasive literature but that they challenged nearly everything previously pious in poetry. For reverent solemnity, they substituted irreverent blasphemy; for impersonality, they put anarchistic egotism; instead of ironic personas and other symbolic artifices, they used man-to-man address and explicit statements. They phased out elegant diction and consistent texture for jagged surfaces and lines of wildly irregular length and mundane words, which were sometimes so profane that Ginsberg's *Howl,* for one, became the subject of an "obscenity" case. Rather than a secondhand world drawn from the history of literature and culture, the beat poets treated their own immediate experience, in specific places and at specific times, often in response to current social malaise; and instead of elliptical associative coherence, they resorted to less obscuring, more accessible kinds of poetic syntax. Moreover, they identified not with the great tradition of English verse but with countertraditions of rebellious, if not mad, poets, from Rimbaud to Artaud, from Whitman to the Ezra Pound of the late *Cantos.* In addition, they eschewed not only classical and mythological allusions but also contrived complexity and obscurity in favor of a public, if not popular, poetry of comparatively simple statements and clear-cut attitudes, all of which was appropriately conducive to public declamation.

Precisely because these poets rejected the established modes so completely, they became an issue over which the activists in poetry chose up sides. Several older figures of a similarly anti-Eliot bent gravitated to the beats' support—among them Kenneth Rexroth, who became their most articulate literary publicist; Charles Olson, whose poetic theory was regarded as relevant; William Carlos Williams, who gave *Howl* a combative introduction that concluded, "Ladies, we're going through hell"; and eventually Karl Shapiro, whose reaction to Eliot-Auden propelled him to an extreme antithesis. Of *Howl*, Rexroth, long an anarchist, wrote "This is the real thing, bona fide revolutionary poetry. Mike Gold [the Communist polemicist] would give his left nut to have written ten lines of it." [*New Directions*, no. 16, (1957)]. By the late fifties, the American poetry scene became split, by observers as well as poets, into two warring camps known variously as square and beat, cooked and uncooked, academic and antiacademic, each of which had its magazines, its critics, its publishers, its students and, inevitably, its anthologists; and in this apocalyptic war, every poet of note was either in one camp or the other. By the middle sixties, however, as even a professor-poet like William Jay Smith emulated Ginsberg's freely formed long poetic line, this dichotomy had less to do with genuine stylistic differences than irrelevant social habits—less what or how a poet wrote than whom he knew and hung around with.

Since Eliot and Pound dealt with large abstractions, spectacularly cosmic concerns and distant places, another reaction was toward a poetry that focused upon immediate perceptions, pedestrian experiences, and natural landscapes. This persuasion not only had its own veteran advocates in William Stafford, Gary Snyder, Richard Eberhart, and Kenneth Rexroth but it also won several talented poets previously in the Eliot-Auden ambience—among them James Wright, David Wagoner, and James Dickey. Nearly all of them produced comparatively short poems, emphasizing image over symbol and subjectivity over objectivity, in lines varying from metered to free, generally in an authentic first-person voice whose tone occasionally echoes Robert Frost. The subject of these poems is usually an experience or quality distinctly of the premachine age. Perhaps because the narrator's intelligence regards things observed as more persuasive than myth and nature as a basically beneficent force, past literature is sometimes seen as threatening his perceptual innocence. Gary Snyder remarks in passing, in "Mid-August at Sourdough Mountain Lookout":

> I cannot remember things
> I once read.

While looking at a newborn child in "Mary Bly," James Wright says:

> I feel the seasons changing beneath me,
> Under the floor.

Between this position and the older one stands a poet like A. R. Ammons, whose most famous work, "Corsons Inlet," perceives a metaphysical dimension in a familiar rural scene. While such modest, mundane approaches to experience are not usually the processes behind inarguably great poetry, this poetic stance, as a reaction in part to earlier excesses, has for this moment an immensely persuasive impact.

A parallel stylistic preoccupation in recent verse deals

unsentimentally with experience in urban environments; and this too is not a poetry of symbols but a literature in which the immediate perception or the scene described symbolizes something larger than itself. This position, generally indebted to William Carlos Williams, informs the best poetry of David Ignatow, Denise Levertov, Harvey Shapiro, Alan Dugan, as well as occasional pieces by Galway Kinnell, Paul Goodman, and Weldon Kees. Their works are usually short in length, informal in language, anecdotal in manner, and swift in development, functioning at minimum to define order or significance in the chaos of the city; and a particular perception, if not a developed theme, usually provides more of the poem's cohering gravity than image or rhythm. In "Get the Gasworks," David Ignatow writes:

> Get the gasworks into a poem,
> and you've got the smoke and smokestacks,
> and mottled red and yellow tenements,
> and grimy kids who curse with the pungency
> of the odor of gas. You've got America, boy.

In one of the late Weldon Kees's poems, the visiting narrator notes of his host's anonymous metropolitan apartment:

> All day the phone rings. It could be Robinson
> Calling. It never rings when he is here.

At times this kind of poetry seems on the verge of what James Dickey calls "metaphysical reportage," investing immense importance in a familiar urban circumstance, usually in New York, such as a Lower East Side street in Galway Kinnell's "The Avenue Bearing the Initial of Christ into the New World" (perhaps echoing the span to Brooklyn in Hart Crane's *The Bridge* [1932]), or the imposing Brooklyn warehouse, near Harvey Shapiro's home, emblazoned "National Cold Storage Company," which becomes a symbolic ash can of American history.

> I myself have dropped into it in seven years
> Midnight tossings, plans for escape, the shakes.
> Add this to the National total—
> Grant's tomb, the Civil War, Arlington,
> The young President dead.

A curious fact is that prior to Eliot the best American poetry avoided the urban scene that so preoccupied, say, Charles Baudelaire; but now that America has become a predominantly urban society and its social and spiritual problems assume an urban focus, it seems appropriate that by the middle sixties an unprecedentedly high percentage of the best poets of all persuasions have gravitated to New York City. This observation in turn suggests that perhaps urban American verse is establishing a historical beachhead for English poetry in an urbanizing world.

One circle of poets mistakenly placed among the anti-academics, primarily because they were abundantly included in Donald Allen's beat anthology *The New American Poets* (1960), collected around John Ashbery, Kenneth Koch, and Frank O'Hara; and to Jonathan Cott, in his 1965 survey of recent efforts, they represented "the most original school of poetry today." Here the professor-proletarian dichotomy simply did not relate to their individual natures; for not only did each of the three have a Harvard B.A., as well as a further degree, but Koch himself, heaven forbid, earned a doctorate and then took a regular teaching position squarely in the enemy's camp, Columbia University. The first mature work of these writers, dating from the middle fifties, followed certain tendencies in modern French literature (where free verse and prose paragraphs typify the major poets) by questioning established concepts of poetic structure through various explorations of *acoherence*— an effort analogous to atonality in music, and this preoccupation continues to inform their work, as well as that of younger poets working in their wake, such as Ted Berrigan and David Shapiro, and perhaps Allen Ginsberg in his 'Wichita Vortex Sutra." Koch's *When the Sun Tries To Go On* (1953) is an interminable nonsense poem in a regularly irregular meter, evenly measured lines and consistent diction that, to Cott, "defies explication or even persistent reading," while his incredible *Ko, or a Season on Earth* (1959) is an absurd narrative in heroic meter. In "Europe" (1960) Ashbery broke through the rectangular format of poetry, using a variety of meters and printed lines, dictions and syntaxes, so that the page became an open field full of fragments—images and remarks, phrases and even single words—whose relation to each other would be tenuous, ambiguous, and perhaps multiple; to Cott, who regards Ashbery as more concerned with connotation than denotation, "Europe" represents the "difficult but adroit construction of a disconnected journey." The fifty-second section in its entirety runs as follows:

> The rose
> > dirt
> > dirt you
>
> pay
> The buildings
> is tree

> Undecided protest This Planet.

In this radical restructuring of poetry's words, the problem, for writer and reader alike, becomes making poetic sense without depending upon the familiar clues provided by either a distinct subject or an expository format; yet what makes such works coherent are the familiar devices of poetry, such as associative imagery, spatial disposition, connotative relation, consistent diction, and sometimes cohesive meter. Precisely because it defies conventional analysis and definite paraphrase, this spatial poetry is extremely obscure by conventional standards, if not inexplicable, and perhaps too precious; yet like all radical writing, these lines ask critical readers to revise not only their standards of coherence in literature but also their strategies for attentive reading. Like so much that is truly adventurous in contemporary art, this kind of poetry asks even the most experienced perceptor to discern structure in what at first seems chaos.

A series of "flank attacks" upon an established style invariably produces a spate of alternative artistic conceptions—witness the diversity of reactions to romanticism in nineteenth-century music. If only to avoid the smug restrictiveness that plagued more parochial eras (and seems embarrassing in retrospect), the more sophisticated readers and critics of poetry today are justifiably reluctant to dismiss one or another stylistic alternative as "not poetry," or simply out of bounds. Such tolerance toward adventurous art and thought is, to my mind, all to the good, if only because in this era of pluralism and upheaval, the currently accepted definitions of reality and potentiality shift, like the seasons, right under our feet.

Some of the more radical possibilities for poetry today deal with its structural essentials—the discrete word, the printed line, and the overall shape. From the Middle Ages to the present, the format of poetry has consisted

of words laid out in horizontal lines of uniform type-
face, usually set in vertical succession in paragraphs of
rectangular shape; and even if, as in Whitman, the poetic
line runs horizontally beyond the margin, the printer
dutifully pulls in the excess and sets it in the lined space
immediately below. Partly to transcend this restricting
tradition, John Cage employs a multiple-font typewriter
to emulate the typographical variety available to the
graphic designer or the preprint scribe, and literary poets
from George Herbert to Dylan Thomas and Gregory
Corso have written poems to be printed in geometrical
shapes, like a vase with indented parabolic sides or a
diamond standing on one point. A step beyond this involves setting the letters in nongeometric shapes, such as
the vertical lines of rain in Apollinaire's "Il Pleut" or
the more unusual and complicated forms in Kenneth
Burke's "Flowerishes," or John Hollander's pieces in
Types of Shape (1969). Another inevitable direction
comes from imposing a severe horizontal limitation
upon the poetic lines, as A. R. Ammons did by composing a book-length poem on vertical adding machine tape
in his *Tape for the Turn of the Year* (1965). However,
all these poems still operate within the tradition of lines
of poetry and, thus, approximately linear syntax.

Another step beyond involves abolishing the line for
the discrete word itself, presented in its printed form for
all the suggestiveness it can muster, as in certain scripts
for "happenings" that George Brecht has written or the
"minimal" poems of Aram Saroyan. From this point the
poet can also design his word into an expressive shape,
as Liam O'Gallagher, Mary Ellen Solt, Robert Indiana,
and Richard Kostelanetz, among others, have done in
"pattern poems" or "word-images" or "poems looked
at not *thru*" that bestow a resonant visual dimension, if
not an "ideographic logic" and spatial prosody upon

words for a quality, a process, or a thing, such as disintegration or sneezing. Of his purposes in this poetic mode, one practitioner identified, "first, the discovery, or the devising, of expressive shapes for individual words or groups of words that particularly haunt me—to create an image appropriate to a certain word—and, second, the adding of words and letters to archetypal or familiar shapes—literally to verbalize an image. In both respects, the ideal result of the poet's ingenuity should be a word-image whose language and shape are so effectively complementary that the entire picture has a unified integrity and an indelible impact." A move beyond this would eschew the rectangular, two-dimensional page for expressive sculptures of words, as Gerd Stern (or the Frenchman Jean-François Bory) has done, or abolish the word itself for an arrangement of letters or even printed symbols that bear no apparent syntactical relationship to each other. These last pieces are generally classified as "concrete," even if done by card-carrying "poets"; but this kind of work usually defines itself as closer to design than poetry.

As the Yeats-Eliot-Auden conventions became the rites of hackneyed verse, an inevitable departure would be poetic parody, at its best not just for a joke but for richly comic, exaggeratedly ironic effects, as in the works of Armand Schwerner and S. Foster Damon, among others. Damon's *Nightmare Cemetery* (1964), a bleak, often parodic sequence of sonnets, struck the critic Yvor Winters as "a kind of abbreviated *Confidence-Man* in verse." However, the masterpiece in this particular vein is clearly Melvin B. Tolson's *Libretto for the Republic of Liberia* (1953), a fantastic, inimitable conglomeration of loaded words written to fulfill Tolson's obligation as poet laureate for the African country's centenary; and among the real achievements of this relatively unknown and, thanks largely to Allen Tate's introduction, usually misunderstood long poem is the scope of its marvelous satire—the political pretensions of the Republic of Liberia (in historical fact, largely a fief of a single American rubber company), the catchall allusive technique of Ezra Pound, the esoteric footnotes to T. S. Eliot (whose *The Waste Land* made all subsequent footnotes to poetry either ironic or ludicrous), certain American Negro myths about a close relationship to Africa, and much else.

The *Höhere* of God's stepchildren
is beyond the sabotaged world, is beyond
das Diktat der Menschenverachtung,
la muerte sobre el esqueleto de la nada,
the pelican's breast rent red to feed the young,
summer's third-class ticket, the *Revue des morts,*
the skulls trepanned to hold ideas plucked from dung,
Dives' crumbs in the church of the unchurched,
absurd life shaking its ass's ears among
the colors of vowels and Harrar blacks
with Nessus shirts from Europe on their backs

Along with their footnotes referring to sources both esoteric and familiar, both classical and contemporary, these lines suggest, as the critic Dan McCall perceived, that "At times Tolson seems to be running wild in the white castle of learning." Even though some of Tolson's satire may not be entirely intentional, it is precisely such pervasive blasphemy over so many sacred terrains, along with a general inscrutability, that makes the *Libretto* a singular contemporary masterpiece.

In short, most major poets of the post-World War II period decisively rejected at least one major stylistic trait of the post-Eliot establishment, and these rejections became a cumulative process, as illustrated, with some irony, on the following table. Its decline paralleled the decreasing influence of the New Criticism, founded in part to institutionalize a taste for such verse. Indeed, so powerful was the cumulative impact of such reactions that certain embittered poets rewrote their own artistic traditions, if not repudiated certain early poems, precisely to exclude all traces of that *bete noire* Eliot. What all these rejections of the past decades, abetted by a succession of willed "fresh starts," have accomplished is the creation of a new collective sensibility and artistic situation for American verse, so that a greater plurality of approaches to the environment of poetry—the tradition and techniques of the art and the material of man's experience—are currently, in principle at least, acceptable. Indeed, although no known measure is finally accurate, there seems today more genuine freedom from restricting convention than at any previous time in Anglo-American poetry—an emancipation from constraint similar to that informing contemporary painting and dance. For one thing, there is now, as Harvey Gross notes, "no apparent dominant metrical convention such as obtained in the centuries previous to this one." For another, "coherence" can currently be defined as any arrangement that creates its own persuasiveness; and contemporary prosody, as Gross continues, "is 'organic,' developed out of the subject and stance of the poem, and not an imposed or adopted style." All subjects from mundane to cosmic, from familiar to obscure, from lofty to earthy, are available to poets, as are words from all realms of discourse, and all kinds of syntactical structures from scrupulously discontinuous to outright narrative; moreover, poetry need not be structured in either rectangular shapes or successive lines, organized by linear syntax or associative imagery, or even be written by accredited members of the Church of Poetry; and the line separating

Characteristics of American Poetry in 1945, and Subsequent Reactions to the Predominant Style

Associational Coherence	Cultural Allusiveness	Consistent Prosody	Persona-Narrator	Complex Thought	Formal Diction	Symmetrical Format	Reverent Solemnity
Ashbery	Koch	Ginsberg	Lowell (late)	Ginsberg	Antoninus	Ashbery	Tolson
Koch	Kunitz	Ashbery	Antoninus	Cage	Ginsberg	Olson	Koch
Ignatow	Ashbery	Antoninus	Ginsberg	Wright	Berryman (late)	Hollander	Ginsberg
H. Shapiro	Antoninus	Stern	Cage	Roethke	Koch	O'Gallagher	Roethke
Ginsberg	Snodgrass	Berrigan	Sexton	Snyder	Ignatow	Stern	Strand
Cage	Ignatow	Koch	Plath	Koch	Giorno	Berrigan	Berryman
D. Shapiro	Plath	Schwerner	Ignatow	Berrigan	Schwerner	Ginsberg	Stern
Antoninus	Snyder	Lamantia	Rexroth		Stern	Schwerner	Giorno
Wagoner	Dickey	Wagoner	Snyder			Duncan	D. Shapiro
Dugan	Wagoner	Dugan	Dugan			Lamantia	Schwerner
Damon	Lamantia						Damon

This rough chart is by no pretense either comprehensive or definitive. Rather than make accurate classifications, it aims to outline tendencies. Not every important poet is included.

poetry from prose has become jagged and fuzzy. "Poetry," writes John Cage, "is not prose by reason of its content or ambiguity but by reason of its allowing musical elements (time, sound) to be introduced into the world of words." (For her own eccentric pieces, Marianne Moore once offered this classic apologia: "The only reason I know for calling my work poetry at all is that there is no other category in which to put it.") It is, I believe, possible for an individual work today to break *all* the old rules and still attain significances familiar to the traditions of poetry.

The lines between one period of art and another cut so deeply that a new poetry and a new scene for poets invariably accompany each other. The major figures of 1920-40 were mostly part-time writers who held regular, nonacademic jobs—Eliot as a publisher, Stevens as an insurance executive, William Carlos Williams as a doctor, Marianne Moore as a librarian and then an editor; only one of their number, John Crowe Ransom, pursued an academic career for his adult life, and his last twenty working years were spent less in the classroom than as the editor of the *Kenyon Review*. The poets of the recent period, in contrast, have mostly been university teachers, often billed as "poet-in-residence"; and while some have assumed permanent positions as professors of writing—among them Tolson, Roethke, John Logan, Robert Kelly, Eberhart, Snodgrass, Ammons, and Wilbur—others drift from school to school—Lowell, Kunitz, Levertov, Ignatow, and Dickey. Some important poets have taken doctorates in English to become professors of literature—Simpson, Stafford, Wright, Hoffman, Hollander, Wagoner, and Koch. Those poets who remain outside the academy tend to work in allied literary trades, such as publishing and journalism—Ashbery and Harvey

Shapiro; and only one respected contemporary poet has long subsisted, albeit in modest circumstances, entirely on royalties and readings, apart from wives or inheritance or editorial work—Allen Ginsberg.

Although the rates paid for poetry have scarcely gone up in recent years—only the *New Yorker* extends three-figure and sometimes even four-figure sums—what has increased spectacularly are, first, the fees offered, mostly by universities, for live readings and guest lectures and, second, the gross number of poets who are asked to perform. Sums as high as, or even over, a thousand dollars are not uncommon, and rumor has it that one respected and talkative poet earned from his trade over fifty thousand dollars in a recent year. Most established poets, I would estimate, have incomes safely in five figures; and between his performing fees and his teaching salary, as well as the anxious and exhausting sessions both jobs demand, many a harassed American poet might suspect that his beneficent society, by offering greater rewards for performing his reliable standards than for creating new songs, is paying him primarily not to write. "Even today," confessed Hayden Carruth, "in this epoch of foundation grants, cushy teaching appointments, reading tours, etc., most of us write out our poems in the worst possible conditions." This unprecedented situation has made more than one poet "on tour" into an ersatz vaudevillian, if not a traveling salesman, enthusiastically delivering his familiar pitch before appreciative but unsophisticated audiences in a succession of unfamiliar settings. Moreover, it is more by public appearances than by publications that established reputations in poetry are sustained, and several well-known poets, thanks to their popularity as performers, have acquired high reputations that are simply not supported by their verse. For another thing, by now the private patron has all but disappeared from the American poetry scene; but partially replacing him have been a number of native foundations which, under a variety of programs, give grants that have provided considerable leisure time for most major American writers. Indeed, perhaps because poetry has traditionally been the least remunerative of the literary arts, foundations have recently shown particular generosity toward poets, one even offering a year's income, not to write for the theater, but merely to attend enough plays to get, perhaps, inspired.

There is a second, more complicated sociology of American poetry, and this shapes the politics of publication and position, reputation and reward. The scene of American poetry is defined by the proliferation of parochial establishments which jell around various common ties—academic connection, geographical location, sexual persuasion, ethnic or religious or racial origins. Nearly, though not every, significant American poet belongs to one or another group, sometimes less by his loyalty to them than by the group's adherence to him; and what announces the existence of a clique is, first, a discernible network of writers who regularly and publicly praise each other's work, regardless of whether it is excellent or abominable, as well as, second, their blatant penchant for ritualistically either dismissing or ignoring poets outside their circle. One particularly voluble school consists of poets whose paths intersected at Black Mountain College well over a decade ago; to Leslie Fiedler, they comprise "a small circle of friends dedicating books to each other, mythicizing each other from poem to poem." A second constellation connects a number of academics teaching at various schools—Richard Wilbur, Daniel Hoffman, John Hollander, Donald Hall, et al.; a third consists of Southern gentlemen, usually teachers at Southern colleges, none of whom, except for the late

Randall Jarrell, are particularly good or well known; Theodore Roethke was kingpin for "the school of the Pacific Northwest," which also includes David Wagoner, Carolyn Kizer, and William Stafford; a fifth coalesces around the figures of Robert Bly and James Wright, as well as a journal called successively *The Fifties* and *The Sixties*. Yet another could be christened "Lowell's descendants," since all its members at one time or another studied with Robert Lowell and adopted his later "confessional" style—Anne Sexton, Snodgrass, Plath, and Frederick Seidel—while Lowell himself succeeded Delmore Schwartz as poet laureate for the New York literary mob. Poets who appear regularly in the *New Yorker* constitute another establishment, whose chief figures are James Dickey, Elizabeth Bishop, John Updike, and Howard Moss; and what is commonly, though presumptuously, known as the New York school comprises Koch, Ashbery, O'Hara, and Berrigan, as well as scores of vociferously parochial younger poets, some of whom were at one time Koch's pupils. And so on and so on.

In sum, this kind of poetry scene encourages stylistic diversity and clearly defined position-taking, as well as competition among informally organized forces, each with its generals, officers, and foot soldiers, all engaged in what James Dickey aptly calls "the pathetic and vicious jostling and literary back-scratching for prizes and favorable notices." In no other literary art, indicatively, is book-reviewing less disinterested and less discriminating—in Lawrence Hart's phrase, "hardly more than an exchange of valentines." (One well-known poetry reviewer once told me that he puffs everything on the grounds that his services are "good for poetry"; another that he reviews only the work of his friends.) Nonetheless, the most reliable measure of ultimate literary success is not the adulation of one's compatriots, whose judgments finally do not count, but recognition by writers connected with other establishments, or by general magazines, or by disaffiliated (as opposed to party-line) anthologists. For instance, the measure of Robert Lowell's incomparable success is not only the persuasive quality of his poetry and his early friendship with his most promising peers (Jarrell, Schwartz), but also his ascension to masterhood with the original group of Southern gentlemen, then the poetry professors, and afterward the New York literary mob as well, in addition to accolades from poets and critics of even other affiliations, such as the young people editing *Salmagundi,* and rewards from all the major prize and fellowship committees, in addition to customary respectful front-page reviews in the *New York Times Book Review,* a cover story from *Time,* and extra publicity from his peace and political activities.

In short, every poetic establishment has a vested interest in the wider recognition of its major figures, just as all teachers of poetry-writing invariably establish an investment in the careers of their pupils; for the acclaim extended to one man enhances the short-term reputations of all those associated with him. On the other hand, the young poet who works either autonomously or in a radically different way is not likely to receive publication in the established presses, let alone fellowships, positions, grants, and other spoils. Finally, however, although the sociology of American poetry greatly influences such transient factors as who gets what fellowship, award, critical notice, or teaching position, once the establishments of the moment disintegrate, or the independent reader or critic ignores the flack of publicity (or perhaps once the writer turns sixty), it is the quality of the poet's work and its impact upon total strangers that earns his ultimate reputation.

No subject earns more discussion than madness when

American poets come together, for many of the major recent figures have, to be frank, spent considerable periods of their lives in certified mental institutions. "Sometimes, indeed, it seems," quipped Leslie Fiedler, in a statement that would be libelous, were it not so true, "as if the path which leads back and forth between the classroom and the madhouse is the one which the modern American muse loves especially to tread." Poets reacting against the willed impersonality of Eliot and Auden inevitably made their own experiences as "mentally ill" a subject of their own work—Robert Lowell in "Waking in the Blue," Allen Ginsberg in *Howl,* and Anne Sexton in *To Bedlam and Part-Way Back,* among others. In his poem "Heard in a Violent Ward," the late Theodore Roethke, who found a permanent academic position only when his sympathetic chairman granted automatic leaves, mystically regards himself as heir to a tradition of mad English poets, as he speaks of entering a heaven,

> With the likes of Blake,
> And Christopher Smart,
> And that sweet man, John Clare.

And in a prose piece he tells of "a kind of psychic shorthand when his protagonist is under great stress." To the late poet Delmore Schwartz, himself a sometime inmate, Robert Lowell attributes this couplet that indicatively echoes as it twists two classic lines in Wordsworth:

> We poets in our youth begin in sadness;
> Thereof in the end come despondency and madness.

"Surely," Fiedler continues elsewhere, "it is not the lucidity and logic of Robert Lowell and Theodore Roethke or John Berryman we admire, but their flirtation with incoherence and disorder." The reasons for such high incidence of mental distress, particularly in important poets born between 1913 and 1917, are inevitably more personal than public; yet among the latter possible causes were experience in World War II (sometimes as noncombatants, if not as imprisoned conscientious objectors) and hardships inherent in the profession of poetry, especially before 1950. There was also the powerful symbolic example of Ezra Pound, incarcerated by his country in St. Elizabeth's Hospital. Poets have come to confess their derangements, almost as a badge of honor, while claims are sometimes made on behalf of insanity as a kind of higher sanity; as Roethke himself once wrote, "Disassociation precedes a new state of clarity." The literary public tolerantly, if not generously, accepts such debilities; yet the specific relations between madness and contemporary poetry have hardly been explored in print. Oddly again, while certain previously taboo subjects have become public, others, such as homosexuality, remain all but universally private, the prime exceptions being Paul Goodman and Allen Ginsberg, the latter concluding his "America" with one of the great lines of contemporary poetry,

America I'm putting my queer shoulder to the wheel.

Conversation around the community of poets never ceases to tell of "unpublished gay poems which are really XYZ's best stuff," and this suggests that in the battle for unashamed, "free" expression, there are still some distinct frontiers to be crossed.

Possibility and change are the crucial words for discussing contemporary American poetry; for not only has poetic writing as a whole changed drastically since the end of World War II, but many major poets, particularly older ones, have decidedly explored alternative possibilities in midcareer. Of certain poets now between forty and sixty, the poet-critic Daniel Hoffman has written, "Different as these poets are from one another, each has passed in his own way through a similar progress: early mastery of received modes and forms, the intensification of these traditional materials, then the struggle to free the tongue from accustomed language, the ear from familiar cadences, the eye from habitual ways of seeing, the sensibility from conventional responses to experience." In the end, however, these particular poets, most of whom were recognized in the late forties, have only epitomized the character of their times; for in no other period of literature did poets and their critics alike, as well as other writers and artists, put such a high value upon stylistic development—upon the necessity of replacing old skins around their imagination with new ones—even if the previous style has brought nothing but personal satisfaction and critical success. (This perhaps explains why so many important recent pieces should take as their subject a particular conception of poetry.) Beyond that, at no time before have writers been so sympathetic toward flirtations with artistic impossibility, to the point that a true innovation is often defended less for its intrinsic excellence than as "an interesting thing to do"; and this seems a particularly opportune moment to launch an adventurous poetic involvement. In sum, it is the numerous breakings of old molds for alternative possibilities that constitute the significant stylistic history of post-World War II American poetry, as well as shapes the current "tradition" that promises to inform poetry written in the near future. Although the qualitative measure of recent verse may seem, in close retrospect, less substantial than poetry of 1920-1940 and the present period seems less blessed with indisputable masterpieces, it may be the absence of overbearing contemporary touchstones, as well as the great number and stylistic variousness of good poets, that grants the current moment an atmosphere of deeply felt freedom and possibility.

Impounding Pound's Milestone

(1970)

Here it is finally, all *The Cantos* (1970) literally fifty-five years in Ezra Pound's making—802 pages, with 154 pages of cantos not included in the earlier retrospective (1956) and 28 pages of cantos, numbered 110-117, not collected before. Everything has been comprehensively repaginated, thankfully, eliminating the clumsy successive paginations of the earlier collected edition; but the cantos that would be numbered 72 and 73 (and reportedly drafted in Italian) are still missing. The errata prefacing the earlier collected edition have been incorporated into the book; but on p. 471 the text still has the archaism "f . . . . n". (Also included, without any explanation, is an "Addendum for Canto C" that hysterically attacks usury.)

These latest cantos are less extreme, less obscure, and ultimately less interesting than their immediate predecessors, the *Thrones* (1959) composed at St. Elizabeth's prison-hospital; and at interludes these new sections are almost lyrical: "That I lost my center / Fighting the world," reads the book's final page, its own bottom line becoming perhaps the work's definitive terminus: "To be men not destroyers." Conceptually and stylistically, these late cantos represent an extension of Pound's earlier poetry, rather than, like Stravinsky's late compositions, a personal metamorphosis into a genuine stylistic breakthrough. It is nonetheless appropriate that at the dock of both poetry and life Pound should have survived his own more cautious contemporaries (Eliot, Stevens, even Williams) in more ways than one.

The technique of *The Cantos* is derived fundamentally from collage (itself the most extraordinary compositional innovation of the early twentieth century), in which an abundance and variety of both experiential and linguistic materials are pulled together into a poetically integral mosaic so that even where striking images are evoked, the effect of their structural principle is unfamiliar, perhaps telling juxtaposition. Otherwise, the overall stance of *The Cantos* is haughty, the perspective impersonal, the vision all-encompassing, the voices various, the form open-ended, the syntax more notational and associational than linear or syllogistic, the rhythm irregular, the metaphors elaborate, the observations condensed, the diction quite formal, the relation between the parts elliptical, and the sensibility awesomely erudite.

Avoiding at all costs the slickness of Victorian verse, *The Cantos* continually flirt with sheer incoherence (and Pound himself has admitted that certain earlier sections now strike him as inscrutable); and it is this characteristic, more than any other (including Pound's nutty politics), that produced this cutting paradox: For all of Pound's influence upon the profession of poetry, his work has scarcely affected the general public, although certain attitudes and linguistic devices have passed through lesser poets to the larger audience. (Some of this circuitous intellectual influence has been lamentable, because neither Pound's thought nor his poetry are especially wise.)

A rereading of *The Cantos* today makes increasingly

clear how close Williams and Eliot finally are to each other, despite their lifelong enmity, and then how much of post-World War II American poetry is indebted to Pound—not only the post-Black Mountain cabal, but even the New York school with its cultivated interest in poetic acoherence. And it is appropriate perhaps that the most sophisticated new anthology of post-1910 U.S. poetry, Hayden Carruth's *The Voice That Is Great Within Us* (1970), should be dedicated to Pound. Poetry magazines are still founded in the Poundian mold, such as *Stony Brook*, begun in 1968, by young George Quasha, who had, according to Noel Stock's recent biography (1970) an audience with the master in New York that year, and whose first issue opened with, cheers, a new canto! (It has been all but slavishly amenable to post-Poundians, abetted by Stony Brook colleagues and some Michigan naturalists, ever since.) That recent revolution in pop song lyrics, away from slick couplets to freer verse, can also be traced partially to Pound. On higher poetic levels, his influence particularly persists in nearly every recent long poem in English, especially those that similarly aim to represent "an intellectual diary"; for rare is the contemporary poet who can write more than twenty pages without appropriating Poundian compositional devices: for examples, such free-ranging, open-ended collages of all kinds of voices and material as William Carlos Williams's *Paterson*, Louis Zukofsky's *"A,"* Charles Olson's *Maximus Poems*, John Cage's *Diaries*, and even Allen Ginsberg's "Wichita Vortex Sutra," which is the first installment of an announced ambition to collage all of America.

By the seventies, this Poundian influence is, alas, fundamentally conservative, as indeed are nearly all post-Poundian poets. It has been academicized, most post-Poundians of note holding professorships and lecturing widely; and undergraduates can now freely write post-Poundian poems for academic credit. *The Cantos* can also be cited to rationalize obscurity, in addition to all kinds of creative self-indulgence, sheer stupidity, and ineffectual formlessness, so that more bad poetry in America today is indebted to Pound than anyone else. (In this tradition, as fomenter of American dreck, has he succeeded Henry Wadsworth Longfellow!) Indeed, collage itself is by now such an exhausted technique that it rarely provides any new illuminations in any art form today; and in this respect, perhaps the greatest implicit weakness of Pound's new cantos stems precisely from his unwillingness to confront at this point (and as Stravinsky did at a comparable age) the problem of stylistic alternatives.

The remaining esthetic truth is that Pound's freedom in handling poetry's materials clearly implies the opportunity to transcend *The Cantos*'s pet compositional techniques; and some of his tentative innovations, such as spatial placement and the use of both visual materials and other languages, all suggest far more elaborate development. Beyond that, let me judge that the quality which is most alive today in *The Cantos* is their encompassing vision (notwithstanding the dominance of romance and oriental cultures); for this dimension, like all examples of continuing relevance, has rarely been imitated successfully and never surpassed. Nonetheless, *The Cantos* are by now such a powerful milestone that perhaps the easiest measure of genuine "newness" in modernist poetry today is this: Whether the work at hand moves beyond not only the old forms of structure and lyricism, but also beyond the compositional vocabulary of *The Cantos*. In this respect, it is as an anthology of things that need no longer be done that this book is most worth reading, or rereading, now.

A Magazine of Worse

(1979)

The reason why I abominate the American Magazines and why I think they should be exterminated in revenge for the damage they have done American poetry is that they specialize in two or three tones. . . . [Ezra Pound, in a letter to Harriet Monroe, Spring, 1915]

Now that the recent chief editor and the present associate editor of *Poetry* have edited an anthology culled from the magazine's sixty-five years, a well-kept secret has been let out of the closet, onto public display—the oppressive amount of bad poetry, indubitably bad poetry, that has appeared in *Poetry*. Perhaps one-third of the poems reprinted in *The Poetry Anthology, 1912-1977,* edited by Daryl Hine and Joseph Parisi, contain such fundamental clinkers as weak lines, clumsy syntax, atrocious ideas, mischievous metaphors, insensitive line breaks, leaden language, overblown rhetoric, uneven tone, etc., etc.

> The dawn was apple-green,
> The sky was green wine held up in the sun,
> The moon was a golden petal between.
> > [which is the opening half of "Green," by
> > D. H. Lawrence, 1914]

Roughly once every five pages I came across passages that were so inept, so gross, so gauche, so amateur that they would not pass untarnished through a "creative writing" course in most of America's universities. A second *Stuffed Owl* could be compiled from *The Poetry Anthology* alone; for if this book is meant to have pedagogical uses, it will be largely as an anthology, a selective collection, of the ways in which "poetry," blessed poetry, should *not* be written.

> Heavenly Evil, holy One,
> You whose work is never done,
> Any visage, any name
> Cannot cloak your single aim.
>> [which opens Louis Ginsberg's
>> "Hymn to Evil," 1927]

> The wave approaching and the wave returning.
> The grave is broken, and the phoenix burning,
> The myrtle blossoms from the twisted pillar,
> Love illuminates a scene of pallor:
> Inevitably to life consigned
> The flame consuming, the by flame consumed,
> Eternally eternally bud and blossom
> Evolve the particulars of doom.
>> [which opens "Sequence,"
>> by George Barker, 1937]

My initial suspicion was that only the opening sections of this chronological anthology were riddled with such bad verse; they would reflect the editorship, from 1912 to 1936, of the magazine's founder, Harriet Monroe, whom Irving Howe characterizes, not unfairly, as "a poor poet, indifferent critic, gifted fundraiser; one of those slightly comic, forever busy middlewomen who edge the literary scene." In her considered critical study of *Poetry*'s initial ten years, *Harriet Monroe and the Poetry Renaissance* (Illinois, 1977), Ellen Williams judges that, after the initial, Pound-abetted flurry of 1912-16, "The magazine began to decline toward relative mediocrity. . . . And by 1917 the magazine falls well below its past standard." In part because of Monroe's editorial high-handedness, advanced American poetry went elsewhere, never to return again.

> What has bent you,
> Warped and twisted you,
> Torn and crippled you?—
> What has embittered you,
> O lonely tree?
>   [which opens "The Pine at
>   Timber-Line," by Harriet Monroe, 1915]

Ellen Williams continues: "*Poetry*'s role in the twenties began to emerge in 1921. First, it was a place for the occasional good poem rejected by a more prestigious magazine. *Poetry*'s history made it an outlet that a poet of reputation could use without disgrace." Later, she adds, "Harriet Monroe's greatest editorial vice [was] her consistent kindness to the polished, well-bred poet who seems to be operating between firmly fixed limits." To judge from the work reprinted here, however, later editors of *Poetry* also had leaden touch, not only in editing but in writing; the badness is continuous, creating *Poetry*'s own inimitable tradition of verse that is worse.

> My mountains, God has company in heaven—
> Crowned saints who sing to him the sun-long day.
> He has no need of speech with you—with you,
> Dust of his foot-stool! No, but I have need.
>   [which opens "In High Places,"
>   by Harriet Monroe, 1922]

The next question is whether a better *Poetry Anthol-*

ogy could have been drawn from its thousands of pages or whether, instead, the magazine has always been so lacking in excellence that a more substantial selection would be impossible? An evident taste for sonnets in this book leads me to suspect its editors; never before have I encountered so many fourteen-liners in an anthology of "modern" poetry. On the other hand, random examination of past issues leads me to believe that, given what Hine and Parisi had to choose from, this may well be the best that could be done. (Indicatively, the critical commentaries in the issues I sampled were as embarrassingly amateur and mediocre as the poems. *The Poetry Criticism Anthology* would likewise be a textbook of how *not* to proceed.) If *Poetry* has indeed always been worse, why should any aspiring poet today want to appear in its pages? Why should he or she want to append the stigma of mediocrity to their biographical notes? Should *Poetry* be censured for exploiting the masochism of opportunistically ambitious poets?

> Through a wild midnight all my mountainous past
> Labored and heaved with all I had forgotten
> Until a poem no bigger than a mouse
> Came forth. And with the darkness finally passed
> We faced each other, begetter and begotten:
> "Monster!" I cried. And "Monster!" cried the mouse
> [which is, in its entirety, "The Monster," by
> Henry Rago, 1950-51]

Indeed, implicit in the magazine's history is a textbook example of editorial nonthinking. One easily verifiable sign of thoughtlessness is the fact that *Poetry* currently has exactly the same format it had sixty years ago—a selection of poems, followed by prose "comment," biographical notes, "news notes," and finally a list of "books received." Similarly, just as none of its succeeding editors have thought to redo Harriet Monroe's austere format, so none can be credited with particularly transcending the tastes of his predecessor—not even the chief editor from 1950 to 1955, Karl Shapiro, who has elsewhere shown professional initiative. No reader of this chronological anthology can tell from internal evidence alone when one editor departed and another began. *Poetry*'s deleterious traditions appear to have overwhelmed everyone ever involved with the magazine. Whether the new editor, John Frederick Nims, can rejuvenate *Poetry* seems doubtful; he served as an associate editor during the forties. *Plus ca change, plus c'est la même chose.*

> The judge who lives impeccably upstairs
> With dull decorum and its implication,
> Has all his servants in to family prayers
> And edifies *his* soul with exhortation.
> > [which opens "Upstairs Downstairs,"
> > a sonnet by Hervey Allen, 1922]

> These lover's inklings which our loves enmesh,
> Lost to the cunning and dimensional eye,
> Though tenemented in the selves we see,
> Not more perforce than azure to the sky,
> Were necromancy-juggled to the flesh,
> And startled from no daylight you or me.
> > [which opens "Counsel to Unreason,"
> > by Léonie Adams, 1927]

The fact that the above lines, along with others quoted here, passed through not just the editor(s) initially accepting it for *Poetry,* but then the anthologists Daryl Hine and Joseph Parisi as well, inevitably raises all sorts of disparaging questions: How many other putative "editorial geniuses" read these poems prior to their publication and the republication? How many editorial assistants, proofreaders, secretaries, and even store-to-store salesmen anxiously flattered their superiors as this went through the publishing house? Who is conning whom? The poets who slip junk past periodical editors? Messrs. Hine and Parisi, who sold a load of baloney to Houghton Mifflin? The poetry editor at Houghton Mifflin, who must have convinced his colleagues that this anthology would "for sure, you know," become a classroom staple?

> When Memory's Fabled Daughter
> Descended to the Word,
> The lapping sound of water
> Was profitably heard.
> Through language set in motion
> By river, stream, or ocean
> Men acted their devotion,
> Both tragic and absurd.
> > [which opens "Notes for a History of Poetry,"
> > by David Daiches, 1961]

All the "famous names" are here, you betcha, mug-shots of them filling both the front cover and the back of the paperback edition. However, nothing but nothing conclusively reveals the editorial celebrity-chasing, combined with the absence of literary taste, than inept poems by Household Names:

> Summer, betray this tree again!
> Bind her, in winding sheets of green;
> With empty promises unlock her lips;
> Sift futile pollen through her finger-tips.
> > [which opens "Misericordia," by Margaret Mead,
> > 1929-30]

> They come not within the tall woods,
> neither they nor their enemies;
> their commerce is but chaffering in
> futilities.
> > [which opens "To One Elect," by S. Ichiyé
> > Hayakawa, 1934]

The abundance of bad poems by War Horses suggests that *Poetry* has double standards in editorial policy, collecting all sorts of garbage by renowned and previous contributors, while begrudgingly admitting anyone new (unless, of course, his or her work comes with a garbage-person's personal recommendation). One hesitates to calculate the amount of editorial anxiety that went into selecting *people,* not poems, for this book. The poems were incidental, one suspects; the selections quoted here raise the question of whether *Poetry*'s poetry was "editorially" read at all.

> As Winter, fleeing,
> Leaves the shreds of its ermine
> To be crunched into murk,
> The fearless leave
> Their names.
> [which is, in its entirety, Mortimer J. Adler's "The Fearless," 1921]

One reason why *Poetry* has remained so mediocre for so long is its complete neglect, since the 1930s, of the dominant experimental tendencies in American poetry. The magazine apparently strangled on its roots in early modernism, while poetry has since changed. Indicatively, one would search *The Poetry Anthology* in vain for the dominant figures of Jerome Rothenberg's anthology of avant-garde poetry from 1914 to 1945, *Revolution of the Word* (1974): Bob Brown, Abraham Lincoln Gillespie, Harry Crosby, Else von Freytag-Loringhoven, et al. Closer to the present, among the conspicuous absences are such consequential North American individuals as Charles Olson, Kenneth Rexroth, Paul Blackburn, Rothenberg himself, Earle Birney, Bill Bissett, all the "beats." Among the currently experimental modes com-

pletely omitted from *The Poetry Anthology* are pure
visual poetry, sound poetry (also known as text-sound),
permutational poetry, neologistic poetry, and asyntac-
tic poetry. There are no poems here in languages other
than English (aside from a single Sidney Goodsir Smith
in Anglo-Scots), implying, falsely, that no one in the
English-language world writes distinguished poems in
other languages. Reflecting current academic fashion,
the anthology includes representatives of *social* minorities, as long as they write in "acceptable" ways, while
excluding *literary* minorities.

> There were five of us within the room
> (Bach's polytechnics beat upon the limpid air)—
> Eliot stretched in a chintz-covered chair,
> While Pound sat around
> Sipping a sloe gin fizz
> And disseminating Italian gloom
> That was peculiarly his.
> [which opens "I Come To Bury Caesar," by Sydney
> Justin Harris, 1935]

Indeed, nothing unusual in contemporary American
poetry ever appears in *Poetry,* which opportunistically
cultivates, or guards, its "establishment" image largely
by totally excluding all language works that its principal audiences of provincial academics and high-school
teachers might dismiss as "not poetry." However, by
genuflecting to the god not of courageous discovery but
of expedient inertia, *Poetry* drives itself headlong into a
cultural cul-de-sac. This is the principal reason why the
magazine has had so little influence upon the recent
history of American poetry (aside from, of course, the
messy business of getting academic poetry jobs). Finally,
nothing reveals editorial mindlessness more surely than

the fact that these conspicuous absences are not acknowledged in the book's otherwise elaborate introduction; one assumes that the possibility of such gross omissions never entered its editors' heads.

> Women have loved before as I love now;
> At least, in lively chronicles of the past—
> Of Irish waters by a Cornish prow
> Or Trojan waters by a Spartan mast
> Much to their cost invaded—here and there,
> Hunting the amorous line, skimming the rest,
> I find some woman bearing as I bear
> Love like a burning city in the breast.
> [which opens Edna St. Vincent Millay's "Sonnet," 1930]

Writing this review took longer, much longer than I expected, I must confess, mostly because I spent countless hours selecting the very worst poems. Initially, I could not believe how many there were. I read them aloud to friends and lovers who were likewise incredulous, as well as amused; and let me encourage readers of this review to do likewise. (Recalcitrant sex objects will fall at your feet in mirth.) I wondered if a super-hoaxer had not actually slipped *The Stuffed Owl* into new covers, fooling not only Houghton Mifflin but countless fawning reviewers (including, typically, Irving Howe in the *New York Times Book Review*). As I read the book more closely, for my own review, I found such a surfeit of baddies that the choice of those to quote here became an agonizing problem. Fearing that the worst of the worst might escape me, I telephoned friends and editors asking for help. Help. As I write, my suspicion is that some whoppers, real whoppers, slipped through my gap-toothed comb.

The will dissolves, the heart becomes excited,
Skull suffers formication; moving words
Fortuitously issue from my hand.
The winter heavens, seen all day alone,
Assume the color of aircraft over the phthisic
Guns.
    [which opens "Soliloquy in an Air-Raid," by Roy
    Fuller, 1941]

(Formication, one should know, perhaps, means "a sensation of the body resembling that made by the creeping of ants on the skin." *Phthisis* is, believe me, "a wasting away of the body, or any of its parts; esp., tuberculosis of the lungs." How Fuller thinks "guns" might be "phthisic" raises further questions.)

The standing guests, a grotesque glade
Dispensing microcosmic gloom,
Make artifice of light and shade
In an eternal drawing room.
    [which opens "The Party," by Margaret
    Avison, 1947]

In passing, I also discovered that the book's index is inept as well, Glenway Wescott and Gertrude Stein being two poets whose works are not where the index says they should be. Also, if the editors actually obtained permission to reprint the Gary Snyder poem on pages 402-3, that fact is not acknowledged in the exhaustive "Credits." Quite frankly, fellow reviewers, it is much harder and more tiresome to identify the worst poems in a bad book than the best poems in a good one.

Granted that what we summon is absurd:
Moustaches and the stick, the New York fake

In cowboy costume grinning for the sake
Of cameras which always just occurred;
                    [which opens "T. R.," a sonnet by
                    Donald Hall, 1958]

The sun is the blind eyes of statues gilded
with lilies and fig leaves, the statues cast
of 20 carat gold, and the side frames
and pillars of gold, and the walls mirrors
recollecting gold and the flash bulbs flashing
to record the slaughter of the camera.
[which opens "The Sun," by Andrew Oerke, 1971]

The Poetry Anthology suggests, to me at least, that
Poetry has probably done more to hinder the development of American literature, as well as to encourage the
publication (and thus the creation) of more utterly awful
writing, than any other literary magazine of its time.
(Perhaps its "hidden" patron is the KGB, exceeding
even the CIA at covert cultural subversion.)

The King's Highway to the Dare-Not-Know
—but I get my rides and oh I know
those boring roads where hundreds and hundreds
of cars fade by in hundred-hundreds
of flashing windows too bright too fast
to see my face. I am steadfast
long hours o' the morning, I am so sad.
   [which opens "Dreams Are the Royal Road to the
   Unconscious," by Paul Goodman, 1947]

Precisely by preempting the best and most inclusive
name a poetry magazine can have, *Poetry* has achieved
the cultural coup, belonging more to the history of
Publicity than to Literature, of coming to represent
"American Poetry," not only before impressionable
highschoolers but also before Europeans who know

enough about contemporary literature to regard *Poetry* (and thus, alas, all American poetry) as a juvenile riot of reaction.

> Dunes are graying that were blackest;
> Truckers catching a quick breakfast
> Where the all-night pinks the cactus
>   Think the morning looks okay;
> But these couples who awaken
> Perched above their eggs and bacon
> Eye with arid eyes the sacred
>   Languors of beginning day.
>   [which opens "Aubade: The Desert,"
>   by Frederick Bock, 1958]

Not only in itself, but also in its influence, *Poetry* is truly a magazine of worse.

> Amazing games that always used to end in mate!
> Precious as sex is, flesh, perennially wretched
>   In fact turns out to be a tourist trap at last.
> The mathematical vision which built this system
>   Of the universe, all-devouring power-house
> (The mysteries of dust are nothing to live up to!)
>   Briefly yields to the weaker tyranny of weeds.
>   You used to choose the rules with superfluous humour:
>   Monotony, the awful drawback of my song,
> Slowly unfolded, like a brocade robe thrown over.
>   Persuaded of the possibility of joy,
> Finally I tried to define why divine silence. . .
>   [which closes "Vowel Movements" [sic],
>   by Daryl Hine, 1974]

The New Class

(1976)

The American Poetry Anthology (1975)—what a pretentious, encompassing title for Daniel Halpern's collection
that, upon closer inspection, appears quite modest and
parochial. At least sixty-five of Halpern's seventy-six contributors have, like himself, worked as college teachers—
not of literature or art or history, to be sure, but of
creative writing. Many of them, to judge from the biographical notes, have also received graduate degrees not
in literature or something else but in "writing," often
from the University of Iowa. This anthology is the end
result of an hermetic system: an M.F.A editing M.F.As'
poems for aspiring M.F.As to study. Its precursor in this
respect is David Allan Evans' *New Voices in American
Poetry* (1973), whose preface acknowledges the aim not
to establish taste but to fall snugly into "courses in creative writing." Are academic "writing" positions becoming the plums (or plots) that indubitably minor poets
pick?

Ever fashionable, *The Ampoant* includes black poets,
Amerindian poets, one Nisei poet, but it does not include
New York school poets, underground poets, avowedly
gay poets, visual poets, sound poets, minimal poets, or

nonsyntactic poets—absolutely none. Why? One reason that comes immediately to mind is that members of the latter groups, unlike the former, are never employed to teach creative writing. Since their work is, for now at least, academically blacklisted, it is not included here.

The book's total exclusion of "undesirables" suggests that a sort of new fascism has struck again. Only a year ago, I suggested in *The American Poetry Review* (which, curiously, exemplifies the sin), "The complete absence of [visual poetry], along with other avant-garde forms, in the poetry magazines and anthologies is one symptom of literary opportunism in its current form, impressing academics by the neglect of what they consider "not poetry."

Indicatively, there is only one full-time writer here, Jim Harrison, but the choice from his work is limited to poems composed some years ago, when he was teaching creative writing, naturally. *The Ampoant* is an act of opportunistic literary politicking, whose heft (506 pages) acknowledges a new establishment whose existence I for one had not previously perceived. Tellingly, this high-priced book comes not from a quality paperbacker, anticipating modest returns, but a mass house, Avon (Hearst Corp.), whose salesmen undoubtedly envision gross sales to, you guessed it, creative writing classes. Bless 'em.

Though Halpern's preface claims "heterogeneity, in terms of form, attitude, and treatment of content," I see an editorial principle that favors not diversity but uniformity—more precisely, miniscule diversity amidst general uniformity: a soft surrealism, image-centered, stylistically prosy, unmetrical, humorless, slightly incoherent, willfully mysterious, structurally flaccid and, of necessity, attitudinally "poetic." The language of these poems is predominantly low-keyed and undistinguished, the diction stilted, the subjects trivial and the tone limp, as words march militarily from flush left-hand margins in unbroken horizontal lines, straight through conventional syntax and unemphatic line breaks to predictable periods. A quiet modesty pervades, as the book eschews encompassing visions, moralistic jeremiads, blatant confessionalism, even strong language; everything extreme is earnestly excised from *The Ampoant*. The contents are so similar that an ingenious reader could easily take lines from one poet and work them into poems by another poet.

Halpern also connects his selections to the "growing internationalism of American poetry," but none of *these* poems were published abroad (unlike more experimental American poetry, which often appears abroad). None of *these* poets relate to their European contemporaries. *These* Americans are importers of a putative European past, rather than exporters of a present American art that participates in European developments. The false claim seems concocted to cater to the American academic sweet tooth for things "European."

The Ampoant has so much prose, artificially chopped into lines of poetry, that the reader would relish some variation, even an interlude of dialect or, yes, a hackneyed rhyme. A typically prosy example comes from Halpern himself: "On the prow, / standing on red planks, / the white maiden holds / hand to temple, / faint, keening. / The fog snags the edge / of her gown, dissolves / it at the ankle, begins / for thighs, for breasts / unlike white stone, her / neck, and then her / lips like white stone." Passages like this make me wonder about the current status of the academic distinction between *poetry*, which is to say heightened language, and irredeemable *prose*? (The review you are now reading is, to my mind, prose. *The Ampoant* suggests that it might well pass as "poetry": The review / you / are now / reading is, / to my mind, prose. . . .)

Given Halpern's preference for murky prose that is difficult to read, but easy to "teach," (and "poetic" prose as an ultimate extension of prosy "poetry"), it is scarcely surprising that, even within the circumscribed class of poets he favors, some of the better practitioners are omitted. Superior post-1934, sometime professor-poets that come to my alphabetical mind include Dick Allen, R. H. W. Dillard, Ray DiPalma, Charles Doria, Albert Drake, Siv Cedering Fox, David Franks, Albert Goldbarth, John Jacob, Joe Johnson, Laurence Lieberman, N. J. Loftus, Richard Mathews, Michael Joseph Phillips, Jonathan Price, Grace Schulman, David Shapiro, Jane Shore, Karen Swenson, Al Young. There are, no doubt, other young poetry professors who, like these, write better poetry than Halpern's weaker colleagues.

Theoretically, academic affiliation has nothing to do with poetic style, but the grim uniformity of Halpern's inclusions, along with the absence of esthetic surprises, suggests that he perceives a direct connection. The implicit critical achievement of *The Ampoant* might be the identification of junior academia's current period style. However, even here Halpern sabotages his literary purposes, for an anthology representing a certain class of once-scorned writers (academic poets) should include only the very best work. Otherwise, skeptical readers will think that the group as a whole is completely undistinguished, while the chosen poets will think their literary cause betrayed. *The Ampoant* is, alas, the sort of anthology from which the better contributors will want to disassociate themselves. Some of those initially blessed will recognize the kiss of death.

Indicatively, the book's biographical notes are nearly

identical, representing an implicit tribute to editorial homogenization. Though many of the contributors' names are unfamiliar, their "credentials" are not. The Halpern bionote usually opens with the chosen poet's year of birth, followed by the universities at which he or she has studied, the places in which he or she has lived, awards received, publications edited, and colleges taught. A typical example, aside from omitting *alma mater,* is the editor's resumé for himself:

> Daniel Halpern(1945) was born in Syracuse and grew up in Los Angeles and Seattle. He spent two years living in Tangier, Morocco [*sic*] where he began the literary magazine *Antaeus.* He has received various awards, including the YMHA Discovery Award in 1971, the Great Lakes Colleges National Book Award for his first book of poems, National Endowment for the Arts Fellowships, and was a Robert Frost Fellow at Bread Loaf. He is the editor of the American Poetry Series for the Ecco Press, and teaches at Princeton University and The New School for Social Research.

These biographical presentations are, like the book itself, colorless and earnestly ambitious, speaking not about poetry but careers. There are no quotations of purposes from the contributors, no critical commentary or even descriptive characterization from the editor. There is nothing as well about husbands, wives, or lovers. It is all so perfunctory that one suspects the presence of a machine. It is hard to remember one biographical note apart from the others; it is nearly as hard to remember individual poems. What is one to make of this fascination with professional positions (which are not poems) and with awards (which are not poems, either)?

It would be neither unflattering nor inaccurate to characterize Halpern as a remarkably sensitive and successful literary politician, whose magazine *Antaeus* has featured well-known writers who have, in turn, made Halpern's reputation as a celebrity-chaser—the Norman Podhoretz of the younger generation. (Thus, the awards and fellowships.) A young literary politician choosing this well-trod opportunistic path generally makes a point of ignoring his chronological contemporaries. In this respect, devoting *The Ampoant* to youngsters represents a creditable editorial departure for Halpern. However, since he has, in the past, exhibited so sure a sense of the real sources of professional power, I take this new anthology to be a fat acknowledgment of the literary-political preeminence of provincial professors. Indeed, at least in poetry, that group, with its magazines and small presses, might by now be more powerful than the literary-industrial complex which, though it publishes some of Halpern's own books, pays increasingly less attention to poetry. The publisher's publicity flier declares, echoing their author-editor Halpern: "Mr. Halpern has chosen the poets for this anthology without regard to 'schools of poetry', current fashion or literary cliques." What egregious nonsense. He has chosen up sides and isolated his own team. Onward, college soldiers.

It seems to me that Richard Howard, himself a master literary politician, single-handedly keeps alive an older generation of academic poets, memorialized in his critical book, *Alone in America* (1969) and his anthology, *Preferences* (1974). If Howard did not exist, let me conjecture, these poets would disappear from public view. Halpern apparently wants to serve a similar function with a younger generation of academics, becoming their Man in Manhattan, who will be amply rewarded with invitations to declaim his own poetry at backwoods universities. Typically again, Halpern, as a sensitive conservative politician, acknowledges in his preface such old-boy powerhouses as Howard Moss, Leonard Randolph,

Stanley Kunitz, and Donald Hall, "without whose help the publication of this book would have been impossible." What, one wonders, is meant by "impossible"?

Back in 1957, three then-young academic poets—Donald Hall, Robert Pack, and Louis Simpson—produced *New Poets of England and America,* a paperback anthology that exploited fifties conservatism on the way to the classroom. The copy I have reads "Seventh Printing October 1962." For nearly a decade, it suggested not how poetry might be written but what sorts of poems will earn a coveted A. Though both editors and contributors to *New Poets* prospered in the academic world, the kind of metrical poetry they practiced has since disappeared from public view. Perhaps the book's success in the classroom, coupled with the general mediocrity of its inclusions, contributed to erasing this once-dominant style from the printed page.

I would wager that *The Ampoant* will have a similar, two-sided career.

Field's Faceless Fusiliers

(1980)

No one should make art unless he or she intends to create something that has not existed before, and one fundamental sign of artistic seriousness is the desire to do work that is securely one's own—work that is so perceptibly different from what everyone else is doing that it is instantly identifiable. Most of us can usually tell after only a few notes that the music is Bach's, from only a few square inches that the painting is Jackson Pollock's, with only a few lines that the poetry is T. S. Eliot's, John Milton's, or William Blake's. It follows that art is not worth doing unless your aim is individual excellence; there is otherwise too much work for rewards that are too meagre. If you do not aim high, the result is likely to be mere amateur exercise in homage and faceless flattery, perhaps "acceptable" and even successful now, but doomed to disappear in the future.

Nearly all the contributors to Edward Field's new contemporary anthology, *A Geography of Poets* (1979), apparently missed this truth—that one basic test of artistic purpose, let alone excellence, is *signature*. To his credit, Field acknowledges its importance in his prefatory discussion of the "masters of modern poetry, each with a distinctive style of his or her own"; but several pages later, he remarks that in his compilation of living poets, "No great figures have emerged yet." Instead of poetry with signature, *A Geography of Poets* is filled with passages like these:

> This cross section, here incorrectly titled,
> "Mechanical Drawing for a Steamboat,"
> is not a steamboat at all.
> This is part of a submarine.

> First there is the student
> who so adores his teacher
> he must satisfy that feeling: he runs
> off with the teacher's wife.

> This dumbbell bee must be working
> the half-dozen highest buttercups on earth.
> Low alpine sun, bright enough to hurt.
> Under my feet a 7-acre snowbank gargles
> like gangster summer, riddled with kitchen taps.

The theme of *A Geography* is that most American poetry today is written outside New York City—a quantitative judgment that no one would dispute—and with 229 contributors, this monolith is certainly the single most populous of the current anthologies. Its editor also claims that *A Geography* presents "the enormous variety of poetry today." To the contrary, I find that the dominant characteristic of the book is an insipid uniformity that smothers the few gems that managed to slip past Field's narrow, homogenizing taste.

The surest sign of the absence of variety, in this or any other putatively comprehensive collection of American poetry, is the complete exclusion of the rough edges—those radically different poems that, precisely because they are formally so unusual, are often dismissed as "not poetry." Thus, there is no place in Field's *Geography* for poems that depend upon the visual enhancement of language, for sound poems, for minimal poems, for abstract poems, for poems exploring permutational ordering or other alternative forms of structure—all of them banished as apparently not only "not poetic" but "un-American" in Field's recruitment of the current scene.

Even in an anthology so populous, there are no poems in languages other than English, or even any glimmer of recognition that within the United States today poetry is written in Spanish, Yiddish, Russian, and yet other languages besides. After all, such acknowledgments, let alone inclusions, would make this voluminous book more various, and that would be contrary to Field's patronizing purposes, which I take to be the definition of this period's most popular minor styles.

> Now in the after play
> I press my fingers against
> these blemishes on your
> warm and beautiful back
> —those little, worm-like, fatty
> masses in your follicles—
> where I have just held your flesh
> in the grip of passion.

> Muramoto knew all this as a child.
> But then he had the old country
> around and behind him,
> the people being whole and natural.

> Long Island springs not much went on
> Except the small plots gave their all
> In weeds and good grass; the mowers mowed
> Up to the half-moon garden crammed
> With anything that grew.

In my opinion, few of Field's inclusions are especially good; few are egregiously bad. Nearly all are simply undistinguished. It is scarcely surprising that most of the most consequential poets working in America today are *not* included here. (The only sure way to substantiate that last judgment, alas, would be another, better anthology.)

The vast majority of the poems here are prosy in language and loose in form, with weak line breaks and mundane subject matter. Rhyme and alliteration are just as scarce here as an unusual word or an inspired metaphor. In lieu of poetic language and poetic tropes, the book is filled with poetic attitudinizing—the authorial voice making the kinds of comments that we associate not with accountants or used car dealers but with the profession of poetry. (A *poet,* by this definition, is someone who writes what "poets" say.)

> This morning Amanda
> lies down during breakfast.
> The hay is hip high.
> The sun sleeps on her back
> as it did on the spine
> of the dinosaur
> the fossil bat
> the first fish with feet
> she was once.

> It was a big boxy wreck of a house
> Owned by a classmate of mine named Rod Usher,
> Who lived in the thing with his twin sister.
> He was a louse and she was a souse.

> German submarines were an idea we watched
> off the south shore of Long Island;
> two newsmen drove and acted suspiciously

all night to prove two spies could;
I spent afternoons at the Bay
watching for unidentified airplanes;

A contemporary literature anthology is theoretically an arena for open competition, where readers can discover which individual artists stand out from the crowd (without the benefit of advertising, publicity, and the other devices that commercial publishers have for their *buying* readership). In anthology, we can observe how well the work of poet X stands in relation to the work of poets Y and Z. However, when so many of the contributors resemble each other, they cancel each other out in an involuntary massacre. Indicatively, influential poets like Robert Bly and Galway Kinnell fall when surrounded (and outnumbered) by imitators who have digested their masters too well. More than once I imagined that six slightly skilled parodists wrote all the poems in this book.

If these poems are "selected" from a larger corpus, one hesitates to calculate how much utterly mediocre poetry is written and, worse, published in America today; one is pained to consider how many American poets there must be who believe, and are encouraged to believe, that they need not be particularly good. Indeed, one senses too often that most of these poets are trying to be undistinguished, if only to be "acceptable" to their teachers and colleagues. (After all, true excellence inevitably generates jealousy and controversy.) It follows that this anthology tries to be acceptable to the largest number of potential buyers mostly by being innocuously mediocre. Therefore, everyone is happy—even the paperback publishers.

No one wants to be discouraging, but there comes a point when the current fashion of artistic populism can

be self-defeating—when the sheer amount of junk smothers the emergence of quality. *A Geography of Poets* suggests, to me at least, that perhaps the "garbage death"
of our cultural entropy has now been reached, and it
might well be time to call out the militia for emergency
sanitation.

> Eggs boiling in a pot.
> They click
> like castanets.
> I put one in a cup
> & slice its head off.

> Beneath the cement foundations
> of the motel, the ancient spirits
> of the people conspire sacred tricks.
> They tell stories and jokes and laugh
> and laugh.

> And when the revolution come
> the militants said
> niggers wake up
> you go to comb yo hair
> the natural way

It is clear that Field aimed to include every sociological group, whether geographic, ethnic, or racial (and
even a token nonogenarian), producing a selection "bal-
anced" with the glib caution typical of an NEA grants
committee. The principal distinctions within this anthology have less to do with styles or even kinds of subject
than with sociological locations and, it follows, with
parochial nostalgia (which Field apparently regards as
the most appropriate subject for poetry today). Thus,
in Field's sense of American poetry, northwest poets

deserve inclusion when they write about the northwest, Nisei poets when they use Japanese names, and so forth. Behind such simpleminded taste is the implicit assumption that poetry should be a surrogate for sociological reportage, but anyone studying literary history can observe that poetry based upon that idea is destined to date and thus to disappear.

One way a publisher can insure a large initial sale for a book is to include an abundance of living poets who had not been anthologized before. Consider this. If each contributor to *A Geography* buys an average of nine copies for his friends and relatives, then over 2,000 copies have been sold. In addition, at least half of the contributors are teachers of poetry and creative writing. Now, if they can get at least forty of their students to buy the book, then there are 5,000 more customers. How nifty.

The final impression created by *A Geography* is that of an army of American poets, in roughly uniform dress, marching blindly to a prosy tune off the end of an esthetic cliff.

> Elephants are born with so much clothing,
> wrinkled and folded,
> and such a cargo of bones, cartilage, nerves—
> only their brains being small, gray jewels—
> and everyone a Cyrano,
> noses curled like vines,
> but tuskless, the sucking mouths open.

> Like thunder they run out, like Holstein thunder—
> These dark females swinging their heavy equipment,
>   these barbarous ladies
> That slip, fall, run with irregular glances
> At us. No one touches them; they keep their separateness,
>   in fear.

My love wants to park
in front of your house.

Thank God.
It's been driving me crazy
going around and around the block.

The ancient reservoir,
an underground lake beneath the city,
has been closed to the public by the government
due to stringent budget cuts.

Readers who keep score might like to know that the above examples are all opening passages—that being the place where the poet's signature is most likely to be established—and that their authors are Marvin Bell, Edward Field, Eloise Klein Healy, Lawson Fusao Inada, Erica Jong, Maxine Kumin, Howard Moss, Simon J. Ortiz, Carolyn M. Rodgers, Reg Saner, Knute Skinner, Ann Stanford, Adrien Stoutenburg, Charles Waterman, Theodore Weiss, and Reed Whittemore. Now that this information is revealed, the reader of this review might like to test himself (and myself) by identifying who authored which excerpt.

Poetry Readings

(1975)

In my observation, remarkably few poets like to go to them, and that is a sentiment I share. Most of us consider it an onerous duty in acknowledgment of friendship, favor, or some other professional obligation. Foreknowledge of a post-party generally helps attendance. Famous poets sometimes make a point of arriving late. The analogy seems to be an academic lecture by a colleague in one's own field; only professional obligation can summon an audience. However, academics know that little of importance is communicated in such situations. Old ideas are reiterated, just as, in poetry readings, old poems are declaimed.

I go to modern music concerts primarily to hear pieces that are not available on records; but while many major contemporary pieces remain unrecorded, nearly all good poems eventually appear in public print.

The implicit theme of most poetry readings is the superior sensitivity of the poet—his *sensitivity,* not his intelligence, his knowledge of poetry, his artistic courage, his conceptual intelligence, his social relevance, his capacity for invention, the style of his language, but his sensitivity. This theme is customarily reinforced by the poet's prefatory remarks. However, little great poetry has personal sensitivity as its principal theme.

Most first-rank poetry cannot be comprehended in a single hearing, and too much flaccid poetry I read in the magazines gives me, at least, the impression that it was written especially to be declaimed. Performance is particularly appropriate for poems that the audience already knows or those that are easily understood, especially if they also appeal to the audience's sentiments, not only about life but about poetry. [Applause.] Nonetheless, poetry at its best has little in common with soapbox oration and other streetcorner entertainments.

Most poets in performance try to be charming and ingratiating; however, most great poems, even of recent years, are more provocative than ameliorating, more challenging than charming, more disturbing than ingratiating. In more respects than one, the values upheld in poetry readings are quite different from those that inform the best contemporary poetry writing.

Nearly every good poet I've heard goes on too long, in part because poets are unashamedly hoggish about time, but also because few poets understand the principle of a concise statement. Last fall, I attended an anthology performance by thirty-five visual and musical artists, each of whom was alotted 2 minutes of playing time. The entire show took 150 minutes, including setups and intermissions, because nearly everyone acknowledged that he could make his artistic statement within a short time. Thirty-five poets, in a similar setup, would never have finished in less than ten hours.

What kills most poetry readings for me is the egomania that seems intrinsic in most contemporary poetic practice—the exploitation of the self, the use of personal experience or sensibility as the principal cohering force, the craving for personal admiration and recognition at any cost, the pervasive opportunism that hinders collective consciousness. However, art at its truest disciplines the ego, rather than exploiting or indulging it.

The idea of trying to win an audience entirely with one's own presence strikes me as tacky, if not vulgar; that sort of thing is strictly for stand-up comics or stripteasers.

The most successful poetry reader I know is Allen Ginsberg, but his effectiveness depends upon familiarity— not only with his work and the sound of his voice, but his genuine celebrity—precisely those qualities that make Dick Gregory, Flo Kennedy, and Mick Jagger such effective performers.

Most of my own poetry is visual, which means that it is intended to be seen, rather than heard; visual poetry at its truest cannot be verbally declaimed. Instead of "readings," I do "illuminated demonstrations" in which two carousel projectors with timing devices automatically throw words up on a wall or screen, while I read a nonsynchronous voice-over narration that explains, in a purposefully flat way, the history and purposes of my visual poetry. The talk is designed to give the audience some verbal terms on which to hang their visual perceptions. I usually deliver this talk from behind the projectors, changing the slide trays when their cycles are complete; for I prefer, for both esthetic and moral reasons, that the audience not look at me. (I'm not the Poetry. Nor do I resemble the Poetry.) I also think that a multimedia presentation makes a more powerful and effective "reading" than individual declamation.

Allen Ginsberg

(1977)

By the time he passed fifty (June 3, 1976), Allen Ginsberg had securely entered the pantheon of American literature. He was no longer considered an *enfant terrible*; he was no more a poet whose name could divide a literate audience or a university visitor capable of awakening the protectiveness of trustees. No, by 1976, Ginsberg had received almost all of the nation's literary prizes and had even been solemnly inducted into the National Institute of Arts and Letters—the American version of the French *Académie*. Today, it is generally agreed that he has been the most influential poet of his generation and surely one of the best as well, who has written one indisputable masterpiece, "Kaddish," and at least one poem, "Howl," whose lines resound in the head of every literate American under the age of fifty.

Ginsberg has had unrivaled *influence*, in contrast to "power," which is the result of position and patronage; and the measures of his influence include not only how he contributed to the remarkably sharp change in American poetry, overthrowing the formal verse that was so predominant in the fifties, but also how he changed the appearance of "the poet" in America. Anyone today

82

picking up the initial Hall-Pack-Simpson anthology, *New Poets of England and America* (1957), will be surprised to find kinds of poetry that scarcely exist today, and it is hard for us to remember now that most well-known poets two decades ago appeared clean-shaven. (*Clean-shaven!*) Some of this influence stems from Ginsberg's poetry, to be sure, but no appreciation of his singular achievement should neglect his talents as both a publicist and participant and his indefatigable competence as a poetry performer and a letter writer. Ginsberg made things happen, not only in the professional world immediate to him, but, as his stones fell into water, in increasingly wider circles around the world.

It was Ginsberg, more than anyone else, who made the "poetry reading" a popular cultural fashion all over the land, even though few can explode off the platform as successfully as he. It was Ginsberg, more than anyone else, who made homosexuality something that a celebrity could safely acknowledge in public. It was Ginsberg, more than his "beat" colleagues, who performed the amazing literary-political feat of overturning the negative stereotype—the "Know-Nothing Bohemians," in Norman Podhoretz's phrase—that encased them twenty years ago. And it was Ginsberg, unlike anyone else, who persuaded younger poets to carry notebooks at all times, "accurately recording on the spot whatever was in the mind's eye," as Gordon Ball put it, and later mining those journals for finished poems. Writing itself became for Ginsberg the process of creation—of discovering the unknown, rather than refining what he already knew; for Ginsberg has been a poet not of invention but of expression, not of construction but of communication, constantly revealing his mind through language.

Now that he is securely in the pantheon, a secondary Ginsberg literature is beginning to appear. Most of it is written by others, ranging from friends to junior professors; much of it comes from Ginsberg himself. Grey Fox, a small press in Bolinas, California, issued a volume of his earliest poems, *The Gates of Wrath,* back in 1972, and Full Court, in New York, has more recently issued his earliest songs, *First Blues* (1976). McGraw-Hill published a collection of impressive intellectual improvisations, *Allen Verbatim* (1974) and then John Tytell's first-class critical study of Burroughs-Ginsberg-Kerouac, *Naked Angels* (1976). Creative Arts in Berkeley, California, promises the Ginsberg-Neal Cassady correspondence, in the wake of the latter's widow's memoir of "Jack and Neal," *Heart Beat* (1976); and Penmaen Press in Lincoln, Massachusetts, just released a curious volume, *To Eberhart from Ginsberg,* which consists of a letter that Ginsberg wrote twenty years ago to the poet Richard Eberhart, who was then commissioned by the *New York Times* to "write a piece about what was happening on the West Coast." This book includes Eberhart's report, which seems embarrassingly tentative today, and Ginsberg's interesting preface, guilelessly entitled, "More Explanations Twenty Years Later."

Gordon Ball, a North Carolina graduate student who had previously compiled *Allen Verbatim*, edited this new book, *Journals: Early Fifties and Early Sixties* (1977), from a stack of notebooks accumulated by Grove Press in 1967, and especially since Ginsberg's handwriting is so scratchy, Ball should first of all be commended for his loving labors. (One caveat: I wish he had at least estimated what percentage of the total notebooks is represented here.) What these *Journals* portray is the early progress of the man, from a private, insecure, self-conscious poet, learning from other poets and sampling mind-bending drugs, unsure of how he might economically survive, to a mature full-time professional in command of his personal powers and aware of his growing eminence. The book's final line, written February 11, 1962, is a testament to his self-realization: "I'm on a trip of my own."

In addition to some illuminating gossip (especially about Dylan Thomas, of all poets), *Journals* also contains uncollected poems, which is to say those first drafts that Ginsberg decided *not* to cull into publishable form. Since these are generally neither as intense nor as coherent as his canonized poems, Ginsberg's *Journals* first of all makes us aware not only of the procedures of Ginsberg's poetic imagination but also of his own self-editing functions. (Two poems worth preserving by themselves, in my judgment, are "Subliminal," a very angry poem from 1960, and "Snicker Snoop," a marvelous sound poem coauthored with Jack Kerouac in 1961.)

The Beat Diary (1977), edited by Arthur and Kit Knight, is another kind of secondary Ginsberg literature. A compendious paperback anthology, 8½-by-11 inches, it includes, in addition to selections from Ginsberg's *Journals,* interviews with Gregory Corso, William S. Burroughs, Philip Whalen, and Gary Snyder (who is especially perceptive), as well as new poems and prose by Michael McClure, Carl Solomon, Herbert Huncke, and Lawrence Ferlinghetti, among others. The best parts, however, are, first, the awesomely exuberant 1948-52 correspondence between Jack Kerouac and John Clellon Holmes and then the full-page photographs, nearly all of which are fresh to print. To each his own, I suppose, but my own favorite, almost at the end of the book, shows Ginsberg conversing earnestly with Diana Trilling on the right, while Lionel Trilling, on the left, stares forward apprehensively. *The Beat Diary* is the kind of sloppily produced, nonetheless invaluable book that typically comes not from commercial publishers but the nation's small presses.

The self-portrait remains a partial one, however, for what the *Journals* scarcely reveals is Ginsberg's competence as a literary politician, organizing his colleagues, overthrowing the negative stereotype and advising people of power, either because he would prefer that such activities not be publicly divulged or, more likely, because he thinks them beneath the dignity of his *Journal.* Our sense of this dimension should not be lost, for one theme I get from Ann Charters' fine biography of *Jack Kerouac* (1973) is that Ginsberg survived, unlike Kerouac, because he knew how to conduct a radical literary career in America.

Perhaps *this* dimension of the total picture should be left to yet another contributor to the secondary literature—Ginsberg's future biographer.

John Ashbery

(1976)

> What I like about music is its ability to be convincing, to carry an argument through successfully to the finish, though the terms of the argument remain unknown qualities. . . . I would like to do this in poetry. [John Ashbery, in a statement, 1964]

John Ashbery's poetry is extremely difficult, if not often impenetrable; it does not "work" or "mean" like traditional verse, or even most contemporary poetry. It scarcely resembles Allen Ginsberg's poetry, or Ezra Pound's, or Sylvia Plath's, or Rod McKuen's. The title poem of his most recent collection, *Self-Portrait in a Convex Mirror,* opens with these lines:

> As Parmigianino did it, the right hand
> Bigger than the head, thrust at the viewer
> And swerving easily away, as though to protect
> What it advertises. A few leaded panes, old beams,
> Fur, pleated muslin, a coral ring run together
> In a movement supporting the face, which swims
> Toward and away like the hand
> Except that it is in repose.

Nonetheless, in February, John Ashbery's latest book was selected for the top prize of the newly formed

National Book Critics Circle. In April, it won the National Book Award; in May, the Pulitzer Prize.

These lines, like other Ashbery poems, are subtle, allusive, indefinite, perhaps obscure. Its title clarifies its subject—the experience of looking at oneself in a perspective-distorting convex mirror. The reader would be wise to know that Parmigianino was a sixteenth-century Italian painter whose most famous work portrayed him looking into a convex mirror. In later passages of this poem, the reader finds the quick transitions from subject to subject and from general observation to personal reminiscence that have always characterized Ashbery's work. His style can be most surely defined by what it is *not*; it is not familiar, not declarative, not rhymed, not sentimental, not accessible. The poet himself is similarly modest, fastidious, tentative, vulnerable, witty, gentle, languid, delightful—initially friendly, but ultimately inscrutable. He has hundreds of friends, but only a few remember having had extended conversations with him.

Not unlike other poets of his age and stature, Ashbery works as a teacher, a professor of English at Brooklyn College, where he conducts an introduction to poetry, an undergraduate writing seminar, and a graduate writing workshop, in addition to supervising several individual tutorials. He is assuredly the most distinguished writer in his department. His graduate class is held not in the formal classroom to which it had been assigned (which everyone dismissed as "dreary") but in an isolated windowless lounge with low brown couches and a noisy ventilator. Six feet tall, slender in build, Ashbery has smartly barbered, graying brown hair, soft blue eyes, an incipiently ruddy complexion, and a luxurious, dark gray, half-moon mustache around the top of his mouth. His handsome face is capped by a long, beakish nose. Except for his new glasses, he has looked roughly the same over the dozen years I have known him. His talk reveals a flat, nasal, western New York accent, and his easy, infectious laughter, wide spaces between his front teeth. One afternoon this spring, when we met at Brooklyn College, he wore a dark blue tennis shirt, light blue jeans, black hightop shoes and a denim jacket.

Having scrutinized the poems that his class had given him the previous session, he had photocopied those he wanted to discuss and passed duplicates around the class. Once a student-author finished reading his poem aloud, the class began to dissect it in a line-by-line evaluation. "I try not to speak first when we discuss the poems," Ashbery whispers to me. He puts his horn-rimmed glasses on to read and takes them off to talk. His own remarks, when his turn comes, tend to be generous in general, but critical about specifics. He speaks in short, simple sentences, an occasional French phrase being his sole affectation. His class assignments, which are mostly exercises with unusual materials (i.e., translate a poem from an unfamiliar language), function largely to stimulate the students to do something different from what they have written before. "They can express themselves better," Ashbery thinks, "when they've gotten their minds off their subject. When I give them an exercise, it is a way of getting toward unconscious areas which they might not use." When not smoking his European cigarettes (Gitanes), he frequently runs his fingers through his hair or scratches the back of his head.

His own comments reveal an unusual sensitivity to nuance and "sound." After a student challenges Ashbery's critique, he defers, "I'm not saying that I'm not obtuse." When another student suggests that the poem at hand "sounds like you, John," the poet-teacher replies, typically again, "I don't enjoy reading poets who sound like me." What the class seems to teach is hypersensitive reading—becoming attuned to the delicacies that distinguish one poet's work from another and superior poetry from mundane; and perhaps the principal reason why students take Ashbery's courses is that this kind of experience—this kind of professional prerequisite—is not readily available elsewhere. After class, we adjourned to dinner at his favorite West Village restaurant, Duff's on Christopher Street.

On the subway back to Manhattan, I learned that, not unlike other prominent poets, Ashbery travels to college campuses a good deal. This past spring, he gave poetry readings at Chicago, Texas (Austin), Barnard, Williams, Amherst, Yale, and Wellesley. Later, back home in my library, I found that works of his are included in nearly every comprehensive anthology of modern American poetry and his name appears in all the contemporary literary histories. By now, even those anthologists and historians unable to comprehend his difficult poetry feel obliged to acknowledge it. (Some however, misspell his surname as "Ashberry.") In the past fifteen years, Ashbery has won two handfuls of stipends—two Guggenheims, two Ingram Merrills, two awards from the National Endowment for the Arts, one from the National Institute of Arts and Letters, two from the Poets Foundation, and the Harriet Monroe Award ($1,000) from the University of Chicago. His works may still be misunderstood, but their author is no longer neglected.

Born in 1927, on July 28 (which is also the birthday of another inscrutable modernist, Marcel Duchamp), John Lawrence Ashbery grew up an only child in Sodus, New York, where his parents had a fruit farm. Thirty miles east of Rochester, a mile south of Lake Ontario, this family farm grew apples, cherries, peaches, and plums. Ashbery spent every summer until he passed twenty either picking cherries or working in the nearby cannery (as a way of avoiding outdoor labor). His mother taught high school biology prior to her marriage. Her father, Henry Lawrence (1864-1954), was then the chairman of the physics department at the University of Rochester. Ashbery remembers that as a child, "I used to spend almost every weekend with him. He was the scholarly member of the family. He had a lot of books I liked to pore over—complete sets of Victorian novelists and poets. I was very fond of him. It's said that I look like him now, and that as a teenager I looked as he looked at the same age."

Initially more interested in visual art than in writing, young John studied painting once a week at the museum school in Rochester. He won a local Quiz-Kid contest in 1941 and appeared on the national radio program. Realizing the educational limitations of his rural high school, his parents sent him to a prep school, the Deerfield Academy, for his junior and senior years, under "a scholarship" anonymously provided by a Sodus neighbor. For college, he chose Harvard. "Having had a lonely and isolated childhood," he told me over dinner, "I've always been drawn to metropolises. Boston was the first."

As a freshman, he took a creative writing course with Theodore Spencer; among his classmates was the incipient novelist John Hawkes. "I remember Spencer once read one of my poems in class and singled it out for praise. It was very thrilling to hear that from a known poet." In his junior year, Ashbery "tried out" for the staff of *The Advocate,* the undergraduate literary magazine. The senior staffer principally supporting Ashbery's candidacy was a slightly older undergraduate named Kenneth Koch, who subsequently became a good friend and, later, a prominent poet. Ashbery majored in English literature and did his honors thesis on W. H. Auden, graduating in 1949.

Koch, who took his A.B. the year before, persuaded Ashbery to move to New York, where he spent his initial postgraduate summer as a reference librarian in the literature section of the Brooklyn Public Library. Though he "loved the heat" of a pre-air-conditioned summer, he spent most of his working day reading, which was not part of the job specification. Retiring from this by the end of summer, he entered Columbia University's graduate school in the fall, thanks to money from home, concentrating on modern literature, eventually doing his M.A. thesis on the British novelist Henry Green. (His alternative choice was another novelist of acidulous sensibility, Ivy Compton-Burnett.)

Ashbery befriended Frank O'Hara, then an aspiring poet, whom he had initially met during his final month at Harvard. Having taken an M.A. at Michigan, O'Hara moved to Manhattan in 1951. "Frank got me interested in contemporary music," Ashbery remembers. "This was before much of this music had been recorded. He used to play it to me on the piano. He was also reading Beckett and Jean Rhys and Flann O'Brien before anybody heard of them. We were all young and ambitious then. American painting seemed the most exciting art around. American poetry was very traditional at that time, and there was no modern poetry in the sense that there was modern painting. So one got one's inspiration and ideas from watching the experiments of others. Much of my feeling for Rothko and Pollock came through Frank. I really didn't get it until he started talking about it." Whereas most Ivy-educated poets of this postwar generation stayed in the academy, Ashbery opted for downtown Manhattan and a different kind of postgraduate education.

We adjourned to his Chelsea apartment. Clearly the residence of a cultivated man, it had antique furniture, fine rugs, Chinese porcelain, exquisite Persian lamps, plants, flowers, shelves of books, hundreds of records, and a glass table filled with fresh literary magazines, in addition to prints and paintings by his friends Larry Rivers, Jane Freilicher, Jean Helion, R. B. Kitaj, Joe Brainard, Anne Dunn, and Willem de Kooning. Ashbery poured himself a scotch and settled into his favorite couch, resuming the narrative. "In the early fifties, I went through a period of intense depression and doubt. I couldn't write for a couple of years. I don't know why. It did coincide with the beginnings of the Korean War, the Rosenbergs case, and McCarthyism. Though I was not an intensely political person, it was impossible to be happy in that kind of climate. It was a nadir.

"I was jolted out of this by going with Frank O'Hara— I think it was New Year's Day, 1952—to a concert by David Tudor of John Cage's *Music of Changes.* Have you ever heard that piece? It hasn't been recorded. It was a series of dissonant chords, mostly loud, with irregular rhythm. It went on for over an hour and seemed infinitely extendable. The feeling was an open determinism—that what happens was meant to happen, no matter how random or rough or patchy it seemed to be. I felt profoundly refreshed after listening to that. I started to write again shortly afterwards. I felt that I could be as singular in my art as Cage was in his." From nine to five, Ashbery was working as a copywriter in the publicity department at Oxford University Press, preparing publicity releases and dust jacket descriptions about new books. Only on Saturday and Sunday did he do his serious writing. "I'm still a weekend poet. It would be pointless to write poetry every day."

His poems had been appearing in little magazines since the late forties; in 1952 he shared the YMHA "Discovery" prize (along with the poets Harvey Shapiro, now the editor of the *Times Book Review,* and Gray Burr); and John Bernard Myers, then the director of the Tibor de Nagy Gallery, published a chapbook, *Turandot and Other Poems* (1953), in a small edition that now sells for as much as $350 per rare copy. Ashbery submitted a larger book length manuscript to the Yale Younger Poets competition in 1955, but it was rejected by the preliminary scanner. W. H. Auden, the sole judge at the time, had decided that none of the manuscripts sub-mitted that year were worthy of the prize. However, having heard of an Ashbery manuscript that had not come to his attention, Auden asked to consider it and then selected it for publication. *Some Trees* appeared in 1956; the reviews were mostly negative and uncompre-hending. Recognition would not come quickly.

Ashbery's poetry at that time was rather exquisite in surface technique, baffling in statement, indefinite in perspective, and disconnected as a reading experience. His titles tended, then as later, to be more declarative than his texts. One poem from this period, "The Picture of Little J. A. in a Prospect of Flowers," had a second section that opens, not untypically for his poetry at that time:

> So far is goodness a mere memory
> Or naming of recent scenes of badness
> That even these lives, children,
> You may pass through to be blessed,
> So fair does each invent his virtue.

The major influences on these early poems were, as Ashbery acknowledges, W. H. Auden (for "making ab-stract things concrete"), Wallace Stevens ("my favorite poet"), Marianne Moore ("her inventions"), William Carlos Williams ("open form and mundane speech"), and Elizabeth Bishop ("seamless language"). "I don't think of my poetry as coming from nowhere. It extends certain traditions."

In 1954, Ashbery, restless in New York, applied for a Fulbright grant to France (where Koch had gone a few years before). Initially rejected, he was belatedly accepted the following summer, after a previous winner had declined to go. He proposed to translate contemporary French poetry. Assigned at first to the University of Montpelier, he felt "lonely and deprived of American talk. It was my first trip to France. I couldn't yet speak French and therefore didn't hear people on the street say things that would move me." By the second semester, he had transferred to the third great metropolis of his life, Paris, where he lived for the next decade.

He returned to New York for 1957-58, teaching elementary French at New York University in the Bronx and taking doctoral courses at the New York University downtown campus. He began to contribute reportage and reviews to *Art News.* Planning to do his doctoral thesis on the French writer Raymond Roussel, Ashbery persuaded his parents to finance his return to Paris. Roussel (1877-1933) was an extreme eccentric, the self-indulgent son of a wealthy stockbroker, whose novels, poems, and plays were dismissed by his contemporaries as wayward curiosities. "I could tell by looking," Ashbery remembers, "that his works were truly bizarre, and I had to find out what this was about. What was valuable, I learned, was that these works seemed totally autonomous. A book like *Nouvelles Impressions d'Afrique* was there, an object without references to anything outside itself. It was completely self-contained as a work of art. Roussel claimed he used nothing real; everything came from his imagination. I'd never seen anything like this before. There are really no antecedents for Roussel." Ashbery is often credited with single-handedly reviving Roussel's reputation in France—a not inconsiderable feat for a farm boy from upper New York state.

"Was Roussel a major influence on your work?" I asked. "No, except in the sense that one wants to be as unique in one's own way as he was in his." It is nonetheless likely that Ashbery's preference for secret subjects and secret systems reflects Roussel.

Depressed by the poor responses to *Some Trees,* Ashbery feared he would never again have a book of his poems published—that the remainder of his professional life would consist entirely of uncollected contributions to miscellaneous magazines. "I also felt I had come to the end of something with that book," he declared between puffs on his cigarette. "It was time to shuffle the cards." The new source of inspiration was yet another piece of contemporary music, Luciano Berio's *Omaggio à Joyce* (1959). "It got me into a fragmentary kind of poetry." I also got the idea from Anton Webern to isolate a particular word, as you would isolate a particular note, to feel it in a new way. It was partly this penchant for making discoveries different from other writers—and for choosing avant-garde musical influences—that made Ashbery's poetry so singular.

One result of this willful change was "Europe" (1960), which I consider one of the great long poems of recent years—a classic of coherent diffuseness. "I remember writing it in a state of confusion about what I wanted to do. I would sit down and cover pages without really knowing what I had written. I'd get American magazines like *Esquire,* open the pages, and get a phrase from it, and then start writing on my own. When I ran out, I'd go back to the magazine. It was pure experimentation. I didn't really consider these to be poems." Several passages in "Europe" were taken intact from a British children's book, *Beryl of the Biplane* by William Le Queux, which Ashbery found in a bookstall on a Parisian quay. As T. S. Eliot put it, in another context, "Immature poets imitate; mature poets steal; bad poets deface what they take and good poets make it into something better, or at least something different."

The fifty-second stanza of "Europe" reads in its entirety:

> The rose
> dirt
> dirt you
> pay
> The buildings
> is tree
> Undecided
> protest
> This planet

To me, this poetry is diffuse and disconnected, to be sure; yet precisely in its refusal to use the traditional crutches of poetic coherence, "Europe" can be characterized as *acoherent,* much as certain early twentieth century music is called *atonal.* Not unlike comparably original composers, Ashbery creates original work that seems totally unfathomable on first impression, but becomes more familiar with continued contact. Reading it closely, on its own terms, is the best preparation for understanding it better; what it implicitly teaches is the greater appreciation of itself.

"I didn't want to write the poetry that was coming naturally to me then," he explained, typically speaking in negatives, "and I succeeded in writing something that wasn't the poetry I didn't want to write, and yet was not the poetry I wanted to write. For me, this was a period of examining my ideas about poetry—sort of tear-

ing it apart with the idea that I would put it back together. I didn't know what I wanted to do, but I did
know what I didn't want to do." This more experimental
poetry, representing a second distinct phase in Ashbery's
stylistic development, flowed into his second collection,
The Tennis Court Oath, which the Wesleyan University
Press, to Ashbery's surprise, published in 1962. The reviews were no better than before, John Simon quipping
in *Hudson Review,* "Mr. Ashbery has perfected his verse
to the point where it never deviates into—nothing so
square as sense!—sensibility, sensuality, or sentences."

While in Paris, Ashbery had further trouble balanc-
ing his accounts. Some money came from the family
farm he declined to "take over," but it was scarcely
sufficient. He translated two French detective novels
into English, under the witty pseudonym "Jonas Berry,"
adding sex scenes that French censorship forbade and
the American market required. Under his own name, he
put into English Jean-Jacques Mayoux's critical essay on
Melville (1960). In June, 1960, he became the regular
art critic for the Paris edition of the New York *Herald-
Tribune,* writing semi-weekly articles on "whatever was
in the galleries or museums." Initially receiving $15 per
piece, he eventually got $30 each. His readers were pri-
marily American tourists. He coedited a little magazine,
Locus Solus (1960-62), financed by his friend Harry
Mathews, the American novelist. In 1964, he cofounded a
more elaborate, sumptuously produced quarterly, called
plainly *Art and Literature* that, unlike *Locus Solus,* paid
not only Ashbery but its contributors as well. In my
opinion, *Art and Literature* (1964-68) was one of the
best literary magazines of its time with a particularly
good record for discovering younger authors. (My 1967
anthology of *Young American Writers* took twice as
many contributions from it than any other magazine.)

When I first met Ashbery, a few days after Easter, 1965, he was a prominent figure on the expatriate literary scene.

Later that year, Chester Ashbery suddenly died, and John, as the sole son, felt obliged to return home. "There was also a sense that ten was a good round number of years to be away." An unknown poet a decade before, he returned a conquering hero, sort of. During Ashbery's absence, he was still a presence in New York. The art dealer Jill Kornblee remembers, "Everybody talked about him as though he were in the room." His reading at the Living Theater, in the summer of 1963, drew a packed house. Kenneth Koch, by then a professor of English at Columbia College, had introduced Ashbery's work to his students, many of whom became appreciative acolytes. One of them, Jonathan Cott, wrote the first extended critical consideration of Ashbery's poetry for an anthology that I edited, *The New American Arts* (1965), in which Cott identified Ashbery as "today's most radically original American poet." (Another sometime Koch student, the poet David Shapiro, finished the first doctoral essay on Ashbery for Columbia University in 1973.) His American eminence grew in his absence (and perhaps because of it), as Ashbery's work became a controversial issue—a litmus test that, a decade or so ago, seemed to separate advanced tastes from retrograde.

"I had a certain reputation as a poet which I didn't have when I left," he told me over dinner at another Italian restaurant the following day. "Poetry itself had become a more flourishing art, thanks largely to Ginsberg and Corso. Readings for younger poets were nonexistent before I left. They were the sort of thing only Robert Frost did. I returned to find them an institution." Later that evening, Ashbery confided in passing, "I really don't like hearing people read their poetry. It's easy to be distracted. You hear three lines and think, did I leave the oven on? And you've missed something important. You get a weird experience of the poem as interrupted by—and interrupting—your own stream of consciousness. The music of meaning comes through only when you see it." That is also true of Ashbery's own poetry; his own unmodulated, rather rigid and unenhancing declamation mutes the music that becomes apparent when you read his lines silently to yourself.

Once settled in New York again, Ashbery took a job as executive editor of *Art News,* where he worked a five-day week for the next seven years, commissioning articles, editing copy, selecting illustrations on a four-person staff. His specialty became the quick preparation of feature articles that commissioned free-lancers failed to deliver. Drawing upon his journalistic experience, Ashbery remains capable of producing coherent first drafts. "I'm a terrific typist," he boasts with a smile. "I can't use an electric. I enjoy typing on broken-down, reconditioned, antique office-model manuals." In addition to reviewing art, he has written about modern poetry and French literature, as well as, once apiece, on music and film.

"I don't think of myself as a critic," he confessed over coffee. "I have pretty good taste, which is eclectic. I like things that are good of their kind, but I have no critical theory." He paused to puff. "Actually, I'm not interested in writing criticism. There is an idea in America that if you don't know how to do something, people will think you do it rather well. If I hadn't displayed a genuine reluctance to write art criticism, people wouldn't have asked me to do it." Nowadays, most of his appreciative prose appears as introductions to exhibition catalogues. One reason why his criticism is not as consequential as his poetry is that it tends to avoid divisory issues, rather than engaging them, but that avoidance is also one reason why his art reportage has also been more acceptable to magazine editors. For Ashbery, not unlike other versatile writers, easy writing earns money; more difficult writing, respect.

His next major book, *Rivers and Mountains* (1966), represents a step away from the disjunctive work of *The Tennis Court Oath.* In "Clepsydra," one of his last Parisian pieces, he remembers "feeling for the first time a strong unity in a particular poem. After my analytic period, I wanted to get into a synthetic period. I wanted to write a new kind of poetry after my dismembering of language. Wouldn't it be nice, I said to myself, to do a long poem that would be a long extended argument, but would have the beauty of a single word. 'Clepsydra' is really a meditation on how time feels as it is passing. The title means a water clock as used in ancient Greece and China. There are a lot of images of water in that poem. It's all of a piece, like a stream." *Rivers and Mountains* also represents a turning point in critical acceptance. The reviews in *Poetry* and the *Times Book Review,* for two indices, were both more favorable than not.

For the longest poem in this book, "The Skaters," Ashbery wanted to do a poem in which he would, as he told me, "put everything in, rather than, as in 'Europe,' leaving things out." Reaching for his own copy, he read me a typically Ashberian passage in his characteristic unemphatic manner. Here, he said, "the poem talks about itself":

This, thus is a portion of the subject of this poem
Which is in the form of falling snow:
That is, the individual flakes are not essential to the
    importance of the whole's becoming so much of a truism
That their importance is again called in question, to be
    denied further out, and again and again like this.
Hence, neither the importance of the individual flake,

> Nor the importance of the whole impression of the storm,
>   if it has any, is what it is,
> But the rhythm of the series of repeated jumps, from
>   abstract into positive and back to a slightly less
>   diluted abstract.

His "source" this time was another children's book, *Three Hundred Things A Bright Boy Can Do* (1911, England), which Ashbery also found in a Parisian quay bookstall. "It reminded me of *The Book of Knowledge,* which I read as a child. Do you want to see it? I have it here." He went back into his bedroom to fetch a copy, which looked interesting, though it did not instantly tell me much about the poem. Here, as elsewhere, Ashbery freely acknowledges the sources of his poems, and even their titles, are frequently borrowed from other authors, such as "Civilization and Its Discontents" (from Freud) and "The Task" (from William Cowper), or even works of visual arts. As he explains, "The title is a takeoff point, a way of getting into a poem. It may not be the subject, but it is an aperture." The more one talks with Ashbery, the clearer it becomes that the principal inspirations for his poems are other books and then works of music or, occasionally, of visual art.

The next transformation of his creative career was a book modestly entitled *Three Poems* (1972), which took the radical, provocative step of being written entirely in prose. "I returned to something like 'Clepsydra' that would be extremely long and involved, and yet would be as one strand. I used prose because I'm constantly trying to think of things I haven't done yet, and prose poetry until that point, as in Baudelaire or Rimbaud, always seemed slightly askew and not quite right. It sort of sounds self-conscious and 'poetic,' which is a quality I dislike in prose. I was wondering: What about writing prose poetry in which the ugliness of prose would be exploited and put to the uses of poetry? And that was hard to do, of course, like everything.

"There is a great deal of prose in *Three Poems* that is pompous, awkward, self-consciously poetic, like the prose poetry I was trying to get away from. I wanted to use those things which were unpoetic materials in something I could consider a poem, and I feel I succeeded there." Among its sources he acknowledges W. H. Auden's "The Sea and the Mirror" and Giorgio de Chirico's novel, *Hebdomeros* (1929), which he partially translated; in the latter, as he puts it, "The protagonist meets people who are much vaguer than he is."

"I have considerable difficulty reading *Three Poems*," I ventured. "Though I understand that these are meditations, rather than arguments, I find these poems even more impenetrable than your other poetry. Didn't one of your closest critics, Harold Bloom of Yale, say of one prose piece, 'It was difficult to see how Ashbery got from point to point, or even determine if there were points'?"

"Okay, you're not alone," the poet replied. "The majority of those who read them seem to feel, as far as I can see, as you do. I'm interested in communicating, but I feel that saying something the reader has already known is not communicating anything. It's a veiled insult to the reader." He took a draw from his Gitanes. "*Three Poems* are my personal favorites." Why? "They're my most extended and elaborated statement in a form I think rather unusual, and there are passages in them that I like very much." His poetry since *Three Poems* has been prosier ˎthan his earlier works and for this reason, in my opinion, too imitable and, thus, less unique.

When *Art News* acquired new owners in 1972, Ashbery found himself precipitously unemployed. Though his poetry books sold well enough to remain in print, none earned him more than $300 per year in royalties. Receipts from anthology permissions helped, as did poetry readings; however, these sources of income were not sufficient. "If one is a famous poet," he jokes, "one still isn't famous." A reading at Brooklyn College produced a job offer which Ashbery accepted for 1974. For the first time in his entire life, he is professionally involved with poetry, rather than editing or art criticism. Just short of his fiftieth year, he has finally "made it" in America.

Just as his poetry falls into several phases, so his influence upon younger poets has taken various forms. Poets associated with the so-called New York school tend to emulate the fragmentary opacity of the early Ashbery, while younger academic poets prefer the oblique discursiveness of his more recent work. (Echoes of this Ashbery resound through Daniel Halpern's recent *American Literary Anthology* [1975].) By contrast, "Europe" has provided a stimulus to further experiments in the tearing apart of syntactical language, such as Clark Coolidge's poems, which are even more fragmented, even more difficult, than Ashbery's. "He's sort of an exemplary person," in Ashbery's estimation, "but I wouldn't want to do it."

Ashbery's life has been busy these past few years. In addition to teaching, he has been touring, as noted before, and spending several weeks each year with his mother. He corrected a book of French translations of his poems, which appeared in Paris in 1975 to favorable reviews. He produced a text, mostly prose, for a book length collaboration with Joe Brainard, entitled *Vermont Notebook* (1975). He helped his friend David K. Kermani compile *John Ashbery: A Comprehensive Bibliography* (1976), an awesomely elaborate and detailed 244-page record. "I am amazed and a little appalled by the voluminousness of this bibliography," the poet wrote in the foreword. "Have I really been that prolific?" He also works with Kermani in collating his unpublished poetry, which is approximately five times the amount of his published work. "It's not going to be published, if I have anything to say about it. I burned all my high school poetry a few years ago." Is he sure he has retained all the good ones? "Yes."

His present principal project is completing a new collection of poems, whose title is yet unchosen, selections from which have appeared prominently in English and American magazines. Ashbery is also drafting a play about which he says only, "it will be very, very long, unlike my previous plays, none of which I want to have performed or reprinted. This new play will be totally unstructured and free-associating." Another project is translating the complete writings of the Belgian surrealist painter René Magritte. Finally, he is collaborating with the composer Elliott Carter on a musical work for voice and orchestra.

What is in this new collection? "We spoke before of my search for problems that I haven't attacked before. It occurred to me that one of these problems might be writing the quite short poem. *There* is something to try and do. Lately I've written a number of quite short poems. There is no intrinsic value in doing one thing or the other, but in doing the recalcitrant thing. That is my present form of experimenting." Ever inquisitive, he once wrote poems initially in French. "I wanted to see if my voice would sound any different. I concluded that it didn't." He also collaborated with the poet James Schuyler in producing a charming novel, each of them writing sections in alternation. *A Nest of Ninnies* (1969) is, as Ashbery quotes Schuyler, "the sort of novel that neither of us could have, or would have, written alone."

Pausing to light another cigarette, Ashbery began to speak about poetry in general: "I have a feeling that in my mind is an underground stream, if you will, that I can have access to when I want it. I want the poetry to come out as freshly and unplanned as possible, but I don't want it to be stream of consciousness. I'm bored by the automatic writing of orthodox surrealism. There is more to one's mind than the unconscious. I have arranged things so that, as this stream is coming out, I make a number of rapid editorial changes. My poetry has an exploratory quality. I don't have it mapped out before I sit down to write.

"What moves me is the irregular form—'the flawed words and stubborn sounds,' as Stevens said—that affect us whenever we try to say something that is important to us—more than the meaning of what we are saying at a particular moment." "Do you mean 'subliminal?' " I suggested. "It's not just subliminal. One is saying something that one intends to be understood. That is always very difficult. I was communicating imperfectly, but still communicating. The inaccuracies and anomalies of common speech are particularly poignant to me. This essence of communication is what interests me in poetry.

"I think I learned about art from music. What I like about music is the persuasion that takes place, though one is not aware of it. At the end of a Bruckner symphony one may rise to one's feet to applaud. One receives a message without knowing one has been told." He extinguished his cigarette. "Talking about this is painful to me, because I'm not used to formulating what the poetry is about. The poetry talks about itself. That is mainly what it does. To talk about it further is unnecessary and, for me, an ungenial gymnastic. It's rather hard to be a good artist and also be able to explain intelligently what your art is about."

In one of his few published statements of intention, prepared for the encyclopedia *Contemporary Poets* (1975), he wrote, "There are no themes or subjects in the usual sense, except the very broad one of an individual consciousness confronting or confronted by a world of external phenomena. The work is a very complex but, I hope, clear and concrete transcript of the impressions left by these phenomena on that consciousness. The outlook is Romantic. . . . Characteristic devices are ellipses, frequent changes of tone, voice (that is, the narrator's voice), point of view, to give an impression of flux." That is a sometime critic's most succinct and fairly accurate descriptive summary of a difficult poet's work.

Ashbery wants his poetry to remain mysterious—to suggest experiences without defining them, to be definitely indefinite; and "mystery" in turn is a key word in his own critical appreciation of art. He vividly remembers how his friend Jane Freilicher introduced him to Léger's painting. "It looked clear, open and straightforward, but you discovered its mystery afterwards." In the Kermani bibliography is the confession that the various sections of "The Skaters" originally had subtitles which were removed prior to publication. "Then I found that the poem was a lot more mysterious." He also speaks of seeing, in Paris, silent films that lacked subtitles. "You would know only somewhat what was happening. In a way, it was more beautiful. Something was being communicated, but you didn't know what it was." I think it Ashbery's most profound heresy to believe that a poem *should* remain mostly inscrutable, no matter how long or closely anyone studies it.

I asked what he thinks when readers tell him, as they often do, that they were unable to "understand" his poetry? "At first I was puzzled and hurt. I try to communicate—make clear, interpret—things which seem mysterious. And what doesn't? Just look at what's going on around you at this moment. The difficulty of my poetry isn't there for its own sake; it is meant to reflect the 'difficulty' of living, the ever-changing minute adjustments that go on around us and which we respond to from moment to moment—the difficulty of living in passing time, which is both difficult and automatic, since we all somehow manage it.

"When I realized that this incomprehension was going to be the reaction to my poetry, I stopped worrying. Cocteau said you should take negative criticism and develop that side of you. After my initial disappointment at the lack of comprehension, I thought I'd better make the best of a bad situation of someone who was destined never to have an audience." He reflected. "I got one, though, *faute de mieux*—for lack of anything better." This audience consists primarily of people professionally involved with poetry, whether as writers or teachers, and then of poetry readers—the numbers of both groups are increasing; for this is poetry especially for readers passionately appreciative of qualities and experiences particular to poetry.

Some reviewers have praised the title poem of *Self-Portrait* as more accessible than his earlier works. Typically, Ashbery insists that it really isn't. "What makes it seem more accessible is an essayistic thrust, but if one sat down and analyzed it closely, it would seem as disjunct and fragmented as 'Europe.' It's really not about the Parmagianino painting, which is a pretext for a lot of reflections and asides which are as tenuously connected to the core as they are in many of my poems which, as you know, tend to spread out from a core idea." American book reviewers apparently prefer *Self-Portrait* to his other books. Jonathan Cott's favorite Ashbery poem is "A Blessing in Disguise" in *Rivers and Mountains.* David Kermani's is "Scheherazade" in *Self-*

Portrait; David Shapiro's, "The Skaters"; John Bernard Myers's, "Clepsydra." Ashbery himself prefers *Three Poems*: I vote for "Europe." In other words, the arguments over Ashbery's poems—and among his several phases—have scarcely come to an end.

Contrary to Ashbery, I find the recurring subjects in his work include a nostalgia for a rural childhood and a sense of time passing, but all of his poems are ultimately about two things: the thoughts in his mind at the moment of composition—a mental self-portraiture—and then the processes of making poems. (Thus, one theme of his total work—and his continuing career—is, quite literally, the possibilities of contemporary English-language poetry.) The dimensions of Ashbery's artistic intelligence include an extraordinary feeling for language tone and rhythm, a powerful memory for his experience of art, an imagination that is more auditory than visual, an apparently limitless capacity for astonishingly fresh verbal combinations, and then an experimental sense of the importance of changing constraints (or self-imposed rules) as an antithesis to one's creative stream.

The real key to Ashbery's genius lies, in my opinion, in the "sound" of his poetry; it is also the quality most likely to elude the hasty reader of his works. His poetry initially communicates as music communicates, at levels that defy conceptual definition. Jonathan Cott told me recently of Ashbery's "unique prosody. There is something about the rhythmic stresses, which cut against the grain of the conversational tone and yet complement it. The lines start moving in a certain direction, and then get pulled back up again. There is a breathing quality." Pressed for an example, Cott read me these lines from "Spring Day":

> The immense hope and forbearance
> Trailing out of night, to sidewalks of the day

Like air breathed into a paper city, exhaled
As night returns bringing doubts

That swarm around the sleeper's head
But are fended off with clubs and knives, so that morning
Installs again in cold hope
The air that was yesterday, is what you are,

Ashbery's poetry demands not only reading with the
highest concentration but persistent rereading; the mas-
tering of it becomes an epitome of poetic experience.

II

The New Poetries

Some arts move in time, like music; others are presented in space, like painting. In both cases the organizing principle is recurrence, which is called rhythm when it is temporal and pattern when it is spatial. . . . Literature seems to be intermediate between music and painting: its words form rhythms which approach a musical sequence of sounds at one of its boundaries, and form patterns which approach the hieroglyphic or pictorial image at the other. The attempts to get as near to these boundaries as possible form the main body of what is called experimental writing. [Northrop Frye, "The Archetypes of Literature," 1951]

Poets are not simply men devoted to the beautiful. They are also and especially devoted to truth, insofar as the unknown can be penetrated, so much that the unexpected, the surprising, is one of the principal sources of poetry today. And who would dare say that, for those who are worthy of joy, what is new is not beautiful? [Guillaume Apollinaire, "The New Spirit and the Poets," 1917]

Instead of *pure poetry* it would perhaps be better to say *absolute poetry,* and it should then be understood in the sense of a search for the effects resulting from the relations between words, or rather the relations of the overtones of words among themselves, which suggests, in short, *an exploration of that whole domain of sensibility which is governed by language.* . . . If the poet could manage to construct works in which nothing of prose ever appeared, poems in which the musical continuity was never broken, in which the relations between meanings were themselves perpetually similar to harmonic relations, in which the transmutation of thoughts into each other appeared more important than any thought, in which the play of figures contained the reality of the subject—then one could speak of *pure poetry* as something that existed. [Paul Valery, "Pure Poetry," 1928]

Imaged Words & Worded Images

(1970)

> Conductors of an enormous orchestra, [modern poets] will have at their disposal the whole world, its sounds and appearances, the thought and the human languages, song, dance, all the arts and all the artifices to compose the book seen and understood by the future. [Guillaume Apollinaire, "The New Spirit and the Poets," 1917]

> The artist sees and feels not only shapes but words as well. We see words everywhere in modern life; we're bombarded by them. But physically words are also shapes. You don't want banal boring words any more than you want banal boring shapes or a banal boring life. [Stuart Davis, as quoted by Katherine Kuh, *The Artist's Voice*, 1960]

A new art necessarily demands a new name, and the art of incorporating word within image has recently inspired a spate of new names: "calligrams," "concrete poetry," "ideograms," "pattern poems," "visual poetry." These epithets all intend to identify artifacts that are neither word nor image alone but somewhere or something between. Since each of the terms in actual usage defines a particular strain of word-image art, there is a need for a more general yet discriminating term. My choice is "word-imagery," which encompasses the two major genres of the form—imaged words and worded images. The distinction depends upon whether word or image is the base. In imaged words, a significant word or phrase is endowed with a visual form, so that language is enhanced through *pictorial* means. In worded images, by contrast, language fills an image, embellishing the shape through *linguistic* means so that a picture of, say, an ice-cream cone filled with words offers an experience considerably different from that of a cone without words. The difference is the difference between visually laying out a poetic nugget (imaged words) and making pictures with words and letters (worded image).

Though our awareness of word-imagery as a distinct art is rather recent, the practice of mixing word with image is very ancient, perhaps older than that of words separate from images. Its postmedieval ancestors include the classic shape-poems by early seventeenth-century English writers, among them George Herbert, whose "Easter Wings" suggests not only birds in flight but the vessels used for the wine of the mass. Subsequent examples of this strain of worded images—where lines of type fill up the image—include the highly representational mouse's tail in the original edition of *Alice in Wonderland* and Dylan Thomas's diamonds and wings in "Vision and Prayer." Guillaume Apollinaire's "Calligrams," as he called them, take a more radical step by eschewing both the custom of solidly filling a form with words and the conventional linear syntax of all earlier poetry; the words in "Coeur et Miroir" *outline* respectively the forms of a heart and a mirror and pursue a syntactically endless circle, while the lines of words in "Le Jet d'Eau" represent a spray of spouting water.

Most of the early word-image artists were poets, but the modernist tradition also includes painters—Raoul Hausmann and Kurt Schwitters, Stuart Davis and Carlo

Carrà—who incorporated words-to-be-read into their paintings and collages. Precursors of recent word-imagery also include the poet-publicist Filippo Marinetti, who not only mixed various faces and sizes of type in *Paroles en Liberté* but also fractured the horizontally linear grids that, then as now, were favored by most poets. Both these traditions, along with current word-imagery, conceptually differ from "illuminated" texts—early Bibles, William Blake, Ben Shahn, et al., and the more contemporary illuminated forms, posters and comic books—where words are physically separate from image. Word-imagery, to introduce another distinction, does not include the purest examples of "concrete poetry," which contain discernible words but in linguistic signs abstractly displayed.

In most imaged words, there are usually only a few words, as well as no image other than that made by those words, because in the word is the beginning of this art— Gay Beste's *Cross* and *Obsess*, Mary Ellen Solt's *Lilacs*, Ian Hamilton Finlay's *Acrobats*, my own *Echo* and *Degenerate*, and Robert Lax's *Quiet/Silence*. As these examples suggest, a word can be pictorially enhanced as effectively by enlargement or repetition as by representational shape; and certain forms are so effective that the layout bestows an autonomous life upon the word, if not actually granting the word-image profoundly iconographic powers—Indiana's much-imitated *Love,* for instance, or the insignia for Coca-Cola. In this respect, the art is concerned with nonsyntactical properties peculiar to words. But what all successful word-images have in common is the sense that without a visual dimension the words convey a completely different, if not esthetically negligible, experience.

In worded images, by contrast, the shape becomes a frame into which words are poured; so that the art's meaning usually depends first of all upon the familiarity and suggestiveness of the shape. Among the best examples of pictures-made-by-words are the labeled wine bottles that Robert P. Brown designed entirely with uniform type laid in horizontal lines, Robert Hollander's soda container, Edwin Morgan's *Pomander,* Ferdinand Kriwet's concentric circles with overlapping words (in both German and English), and Jonathan Price's *Ice Cream Poem* which, in addition to outlining the shape and even the drip of the original, realizes a nonlinear syntax. John Cage and Calvin Sumsion's *Not Wanting To Say Anything About Marcel* favors a more diffuse visual space (to accord with Cage's esthetic predilections), in addition to an aleatory or "chance" bias that makes the preselected individual words less than decipherable. Perhaps the single most spectacular example in the worded-image strain is John Furnival's *Tours de Babel Changées en Ponts,* in which legible words in several languages are piled into shapes, particularly towers, over six panels—each in the original version over six feet high, with the work as a whole running over twelve feet across. From right to left, the panels seem to tell of the evolution of language; from left to right, of its decline and decay.

While imaged words and worded images are distinct forms, many examples of the art fall across and between. Sequence introduces another dimension, as in several pieces that have more than one image and so depend, to different degrees, upon the reader's turning of pages. Examples are Jean-François Bory's *Christina Story* and Tom Phillips's *A Humument,* which imposes cutout page designs upon a historic Victorian novel. As word-imagery assimilates poetic forms, so it also exploits novelistic ones; an example is Emmett Williams's *Sweethearts* in which the title word is typeset in various shapes that sequentially generate a narrative. Word-imagery can extend also into three dimensions, as in Gerd Stern's *Contact Is the Only Love,* Henry H. Clyne's *Zen II,* and Robert Indiana's *Love* sculpture. Allan Kaprow's *Words* is a four-dimensional work, extending the art around an area and into time as well—a collaborative environment that the spectators continually create within a circumscribed space.

No word-image can be understood with respect solely either to language or design; for in this medium, there is no art or experience in one dimension without the other. Moreover, a richly verbal field, like Furnival's masterpiece, should not, as indicated before, be read just from left to right as literature. Read also from right to left, top to bottom, bottom to top, and perhaps around the circumference as well; and even in the most elegantly painted example, like Indiana's *Love,* it is a certain word, rather than another, that must be acknowledged and understood. (Many paintings with words, by contrast, suffer from indubitably inconsequential or arbitrary language.) One should keep in mind that this art is more constructivist than expressionist, which should explain why individual works are rarely signed; and they rarely reveal anything about the emotional orientation of their creators.

The visual dimension also bestows an aural rhythm—which is to say, an element of time—upon the words portrayed:

SEQUENCE

must be pronounced as well as understood differently from

SE   QUENCE

For just as all words exist in visual space, so in space exist audible words.

"Typographical devices, employed with great daring," wrote Apollinaire, "have given rise to a visual lyricism almost unknown before our time"; and in the best word-imagery are both profound perceptual experiences and unprecedented forms of art-communication which in sum realize the classic ideal of the possible fusion, within one inclusive form, of both poetry and painting.

The New Poetries

(1973)

I

Art is constantly making itself; its definition is in the future. Criticism cannot therefore be a single developing theory; *it must be partisan and polemical in order to join art in asserting what art is to become.* [Harold Rosenberg, *The Tradition of the New*, 1960]

This is the sum and sum again for the publishing situation. Plain it is and has always been and must be to anyone that the best is untimely as well as rare, new and therefore difficult of recognition, without immediate general interest (any more than a tomato was until prejudice had been knocked down), therefore dependent on discerning support (without expectation of money benefit) from the able; scantily saleable—and without attraction for the book trade, while wonders are advertised. And it is at the same time true that the only thing of worth in writing is this difficult, priceless thing that refreshes the whole field, which it enters, perenially, when it will, the new. [William Carlos Williams, "The Somnambulists," 1929]

"New" has become such a disreputable term in discourse about recent American poetry that most of us under thirty-five are initially reluctant to use it. There are "new" anthologies with sections devoted not only to "black poetry," "women poets," and "young poets" but also to "protest poetry" and "poetry of survival," even though examples collected under these author-determined or content-determined rubrics are scarcely new with respect to poetry in general or even to their parochial categories. Unless the word "new" is used to refer particularly to form and style, it becomes a platitude. This debasement of critical language, mostly in the interest of exploiting the prestige of the avant-garde without delivering the goods, regrettably obscures the emergence of genuinely new poetries in North America.

Indeed, some innovative work is so different from traditional poetry that traditionalist mentalities are apt to question whether it can be called "poetry" at all. However, one truth, illustrated repeatedly in the history of innovative literature, is that radically new work upon its first appearance is usually dismissed as "not poetry" or "not art." (The most prominent recent example is Ginsberg's "Howl.") This charge is generally as ignorant as the similarly conservative contention of the new art's "formlessness," even though any sort of definable coherence (as in the following examples) establishes the existence of artistic selection and thus a particular form. In my judgment, poetry is any verbal creation that descends from accepted poetry or more closely resembles accepted poetry than anything else. It is perilous to forget Marianne Moore's contention, radical in its time, that her own pieces are poetry because she finds no other classification more appropriate. Once again, in judgments of evaluation, only the good ones count.

These new poetries move, by definition, decidedly beyond the old poetries which in America cluster around several definable milestones. One is that tradition of lyricism which runs from Yeats through early Pound through Theodore Roethke, who was, in my opinion, the single greatest American poet of the early post-World War II period. Lyricism's more recent heirs include the poetries of nature perception (Bly, Dickey), of urban commentary (David Ignatow, Harvey Shapiro), of personal confession (middle Lowell, late Sylvia Plath), and more freely cadenced dark expressionism (early Ginsberg, Philip Lamantia, LeRoi Jones). A second tradition which deals with alternative kinds of poetic coherence runs from Pound of the *Cantos* through Charles Olson into the New York school of John Ashbery, Frank O'Hara, and their self-congratulatory descendants, as well as the post-Black Mountain school. This tradition includes all poetries based upon isolated notations elliptically laid out in rectilinear space (exemplifying Olson's "composition by field") or upon verbal pastiche with its collage-like penchants for striking juxtaposition and leaps in rhythm and diction. American literary magazines nowadays are filled with derivatives, some more eclectic than others, of these two dominant traditions.

A third sort of old new poetry, considerably less influential than the others, consists of physically separate words and images (or photographs), which are usually the work of two artists in collaboration, but have sometimes been done, as in the examples of William Blake and Kenneth Patchen, by one man alone. A fourth milestone is the "prose poem," developed most brilliantly in early modern France, which customarily consists of a few strikingly crafted, highly "poetic" sentences. Truly new poetry moves beyond such typically contemporary concerns as associational syntax, jaggedly irregular rhythms, rhetorical elisions, imagistic repetition, pointed pastiche, and individual voice (whose most appropriate medium is the essay or the personal letter), along with transcending the subjects and sentiments (and egotisms) typical of those techniques. It moves well beyond the current practice of Lowell, Ginsberg, Dickey, Creeley, Bly—all of whom are frequently imitated in "creative writing" courses. Nonetheless, the works described below selectively reflect certain modern precedents, at the same time as they collectively enhance the great twentieth-century theme of expanding the language of human communication. For, as Vladimir Mayakovsky formulated it, there can be no truly revolutionary poetry without a revolutionary form. Should these examples seem initially incomprehensible, one reason is that they are formally different rather than intrinsically difficult; and that difference may also account for why they may initially seem "unpoetic." Many of them resemble the classics of modernism in challenging and hopefully refashioning our habitual ways of poetic reading.

There is not one kind of new poetry but several which collectively display clear steps beyond previous work. These several directions can in turn be divided into those that emphasize the basic materials of poetry and works that miscegenate them with other arts and concerns. The purist preoccupations of poetry include special kinds of diction (the vocabulary reflected in the selection of individual words) and unusual ways of putting words together; so that either new languages or new syntaxes can be a measure of innovation. In his poem "One Talk One" (1967), Jan Herman draws upon the vocabulary of the medical sciences, shrewdly weaving a lingo previously unknown to poetry:

> energy systems gone/requires no plumbing
> pulse amplitude continuous
> > > eliminates the need for arterial cutdowns
> > > the nursing word station set
> *"like a bilumen tube to which a stomach has been fastened"*
> the required function of each machine the same

His lines realize an encompassing diction that successfully

transcends the collage methods actually used in the work's composition.

The Canadian poet Bill Bissett has developed a personal orthography that, along with other devices, poetically transforms simple statements:

an whn yu cum
an whn yu cum an whn
yu cum an whn yu cum
an whn yu cum an
whn yu cum an
whn yu cum
an whn yu
cum an
whn
yu
cum

CPGraham mixes coined words with familiar ones:

Heroin is the nymphomaniacish
Orgaming in the veins

These examples echo Mayakovsky's dictum: "Neologisms are obligatory in writing poetry."

Rather than evolve new systems of syntax as James Joyce did in *Finnegans Wake,* American countersyntactical poets strive to eschew the old ways of putting words together. One successful device is horizontal minimalism—one word to a line—that repudiates the function of syntax by giving each word (except the two articles and "of") equal weight in poetic exposition:

kids
bounding
down
from
rocks

```
                    hit
                    the
                    shore
                    forcefully
                    and
                    then
                    run
                    the
                    length
                    of
                    it
                       Frank Samperi, "Intaglio"
                       (1973)
```

Several works in Kenneth Gangemi's initial collection, *Lydia,* are unpunctuated, nonsyntactic, simplistically constructed lists whose parts are nonetheless skillfully (which is to say poetically) selected and structurally connected; his poem entitled "National Parks" begins:

> Big Bend
> Bryce Canyon
>
> Crater Lake
>
> Everglades

and continues uninflected in alphabetical order through "Yosemite" down to "Zion," all the chosen names being poetically evocative to varying (and idiosyncratic) degrees. Gangemi's form and taste enable him to realize, paradoxically, highly individual poems with a minimum of self-generated words.

The most impressive of Dick Higgins's poems, many of which are collected in *Foew&ombwhnw* (1969), favor the permutational organization of poetry's materials as one alternative to worn-out associational forms. A work entitled "empty streets" (1967) represents an elementary version of this compositional principle, permuting three separate phrases into three different pairs:

<pre>
                    many boxes
                    many rooms
                    many sounds

                    many boxes
                    many sounds

                    many rooms
                    many sounds

                    many boxes
                    many rooms
</pre>

Higgins's "Thrice Seven" (1968, also reprinted in *Foew&-ombwhnw*) is, thanks to its unusual substructures, one of the few recent long poems in English to avoid any formal echoes of the *Cantos*.

Pedro Pietri, a Puerto Rican poet (b. 1944) living in New York, has also worked in permutational forms as in "Prologue for Ode to Road Runner (1969)" which reads in part:

<pre>
                    train A town down
                    down A train down
                    A downtown train
                    A train downtown
</pre>

And so have such older poets as Jerome Rothenberg and Emmett Williams, along with Donald Burgy, a younger "conceptual artist" whose "Time Exchange #1" reads in its entirety:

<pre>
                Put your then in someone's now
                Take someone's then in your now
</pre>

Put your now in someone's then
Take someone's now in your then.

Back in the middle sixties, John Giorno introduced his remarkable experiments in repetition and line breaking which demonstrated an old poetic truth—that varying placement can give different meanings to the same words:

It is
there
It is there
because
we think
it is
there
because we think
it is there,
and it is
not
there
and it is not there
when
we do not
think
at all
when we do not think
at all.

Though stunning at first, particularly for its exploitation of mundane materials, this device becomes dulled by repetition. Nearly all of Giorno's poems express the same structural theme (while revealing morbid obsessions), and nothing else of his has been comparably distinguished. Another, more adventurous pioneer in this vein, Jackson Mac Low (b. 1922), has been experimenting for over twenty years with a variety of radically alternative structures, some of which have been more effective than others; but since most of his work remains unpublished or scattered through little magazines, it is hard to generalize about it.

Other Dick Higgins poems draw upon his experience in both Cagean musical and mixed-means theatrical composition to create an aleatory structure in which the reader may vary the poem's parts to his choice; the whole of the poet's inversely titled "New Song in the Old Style" (1967) remains, however, artistically superior to any of its comparatively prosaic realizations:

                    (check one)
              ------speak
              ------dance
    When I ------fall in love
              ------grow up
              ------grow old

                        (check one)
                  ------I'm going to be
                  ------it'll be with

                            (check one)
                      ------an apple.
                      ------a lover.
                      ------a smile.
                      ------you.

Higgins has also contributed to another new form, which is less definite and less realized so far, though still distinct, that I call suggestive poetry, to use that adjective in an especially Elizabethan sense of goading a response. In this strain of poetry, an imperative statement intends to initiate an unusual process of imaginative contemplation that is rather romantic and inevitably idiosyncratic. Some of this verges upon what I call Inferential Art—where little is made or said, though much is im-

plied. Take, for instance, Stephen M. Katcher's classically
enigmatic:

> The reuse of this sentence is forbidden.

Or Higgins's "Danger Music No. Twelve (March 1962)"
which reads in its entirety:

> Write a thousand symphonies.

The text gains poetically from the sense that the com-
mandment—not ten but a thousand—is clearly impossible
by normal means. A more concise example (that depends
nonetheless upon unlimited generality) is his "Danger
Music No. Thirteen":

> Choose.

It should be noted that actually following the poet's
instructions introduces a nonpoetic dimension quite
different from the strictly poetic experience of just the
statement itself.

Perhaps the easiest ways to overcome the old forms
of poetic organization are through vertical reductionism,
such as the one-line poems of George Brecht which
customarily are not writ large but set in mundane type:

> o is at least one egg

The only precedent I know in American poetry for this
quality of poetic compression appears in several poems
that the noted critic Yvor Winters, of all people, wrote
in the early twenties, such as "Aspen Song" which reads
in its entirety:

> The summer holds me here.

More extreme forms of poetic reductionism include Robert Lax's great long poem, *Black and White* (1966), whose total vocabulary consists of only three different words and an ampersand; Gangemi's "Guatemala," which reads in its entirety, "Quetzal!"; and the minimal manipulations of Aram Saroyan whose most memorable single poem is:

eyeye

II

My structures are reductive. Syntax—the systems of articulation, connection and relation between words that give linear discourse its quality of extended meaning—is simply removed. . . . What is happening is a reversal of the normal reading experience. When the cumulative process of linear understanding is frustrated, the mind turns back toward the unitary experience of words as structure. . . . My experiments invite you to regard words as an object—or more exactly, as an organism, with patterns of existing that are specific to itself, inexplicable and marvelous. [Clark Coolidge, as quoted in Tom Clark, *John's Heart*, 1972]

None of the younger experimental poets has been as various, intelligent, and prolific as Clark Coolidge (b. 1939) who also edited one of the few genuinely avant-garde magazines of the sixties, *Joglars* (1964-66), in addition to playing drums for a poetry-conscious rock group, Serpent Power. His opening book, *Flag Flutter & U.S. Electric* (1966), collected his early forays into post-Ashberyian poetic acoherence where he attempted to realize the semblance of literary coherence without using such traditional organizing devices as meter, metaphor, exposition, symbolism, consistent allusion, declarative statements, or autobiographical reference. This effort is somewhat analogous to atonality in early twentieth-century music, where the composer likewise eschewed obvious coherences based upon tonics and dominants for more subtle forms of order; but just as successful atonal music never disintegrates into disordered noise—indeed, that is a fundamental measure of artistry —poetic acoherence must consistently distinguish itself from sheer incoherence. In a statement contributed to *The Young American Poets* (1968), Coolidge wrote that "Words have a universe of qualities other than those of descriptive relation: Hardness, Density, Sound-Shape, Vector-Force, & Degrees of Transparency/Opacity." His earliest poems reveal rather extraordinary linguistic sensitivities, especially regarding the selection and placement of words.

In the course of willfully avoiding the crutches upon which the old poetry depended, in addition to the esoteric vocabulary he once favored, Coolidge pursued not just varieties of acoherence but reductionism, joining Gangemi, Lax, and Knott as one of America's most superior minimalists. This is the opening stanza of "The Next":

> the in will
> over from
> as also into as
> in is   .
> of as as an
> in as or
> as is as as and
> as have as is

In the back sections of Coolidge's fullest retrospective, *Space* (1970), are yet more severe examples, such as an untitled poem beginning "by a I" that contains individually isolated words no more than two letters long, scattered across the space of the page (which has so far been Coolidge's primary compositional unit). These words are nonetheless related to each other—not only in terms of diction and corresponding length (both visually and verbally) but in spatial proximity; for if they resemble musical notes, to raise that analogy again, they resound not melodies but atonal constellations of similar timbre. Above that is a visual coherence that is obvious, even if unusual and essential; for if the individual words were arranged in another way, the poem would be different. Distinctions between little and too little are admittedly subtle, if not extremely fine; but sufficient experience with this kind of poetry leads me to regard this particular work among the very best in its mode. (Indeed, most other poetry seems egregiously prolix by comparison.) Incidentally, Coolidge's work also extends radically the Olsonian traditions both of "composition by field" as opposed to lines, and of emphasis upon syllables, rather than rhyme and meter.

Another Coolidge work epitomizes a different kind of poetic reductionism—the poem composed of one and only one unmalleable word which, when read aloud, continually changes not only denotatively but connotatively:

> Which, which which which which—
> which which.
> Which which which which,
> which which which which.
>
> Which which which which,
> which which which which which which,
> Which which which which
> which which which which.
>
> Which which which,
> which—which which which.
> Which which which
> which which which which.

The midwestern poet Michael Joseph Phillips has also been obsessed by this form—the repetition of minimal material—in addition to other experimental structures; the Canadian poet Bill Bissett has used repetition, either of a key phrase written in his personal orthography ("th tempul") or even an entire sentence ("Dinahshoremeets-thocean"), which is distributed with strict regularity but without hyphens or other punctuation through a pyramid shape and then its inversion. Pedro Pietri, also mentioned before, has published poems like "The Broken English Dream" which consist entirely of repeated, evocatively-organized punctuation marks whose "Spanish" forms differ from the original English.

Like all genuinely experimental artists, Coolidge accepted the challenge of an inevitable next step—extending his delicate reductionist techniques into longer works; and among the results are two of the most consequential long poems of the past decade: "A D," originally published in *Ing* (1968) and then reprinted in *Space*; and *Suite V*, which appeared in 1972 although it was composed several years before. "A D" begins in the familiar Coolidgean way with stanzas of superficially unrelated lines, but the poetic material is progressively reduced over twenty pages (thereby recapitulating Coolidge's own poetic development in a kind of formalist autobiography) until the poem's final pages display just vertically ordered fragments of words. *Suite V* is yet more outrageously spartan, containing nothing more than pairs of three-letter words in their plural forms with one four-letter word at the top and the other at the bottom of otherwise blank pages. This poem succeeds brilliantly in my judgment, thanks in part to the consistency imposed by its severely minimal constraint; and though lacking certain virtues of Coolidge's other long poems, such as verbal variety, it clearly ranks among the most awesome works of recent literature. The best introduction to Coolidge's excellence, incidentally, is not *Space* (which suffers from tiny typography), but the third issue of *Big Sky,* a periodical edited by Bill Berkson. While much of Coolidge's work remains unpublished, the work collected in Berkson's periodical is far more various than anywhere else. The collection in *Big Sky* also displays far better than *Space* the extent of Coolidge's poetic intelligence which is revealed not through the complexity of intellectual constructions, but through the remarkable absence of stupidities. It also shows his erudition which is expressed not through allusions but through the scrupulous lack of them, signifying an implicit awareness of styles of poetry that need no longer be done.

III

Returning the word to its status as thing, and us to our senses, is the project of [the] movement.... Representation/ emotional /intellectual messages in the arts engage attention and obscure the medium. Therefore, to maximize awareness of medium and materials, minimize the message; in poetry, minimize semantic freight. Place up front, where nobody can fail to apprehend, consonants and vowels. Appeal through typography and spacing on page—not taking left-to-right for granted, taking nothing for granted—*first of all* to eyes, ears, the kinetic sense of this momentous act of turning the page. Capture the reader with simplicity and, though one blushes to say it, with beauty. [Alicia Ostriker, "Poem Objects," 1973]

Some of these poems broach visualization and thus the other encompassing inclination of new poetry—into intermedia where words are blended with design, or music, or film, or philosophy, or theater. Since some of these language artists were originally trained in music and the visual arts, their poetry reveals radically different attitudes toward words. The first intermedium, which I have also called "word-imagery," depends primarily upon the visual enhancement of language, so that (given Pound's definition of literature as "language charged with meaning") the layout on the page endows words with poetic connotations that they would not otherwise have. Some visual poems are drawn by hand, occasional sloppiness in draftsmanship signifying their origins as "poetry" (in contrast to the technical slickness of "design"), while others depend upon stencils, rubbed-off letters, special typography, photographic enlargers, and other graphic devices. Some are multicolored while others use only black and white. Some are done with technically skilled collaborators, though most visual poets function as their own artists, typically preferring visual solutions that "designers" would not (or could not) do. Most work primarily with rectangular pages, but a few have made paintings and sculptures. The strategies of visual poetry include imagistic distillation that is mimetic such as my own "Concentric" (1967); nonmimetic enhancement that is nonetheless memorably iconographic, such as Robert Indiana's much-reprinted and much-plagiarized *Love* (1966) or Norman Henry Pritchard's "Peace" (1970); or representational shapes filled with words as in Jonathan Price's "Ice Cream Poem" (1968). What distinguishes these examples, except the last, from most poetry is that visual and verbal perceptions are made simultaneously; so that their language can be perceived only in its visual form.

This art is winning so many converts that it is impossible to keep track of all the talented new names; almost every issue of the few periodicals predisposed to such

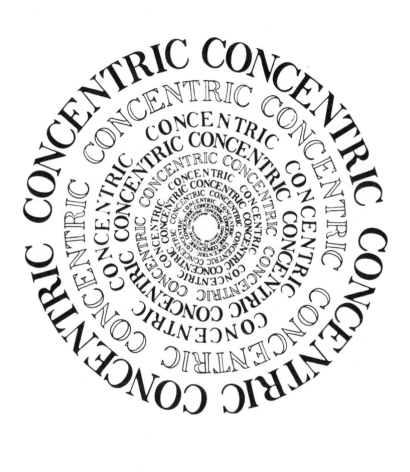

PEACE

PPPPPPEEEEEEEEAAAAAACCCCCC EEEEEE
PPPPPPEEEEEEEEAAAAAACCCCCC EEEEEE
PPPPPPEEEEEEEEAAAAAACCCCCC EEEEEE
PPPPPPEEEEEEEEAAAAAACCCCCC EEEEEE
PPPPPPPPPPPPPPPPPPPPPPPPPPPPPPPPPPPP
PPPPPPEEEEEEEEAAAAAACCCCCC EEEEEE
PPPPPPEEEEEEEEAAAAAACCCCCC EEEEEE
PPPPPPEEEEEEEEAAAAAACCCCCC EEEEEE
PPPPPPEEEEEEEEAAAAAACCCCCCEEEEEE
EEEEEEEEEEEEEEEEEEEEEEEEEEEEEEE
PPPPPPEEEEEEEEAAAAAACCCCCC EEEEEE
PPPPPPEEEEEEEEAAAAAACCCCCC EEEEEE
PPPPPPEEEEEEEEAAAAAACCCCCC EEEEEE
PPPPPPEEEEEEEEAAAAAACCCCCC EEEEEE
AAAAAAAAAAAAAAAAAAAAAAAAAAAAAAAA
PPPPPPEEEEEEEEAAAAAACCCCCC EEEEEE
PPPPPPEEEEEEEEAAAAAACCCCCC EEEEEE
PPPPPPEEEEEEEEAAAAAACCCCCC EEEEEE
PPPPPPEEEEEEEEAAAAAACCCCCC EEEEEE
CCCCCCCCCCCCCCCCCCCCCCCCCCCCC
PPPPPPEEEEEEEEAAAAAACCCCCC EEEEEE
PPPPPPEEEEEEEEAAAAAACCCCCC EEEEEE
PPPPPPEEEEEEEEAAAAAACCCCCC EEEEEE
PPPPPPEEEEEEEEAAAAAACCCCCC EEEEEE
EEEEEEEEEEEE EEEEEEEEEEEEEEEEEE
PPPPPPEEEEEEEEAAAAAACCCCCC EEEEEE
PPPPPPEEEEEEEEAAAAAACCCCCC EEEEEE
PPPPPPEEEEEEEEAAAAAACCCCCC EEEEEE
PPPPPPEEEEEEEEAAAAAACCCCCC EEEEEE

                    ice cream
                    i scream
                    ice cream

        bright   blurred
        chosen   rounded off
        lucent   made indefinite
        sharp   The side
                                                          nubbled
        uneven   syrup-slow
          curving   the image   the taste
          but willed   the transformation   glyceride
        jagged   the memory
                               eating it   smirched
    silent   shimmering
    magical, one   insatiable
moment only

                                                        accumulating,
      melting   dribbling, about
                                                    the cone   to drop
          the shape itself   cardboard
          the texture   the surface
          a test   sticky as plastic
          an admission

            the recognition   immediate and
              deceiving the mind   unknown
              the lettering on the rim   trivial
              arguing sugar crystals,   enormous
                blatant, gummy, broken

                the patchwork grill   licked
                intensifying   moist
                curving   still
                                                    firm

                  outline   yet
                  curling its   dis-
                  fingers   appear-
                  around,   ing
                  and down

                    possessing

                      to draw, to take
                      in the hand,
                      to crunch
                      its one
                      point

work presents a new "discovery." My own list of notable North American visual poets includes Gay Beste Reineck, Tom Ockerse, Bern Porter, Mary Ellen Solt, Ruth Jacoby, Adele Aldridge, Liam O'Gallagher, Aaron Marcus, Gerd Stern, Thomas Merton (just before his premature death), bpNichol, Steve McCaffery, David Uu, Jane Augustine, John Cage, Jos C. Brilliantes, Edwin Schlossberg, Dana Atchley, Paul Zelevansky, Carol Bankerd, Carolyn Stoloff. Some of them are better known as "painters" (and even "composers"), but their use of language, at minimum, reveals a commitment to poetry. Given all the American resistances to this art, it is scarcely surprising that much of their work so far has appeared in European magazines and that most books of their own work are self-published. "The wondrous thing here," to quote Alicia Ostriker, a lyric poet and Blake scholar, "is simply that absolute fresh experiences can emerge when the word is liberated from its context of phrase and sentence, as if some energy customarily compressed into syntactic forms could be freed like the energy locked into an atom, when that atom is split."

As one kind of poetic intermedium depends upon visualization, sound poetry, another kind, depends upon aural manipulations more typical of music, so that the words heard aloud become radically different from those on the printed page. It is true that all great poetic declamation such as Dylan Thomas's or Allen Ginsberg's reveals an attention to the musicality of poetry; but genuine sound poetry draws upon the musical techniques of rhythm, timbre, and amplitude (loudness) to a yet further degree, poetically charging the words with meanings they would not otherwise have. Customarily chanted rather than sung, this kind of poetry depends primarily upon the sounds made by comprehensible words aurally interacting with each other. A more radical strain, even closer to music, consists of linguistically incomprehensible phonetic sounds that nonetheless *resemble* language (and thus sound superficially like a foreign tongue), such as this excerpt from Armand Schwerner's on-going *The Tablets* (1969, 1971):

> min-na-ne-ne Dingir En-lil-ra mun-na-nib-gi-gi
> uzu-mu-a-ki dur-an-ki-ge
> Dingir nagar Dingir nagar im-man-tag-en-zen
> mu-mud-e-ne nam-lu-galu mu-mu-e-de

The work also incorporates visualization and other innovative devices. (However, if such sounds lack even this much linguistic semblance, the result, even if verbally produced, is *not* sound poetry but abstract music and experienced as such, rationalizations to the contrary notwithstanding.) Musical instruments, if used at all, are minimal, such as the single drum accompanying the angry, inflammatory words of Abiodun Oyewole, Alafia Pudim, and Omar Ben Hassen, three New York blacks calling themselves "The Last Poets," who made a spectacular long-playing record. (Words that follow a musical line are experienced as *song* rather than as poetry.) Cage, Pritchard, Giorno, Mac Low, Higgins have all done notable sound poetry, as have such New Yorkers as W. Bliem Kern, CPGraham, and Steve Reich, as well as Toby Lurie in Santa Barbara, David Franks in Baltimore, bpNichol in Toronto, Charles Amirkhanian in Berkeley, and Brion Gysin in Tangier. Other sound poets depend on electronic tape manipulations to produce not only collage (that old-fashioned staple) but also echoes and overdubs. The composer Terry Riley has created artistic environments filled with tape-delay systems that pick up the spectator's own words which are then electronically fed back into the environment in stunningly distorted (and yet recognizable) forms. Since printed quotations are insufficient, it is hard to talk about sound poetry without listening to examples which, like so much else in avant-garde art, must be experienced to be believed; and it is unfortunate that American record companies and radio producers are far less hospitable to this new art than comparable Europeans. Another intermedium for poetry is film, and among the notable American filmmakers working poetically with words are Stan VanDerBeek, Hollis Frampton, and Paul Sharits.

Much that seems at first to be "antipoetry" is, instead, a radically different kind of literary expression that must be regarded as "poetry" because it cannot be defined as anything else (narrow definitions of anything as indefinable by definition as "poetry" are especially ludicrous). Though echoing the neglected eccentricities of the Dada poets, the Russian futurists, E. E. Cummings (rather than Pound or Eliot), the new poetries define their current separateness by a complete rejection of some (and only some) aspects of most earlier poetry. Similar to avant-garde milestones in other contemporary arts, radically new poetry tends to emphasize one dimension at the expense (or neglect) of others. If exploiting all the possible suggestiveness of language was one of poetry's traditional motives, then the radical form that I call empirical poetry echoes a central theme of modern philosophy by completely exorcising such resonances, implicitly raising the old question of whether poetry can be as "true" as physics. It strives to offer nothing more than unadulterated, verifiable information and yet generate that language-created mystery we call "poetic." A similar esthetic motive informs much minimal sculpture such as those pieces which attempt to expunge shapes (even "abstract" ones) of their traditional suggestiveness. It is indicative that the author of the classic example of empirical poetry, Dan Graham's "March 31,

1966," was himself an early theorist of that new artistic direction. If Kenneth Gangemi's chosen facts are highly suggestive, the lines of Graham's poem remain doggedly factual, nonetheless conveying poetically in sum an overwhelming sense of man's modest scale in the cosmos. Although poetry made in this way draws upon compositional techniques that could be called "impersonal," the best examples of this style inevitably reveal, especially to a knowledgeable audience, an artistic signature that is highly personal.

MARCH 31, 1966   by Dan Graham

```
1,000,000,000,000,000,000,000,000.00000000  miles to edge of known universe
  100,000,000,000,000,000,000.00000000  miles to edge of galaxy (Milky Way)
        3,573,000,000.00000000  miles to edge of solar system (Pluto)
             205.00000000  miles to Washington, D.C.
               2.85000000  miles to Times Square, New York City
                .38600000  miles to Union Square subway stop
                .11820000  miles to corner of 14th Street and First Avenue
                .00367000  miles to front door of Apartment 1D, 153 First Avenue
                .00000700  miles to lens of glasses
                .00000098  miles to cornea from retinal wall
```

Historically, minimal sculpture led to what I have elsewhere called "situational sculpture" where rather minimalistic objects are placed in ways that enhance or reflect their surrounding space, the work of art thus encompassing both the object and its situation, as well as relations between. It is assumed that apart (or once removed) from its appropriate space the sculpture is incomplete—a mere concept demanding realization. The prime poetic example of this powerful esthetic idea is Dan Graham's "Schema," originally conceived in 1966 and first published in 1967 a year or two before the flowering of situational sculpture:

(number of)   adjectives
(number of)   adverbs

(percentage of)	area not occupied by type
(percentage of)	area occupied by type
(number of)	columns
(number of)	conjunctions
(number of)	depressions of type into surface of page
(number of)	gerunds
(number of)	infinitives
(number of)	letters of alphabet
(number of)	lines
(number of)	mathematical symbols
(number of)	nouns
(number of)	numbers
(number of)	participles
(perimeter of)	page
(weight of)	paper sheet
(type)	paper stock
(thinness of)	paper stock
(number of)	prepositions
(number of)	pronouns
(number of point)	size type
(name of)	typeface
(number of)	words
(number of)	words capitalized
(number of)	words italicized
(number of)	words not capitalized
(number of)	words not italicized

The data required by the scheme should be deduced from the page on which the work is printed, the work's publisher ideally inserting the accurate information in the left-hand column of a second page in which the right-hand column of items is reprinted; that second page becomes both a self-portrait, so to speak, of itself and an individual variant of the original scheme. (The crucial point is that these variations are not determined by personal choice as in the Higgins poem, but by verifiable measurement of the physical situation in which the poem is printed.) As Graham puts it, the scheme exists "only as information, deriving its value from the specific contingencies related to its placement on the two-dimensional surface (or medium) upholding their appearance." All correctly published versions represent, therefore, a collaboration—not only between the immutable schema and the variable page on which it is printed, but also between the poet and the book's production specialist. (It would follow, therefore, that the scheme quoted before remains incomplete; for unlike suggestive poetry, but like comparable sculpture, situational work demands its realization.)

The new theatrical poetry surpasses both "dramatic readings," with performers sitting stiffly on stools, and even that archaic (and somewhat decadent) form of a one-man literary recital; for poetic performances, as I shall call them, are theatrical events in which some-time poets (that fact alone establishing an esthetic context) turn essentially poetic impulses into performances. Vito Acconci, who began as a poet, art critic, and translator (and even took his *pro forma* M.F.A. at Iowa), developed a self-conscious disinterest in vocabulary, progressing through poems composed primarily of unfilled parentheses or of snippets found in newspapers and other public print, to poetry revealing mechanical operations in the countersyntactical handling of words and sometimes just letters. One 350-line poem, for instance, was distributed one line per page over 350 separate sheets of papers which were then bound into 350 copies of Acconci's otherwise uniform magazine, *0 to 9*. Another work reproduced only those letters along the vertical margins of selected pages of *Roget's Thesaurus*. He then progressed to empirical lists simply itemizing events in his own experience; but by this point he realized, "There were no clues to where I wanted to go in any poetry I read."

The obvious next step led Acconci out of words into empiricist presentations of himself and his own physical processes, the themes of his performances clearly growing out of his poetic ideas. In *Performance Test* (1969), he stared at each member of the audience for fifteen seconds apiece, while *Breathing Space* (1970) consisted of nothing more than himself and another man deep-breathing into amplified microphones, thereby exposing the characteristic timbres and rhythms of that essential form of human expression (and yet suggesting nothing more than breathing). Treating himself as material whose "vocabulary" can be turned to expressive uses, Acconci has created a series of stunning, self-obsessive (if not masochistic), conceptually indefinable performances that have won him international acclaim. His postpoetic evolution was best documented not in a poetry magazine, to be sure, but in a recent issue of a new art journal, *Avalanche* (Fall, 1972).

The crucial point is that just as one extreme, miscegenated possibility for 1960s painters was the rejection of painting for other forms of art (including at times the use of language), so the freedom available to the poet today includes the rejection of words for all kinds of activities that, at their best and truest, reveal their author's origins (and thus the work's context) in poetry. Pieces of this kind, like most other forms of new poetry, are also more international than earlier verse, since they offer much less resistance to the perennial problems of translation. (And some would seem to repudiate Paul Verlaine's haughty motto: "To be understood is the worst disaster.") The new poetries also tend to be less egotistical as most of them avoid self-projection and other pretenses of superior "sensitivity" (while the authors are themselves less egomaniacal), for its creative processes are primarily not expressionist but constructivist, as well as classically self-restrained. Most of this poetry is nonobjective, to use a critical term developed in the criticism of modernist painting, as the works emphasize properties intrinsic in the art while references to outside phenomena are either implicit or unintended. Many kinds of new poetry reflect both advanced ideas in music (i.e., permutational form) and in visual art; and not only are some of its creators also proficient in nonliterary arts, but a knowledge of current concerns in those fields is partially prerequisite to contemporary poetic literacy. A final point is that the new poetries represent not "games with language," to quote a standard objection, but genuine explorations of alternative communication forms that are as linguistically meaningful as poetry has always been.

Since the new poetries described here are all but totally unknown to the larger reading public, sympathetic critics feel obliged, for now, primarily to introduce what might later be discussed with more subtlety and discrimination. These poets testify that a profound faith in what they do, the interest of intelligent Europeans, and the energy gained from hard-won artistic triumphs, as well as the radical's instinctive commitment to change, all keep their poetic adventure going. Perhaps the fate of literature's future depends, to a degree, upon the public fortunes of postsymbolic, postexpressionistic, postcollage poetries. What does not evolve is imperiled.

References

Acconci, Vito. *Book Four*. New York: 0 to 9, 1968.

———. "Notes and an Interview," *Avalanche* 6 (1972).

Aldridge, Adele. *Notpoems*. Riverside, Connecticut: Magic Circle, 1972.

Antin, David. "Modernism and Postmodernism," *Boundary* 2 (1972).

Bankerd, Carol. *Graphic Poems*. Princeton, N. J.: Privately published,1969.

Bissett, Bill. *nobody owns the earth*. Toronto: House of Anansi, 1971.

———. *poems for yoshi*. Vancouver: Blewointment, 1972.

Brecht, George. Various "Fluxus" publications (New York, c. 1965).

Brilliantes, Jos C. *Sonnets in Concrete*. Washington, D.C.: Privately published, 1968.

Burgy, Donald. *Art Ideas for the Year 4000*. Andover, Mass.: Addison Gallery of American Art, 1970.

Colombo, John Robert, ed. *New Direction in Canadian Poetry*. Toronto: Holt-Canada, 1971.

Coolidge, Clark. *Flag Flutter and U.S. Electric*. New York: Lines, 1966.

——. *Clark Coolidge*. New York: Lines, 1967.

——. *Ing*. New York: Angel Hair, 1968.

——. *Amount*. New York: Adventures in Poetry, 1969.

——. *Space*. New York: Harper & Row, 1970.

——. *The So*. New York: Adventures in Poetry, 1971

——. *Suite V*. New York: Adventures in Poetry, 1972.

——. "The Clark Coolidge Issue," *Big Sky* 3 (1972).

Clark, Tom. *John's Heart*. New York: Grossman Goliard—Santa Fe, 1972.

Gangemi, Kenneth. *Lydia*. Los Angeles: Black Sparrow Press, 1970.

Giorno, John. *Balling Buddha*. New York: Kulchur Foundation, 1970.

Graham, Dan. *"End Moments."* New York: Privately published, 1969.

Gross, Ronald, and George Quasha, eds. *Open Poetry*. New York: Simon & Schuster, 1973.

Higgins, Dick. *Jefferson's Birthday*. New York: Something Else, 1964.

——. *Foew&ombwhnw*. New York: Something Else, 1969.

Hompson, Davi Det. *Davi Det Hompson*. New York: Alexandre Iolas Gallery, 1970.

Indiana, Robert. *Robert Indiana*. Philadelphia: University of Pennsylvania Press, 1968.

——. *Graphics*. Notre Dame, Indiana: St. Mary's College, 1969.

Kaprow, Allan. "O.K.," *Manifesto*. New York: Something Else, 1966.

Kostelanetz, Richard. *Visual Language*. New York: Assembling, 1970.

——. "Words and Images Artfully Entwined," *Art International*, XIV/7 (Sept. 20, 1970).

——, ed. *Imaged Words & Worded Images*. New York: Outerbridge & Dienstfrey, 1970.

Lax, Robert. *Black & White.* New York: Journeyman, 1971.

Mac Low, Jackson. *22 Light Poems.* Los Angeles: Black Sparrow Press, 1970.

——. *Stanzas for Iris Lezak.* West Glover, Vermont: Something Else, 1972.

Nichol, bp et al. ("The Four Horsemen"). *Canadada* (ST 88760 036 0).

Ockerse, Tom. *T. O. P.* Bloomington, Indiana: Privately published, 1971.

O'Gallagher, Liam. *Planet Noise.* San Francisco: Nova Broadcast, 1969.

——. *The Blue Planet Notebooks.* San Francisco: X-Communications, 1972.

Ostriker, Alicia. "Poem Objects," *Partisan Review,* XL/1 (Winter, 1973).

Oyewole, Abiodum et al. *The Last Poets* (Douglas 3).

Pietri, Pedro. "Prologue for Ode to Road Runner," *Revista del Instituto de Estudios Puertorriqueños,* I/1 (1971).

——. "The Broken Spanish Dream." In *The Puerto Rican Poets,* edited by Alfredo Matilla and Iván Silén. New York: Bantam Books, 1972.

Phillips, Michael Joseph. *The Concrete Book.* Milwaukee: Privately published, 1971.

——. *Concrete Sonnets.* Indianapolis: Privately published, 1972.

Pritchard, Norman Henry II. *The Matrix.* Garden City: Doubleday, 1970.

——. *Eecchhooeess.* New York: New York University Press, 1971.

Rosenberg, Harold. *The Tradition of the New.* 2d ed. New York: Horizon Press, 1960.

Samperi, Frank. *Quadrifariam.* New York: Grossman, 1973.

Saroyan, Aram. *Aram Saroyan.* New York: Random House, 1968.

Schwerner, Armand. *The Tablets, I-VIII.* West Branch, Iowa: Cummington, 1969.

——. *The Tablets I-XV.* New York: Grossman, 1971.

Williams, William Carlos. "The Somnambulists," *transition* 18 (Nov., 1929).

Young, La Monte, ed. *An Anthology.* 2d ed. Munich: Heinar Friedrich, 1969.

Sabotaging the New Poetry

(1970)

The phrase "concrete poetry" has been drifting through knowledgeable literary talk for nearly a decade now, and within the past few years several anthologies have appeared collectively propagating this new faith. Although the art has converted at least one hundred practitioners who are known to each other, as well as several editors, it has scarcely matured to the point that even its anthologists would agree on common definitions; and those who might want to learn from these books what is and, more important, what isn't "concrete poetry" will be more confused than edified. To Emmett Williams, "concrete poetry, then, is what poets in this anthology make," and with that circular reasoning no one dares risk an extended debate. Jean-François Bory reserves his definition for page 79 of his anthology and then admits its vacuousness: "Concrete writing is real writing, only writing, writing itself." Uh huh. Eugene Wildman, the only anthologist not to include his own work, evades any definition more explicit than this descriptive statement: "Concrete poetry aims, in general, at the ideogrammatic state. The poets pattern the letters of words in much the same way that a Japanese calligrapher patterns the strokes of a character." Mary Ellen Solt, in the most usable definition, speaks of "a fundamental requirement which the various kinds of concrete poetry meet: concentration upon the physical material from which the poem or text is made. . . . The essential is *reduced language*." (This echoes the more precise definition by the English art critic Jasia Reichardt: "Language is used as material rather than the means of emotive personal expression—spatial arrangement and phonetic possibility, rather than syntax, being the connecting link between the different elements.") However, these anthologists hardly expire the collection of extant definitions; perhaps because the British theorist-poet Dom Sylvester Houédard takes the word "concrete" more seriously than his peers, as well as possessing a more fertile intellect, he wrote in 1963, "New poetry is CONCRETE because it is a poetry of nouns, words for concrete things; also because it makes poems that are concrete objects themselves, not windows into souls. . . . Concrete poems just ARE; have no outside reference." And so on and so on.

The phrase is unquestionably more disquieting than ecumenical; and as Mary Ellen Solt reports, poets working more or less in these ways (including myself) habitually deny that they are "concretists." The word stems from artistically parochial origins—a meeting in 1956 between the Brazilian poet Decio Pignatari and a Swiss named Eugen Gomringer; and upon discovering common concerns and ambitions, they decided to call their poetry "concrete," partially in deference to the Swiss "concrete" painter Max Bill, for whom Gomringer then worked as a secretary. (However, it is a curious fact that in Sweden a few years before, Oyvind Fahlstrom, who has since become a painter of note, published a mimeographed and unnoticed essay prophetically entitled *Manifest for Conkret Poesie*.) Then, as Emmett Williams remembers, "In 1957, the year Haroldo de Campos of

Brazil introduced concrete poetry to Kitasano Katue of Japan, a Romanian-born artist Daniel Spoerri, leader of the Darmstadt Circle of concrete poets (which included a German dramaturgist, Claus Bremer, and an American expatriate, Emmett Williams), published the first international anthology of concrete poetry." Imprisoned by this pseudohistoricism, Williams adheres more strictly than other anthologists to a conception of "concrete poetry" as not an autonomous artform but the produce of accredited members of a discrete movement, which is to say those impregnated with the familial seed at an earlier, as opposed to a more recent, time. However, the practice of attributing a new art exclusively to a certain group, rather than anyone who chooses (or has chosen) to create it, is a kind of European duplicity (e.g., "surrealism") that, thankfully, does not survive too long in America.

The word "concrete" is finally so inapplicable—not even Williams explains why his selections should be more *concrete* than other poetry—that there is every reason to discard it entirely for something more general and yet discriminating (or reserve it for those wishing to retain "concrete" for themselves). As the typographer Jan Tschichold observed in *Asymmetrical Typography* (1967), even the term "concrete painting," coined by van Doesburg in 1930, "is not suitable in the English language." The best pieces included in these anthologies—those most meaningful at least to this open-minded and experienced observer—realize their identity at points where word and image enhance each other; and remembering that much that is new in contemporary art stands as an intermedium between older art forms, let me propose the phrase "word-imagery" to circumscribe the area between poetry and visual art. In true word-imagery, then the word (usually isolated from syntactical context) and image are so inextricably complementary that one dimension cannot be separated from the other without destroying the art, and the work usually reveals that artistic attention has been paid to each dimension. There is, for instance, all the difference in art and communication between "Disintegration" and, to quote my own work:

DISINTEGRATION
DISINTEGRATION
DISINTEGRATION
DISINTEGRATION

And in that enhancement lies the most elementary strategy and interest in this new poetry. In this case, the tradition of the art extends beyond the parochial history of the concretists to include those modern painters who successfully incorporate recognizable words into their visual fields—Paul Klee, Carlo Carrà, Kurt Schwitters, Stuart Davis—and poets whose words are laid out into expressive designs—Christian Morgenstern, Filippo Marinetti, Vladimir Mayakovsky, E. E. Cummings, and, most influentially, Guillaume Apollinaire.

There is a difference between anthologies selecting from a body of more or less established works and those presenting pieces likely to be unfamiliar to their audiences. Indubitably of the second type, these four collections all function as introductions to this new poetic art. Though each has something of importance not found in the others, none will go down in this art's history as definitive. Eugene Wildman's *The Chicago Review Anthology of Concretism* (1968) is the least consequential of those released here, partly because it contains the fewest selections, mostly because something less than mature critical intelligence seems to inform the editor's fishings from the sea. Fortuitously, this edition corrects several errors embarrassing its original printing as an issue of the *Chicago Review,* such as attributing to "anonymous" Decio Pignatari's much reprinted *Life* (1958); but Wildman still inaccurately identifies the pictures attributed to the Englishman John Furnival. They are actually small sections of a larger work in six panels, *Tours de Babel Changées en Ponts* (1965) that, as the excerpts suggest, is extremely rich in verbal detail. Nonetheless, this anthology reprints in its entirety on successive right-hand pages Jean-François Bory's *Spot,* one of the best examples of sequential forms. Here the same image of letters is progressively magnified through seven images until the black joint of a small "e" all but fills the final page, bestowing an ironic twist upon a linear process. Wildman's own afterword is a frustrating mixture of evasive platitudes with some genuine original insights, particularly about the intrinsic characteristics of the form and the purposes of a relevant criticism. For instance, at one turn, he writes perceptively that the stuff of his anthology "is profoundly literary, because it deals expressly with the effects of writing (as opposed to telling)," yet a few lines later he can declare such nonsense as, "There is a definite folk aspect to Concretism. Concrete poetry is the poetry of how we think, a poetry that works with what is irreducible in the language that we think in."

Emmett Williams's *An Anthology of Concrete Poetry* (1967) has received the most publicity, which is to say puffy articles in the slickest press; and particularly since ninety percent of this fat book is unjustifiably trivial, most of it by card-carrying members of the "concrete" movement mentioned before, and the introduction is more obscuring than enlightening, all this attention may ultimately not be a blessing to the art. Williams has elsewhere espoused a principle also evident behind his selections here—that not the word but the linguistic sign is the basic material of the "concrete" art (which includes aural *sound* poetry, along with visual); and many of the least ingratiating poems can be summarily dismissed as abstract arrangements of letters that are neither particularly distinguished as design nor communicative as language. Nonetheless, *An Anthology* is compendious enough to include a number of first-rate word-images, mostly by authors who came to the art after 1962—Edwin Morgan's *Pomander* (with a useful explanatory gloss by the author), Reinhard Dohl's much-reproduced *Pattern Poem with an Elusive Intruder* (which is a "Wurm" buried in a sea of "Apfel"), Mary Ellen Solt's *Forsythia,* Ian Hamilton Finlay's *Acrobats* (in one of its weaker typographical realizations), Pedro Xisto's *Zen: A Logogram* (1966), and John Furnival's *The Fall of the Tower of Babel* (1964), illustrated in a series of three progressive enlargements that display his meticulous craftsmanship within an epic format.

However, if an anthology, which supposedly represents an intelligent and tasteful selection, contains so little that is first-rate, then its discriminating reader can assume, not unreasonably, that all "concrete poetry" is similarly beneath his interest. And if this weak anthology becomes the occasion for a television program, as Emmett Williams's once served a New York educational station (whose academic imprimateur supposedly represents selectivity too), then an even larger audience will judge that all new poetry is comparably dreadful, and so on. It is perilous to forget that when public attention goes to anything less than the best, then a new art is badly served, for many possibly sympathetic readers will conclude that all work in this vein need not be considered seriously again. I personally know a half-dozen fairly literate and openminded people who trace their own contempt for word-imagery to this television show, and several others who cite only the Williams anthology. In art, unlike commerce, not all publicity is good publicity, as bad publicity can usher the public death of an artistic enterprise. Since the new art's self-appointed friends can be as murderous as its enemies, one wonders what might have happened to the new modernist poetry if, in the 1920s, Robert Hillyer and Dame Edith Sitwell, say, rather that T. S. Eliot and Ezra Pound, became widely accepted as major spokesmen for the new art?

Jean-François Bory's *Once Again* (1968) is most consistently tasteful in its selections (or at least includes the fewest duds), probably because Bory, a young Frenchman, owes no debts to the accredited celebrities of the "concrete" movement; and not only are many of the pieces more imaginatively designed than those in other collections, and more various as well—here are chaotic fields of words, photomontages, aggressive imagery, sculptured letters, even constructions (photographed for reproduction)—but the book as a whole exhibits an innovative presentation, opening with an occasionally insightful (but stylistically odd) essay that leads into illustrations and then skilfully arranged full-page poems marked only by page numbers and interrupted by occasional editorial comments. (In the back is an index identifying the authors of each page and their respective nationalities; and though edited by a Parisian, it includes more Americans than the other volumes.) The result is a well-modulated trip through a strange art that the reader is forced to understand on its own terms, without the distraction of names and statements. (However, contrary to Bory's assertion, *Once Again* is not at all a "happening," because no example of that new mixed-media art would present itself, as a book usually does, in a permanently fixed form.) It is *Once Again,* more than the other anthologies, that I would recommend to those more visually inclined as the best introduction to the possible styles and syntax of the new art; but since many pieces here strike me as discouraging and inscrutable, while a few reveal no discernible words, and the five-by-eight-inch format is really too small for some of the illustrations, may I particularly recommend those selections by Ferdinand Kriwet, Ronald Johnson (with the assistance of John Furnival, whose name goes uncredited), and the editor himself.

Mary Ellen Solt's *Concrete Poetry: A World View* (1969) is indubitably the most responsible anthology, and probably the most valuable too. Her book opens with a critical introduction that is levels beyond anything previously written on the subject—it is particularly recommended to those who prefer reading the most substantial commentary before sampling an unfamiliar art. Not only does she reprint several important manifestoes, most of them especially translated for her book, but the book closes with an extensive collection of notes, which include translations of unfamiliar words. The poems are printed in extremely clear reproductions, on the largest pages of all the anthologies here; and a few are even reproduced in color. Nonpartisan in her enthusiasms, she includes both Emmett Williams and Jean-François Bory, each of whom eschews the other. The book also represents practically everyone of note ever associated with the organized concretists, in addition to poetic precursors, such as shrewdly selected examples by Louise Bogan, Louis Zukofsky and E. E. Cummings (though not painters who incorporated words); and although Solt retells the parochial history of "concrete poetry," she also knows that the organized movement has no monopoly of precursors or practitioners. Nearly everything about this book testifies to Mrs. Solt's responsible critical intelligence—a quality rare in someone who is also one of a new art's best American practitioners.

Her book's most glaring deficiency lies in her selections of individual works; for while she invariably picks the best pieces by the second-level poets, such as Emmett Williams and Carlo Belloli, as well as such third-rate figures as Aram Saroyan, her choices from the few truly excellent creators—Bory, Furnival, Kriwet—are invariably weaker than their very best. This fault in anthological taste seriously compromises, in my judgment, the book's introductory purposes and persuasive powers. Furnival, for instance, is represented by only one image, in which she finds the word-artist "abandoning the traditional tower symbol for the Mobius strip," but the image is in fact just a section from the second panel of his six-towered *Tours de Babel Changées en Ponts*. Ferdinand Kriwet is represented by an image of letters so indistinct, untypically, that one suspects faulty reproduction; and Jean-François Bory by something levels below his best.

Although Mrs. Solt's text is, thankfully, indebted less to bombastic impressionism than to the New Criticism, with its bias toward the close reading of extant texts, some of her interpretations, while admirable for their courage, court excess and incredulity (e.g., of Dick

Higgins's work); and the abundant appendix sometimes provides translations of what need not be translated at all. Moreover, she organizes her contributors not by alphabetical order but, curiously, by cultural nationality; and the absence of either an index or an itemized table of contents forces the reader to flip several pages every time he needs to find a particular poet or piece. Nonetheless, *Concrete Poetry: A World View* is more than just a collection of friends and favorites but a courageous and substantial comprehensive introduction, where a book's worth of well-illustrated quotations is prefaced by much of the best criticism written so far on the new poetic art.

It is nothing short of scandalous, and yet indicative, that these books went generally unnoticed, even in the more serious reviewing press, for the truth is that the established "critical" media are fundamentally not interested in anything different from the "new poetry" they and others certified five (or more) years ago. I cannot think of an established literary critic who would *know* more about such work than what the anthologies' introductions tell him, and there really are not more than a handful of regular literary reviewers in America capable (or willing) of handling anything this different from what they learned in college, or mastered in their youth. These books are the kind that most poetry critics, let alone poets, try *not* to understand, much as neo-Eliot poets were forever trying not to understand William Carlos Williams or Allen Ginsberg; and I have yet to see anywhere a review of "concretism" that displayed the comprehension and discrimination generally associated with mature criticism. Just the other day, for instance, I came across in *The Village Voice,* where book notices are usually more shabby than not, a review of Paul Carroll's *The Young American Poets* by an incredibly (or cynically) obtuse poet named "Al Lee," who characterizes my own "Tributes to Henry Ford," three patterns incorporating the rather obviously allusive letters "T" and "A" as "charming if framed and hung in the Riviera [a West Village eatery], or printed in a book of cartoons. He occupied three pages with the word 'at'." The old truth, repeated over and over again in the history of modernism, is that for every new style there shall always be new philistines, some of whom, alas, are even young, educated and outspoken.

One is told that visual poetry is "hot" or "faddish" or the like, but not by any criterion known to me is this true. Not a single one-man collection has yet been commercially published in this country, and all the anthologies so far have been done by "small" or university presses. Only one anthology of recent poetry so far has included visual work—the Paul Carroll volume cited above—and few established literary magazines have ever published or recognized the new style. (More of my own works, for instance, have appeared abroad than here.) Exhibitions have been few and far between, and of the dozen or so regular poetry-reading platforms in New York City, none—absolutely none—are open to the new poetry, whether visual or aural. Every time I receive queries from fellow experimental poets asking me to arrange a "reading" in New York, I must reply that no program here is particularly open to our kind of work. (Some have responded with disbelief, nonetheless.) Obtuse criticism, as always, is more of a hindrance than a help.

It should be understood, first of all, that the best examples of word-imagery express what cannot be said as effectively in any other way; and that rule should stand as the most immediate measure of the integrity of both the medium itself and an individual work. Just as great poetry articulates what cannot be said as well in prose, so truly effective word-imagery conveys what cannot be said in either word or image alone. For that reason, just as none of these works can be declaimed, so most are perceived as they are visually read, which is to say that when one assimilates the word he should simultaneously comprehend the import of its shape. Precisely by mixing modes of creation and perception does word-imagery free both design and verbiage from the clichés of each other's medium. That observation, in turn, persuades me to recommend that strictly literary poets try working in visual modes, if only as an exercise to discover what individual words can evoke on the page. Poetry, after all, has always been partially about using familiar words in unfamiliar ways. Mention of traditional poets reminds me of their most common complaint—that few practitioners of word-imagery have "paid their dues" as more conventional poets. However, this does not constitute a valid criticism of anything, except, inadvertently, the deleterious initiation fees of their craft union. On one hand, word-imagery is another way of doing poetry; yet the most realized examples of the art are perhaps not "poetry" at all in the end, but something else.

Each of these preliminary "concrete" anthologies contains as well as lacks something important that can instead be found in one of the others, and even as a foursome they fail to close the circle around the new art. Completely omitted are the two older American image-poets Liam O'Gallagher and Gerd Stern (both anthologized in my own *Possibilities of Poetry*) as well as two younger people only beginning to do distinguished work in the medium—Gay Beste and N. H. Pritchard; and the concept of word-imagery should, to my mind, include many of the classic paintings of Americanisms by Robert Indiana. Also omitted from these four anthologies, more on grounds of practicality than ignorance or malice, are what I take to be the two genuine masterpieces of the art—John Furnival's *Tours de Babel Changées en Ponts* (1965), much reprinted in part (as noted before), but never in its entirety, which consists of six panels, originally wooden doors six and one-half feet high, meticulously filled with expressive words in a style composed of irony, aphorism, and visual distortion; and Jean-François Bory's *Saga* (1968), actually a "fiction" in thirty-two pages of word-imagery. They are the only two works I know in the medium to approach both the step-ahead profundity and absolute perfection characteristic of great avant-garde art and literature. The omission of all these works from these four anthologies suggests the need for a more discriminating collection that culls nothing but the best from a large body of work; for as dreadful and boring as most efforts in this new (or any) form are, critics of word-imagery should never forget that it is by the best work and the very best alone that we ultimately measure the achievement of a particular style or a new art.

A Conversation on Visual Poetry

With Keith Rahmmings

(1978)

Do you think that visual/language forms will ever achieve acceptance in the mass markets? Do you think they should?

Eventually they will; most first-rank writing finally does, if only in the mass market of the North American classrooms. However, your question puts the cart before the horse. For now, the principal problem is breaking down the stubborn resistances of so-called literary editors and funding agencies. Nonvulgar innovative writing cannot break through into mass-markets until a secure professional beachhead is established in the literary magazines and publishing houses.

Name five or more contemporary poets/writers exploring visual/language (and related) concerns whose efforts are in your opinion particularly worthy of attention. Briefly elaborate.

Loris Essary, not only in his own visual poems and stories, but in the brilliant verbal-visual essays that he co-authored with Carl D. Clark; these latter pieces appeared as prefaces to their magazine *Interstate,* and one will be included in my anthology *Esthetics Contemporary* (1978). The Future Press applied to the National Endowment for the Arts to do a book of them; but this, like everything else experimental, was turned down by those shameless philistines. My next creative book, *Foreshortenings* (1978), is dedicated to Essary.

Fred Truck, a poet-printer in Des Moines, Iowa, who has developed an encompassing myth that expresses itself in words, images, sculptures and even a proposed artistic machine. My own latest collection of visual poetry, *Illuminations* (1977), is dedicated to Truck.

Paul Zelevansky, whose *Book of Takes* (1976) ranks among the richest, more difficult, and most elegantly produced visual-verbal books of the past few years. If you don't already know it, you should.

Ian Tarnman, a Nevada poet, working with words as objects, much in the tradition of what is called "concrete poetry." The Future Press, whose literature program I direct, published his initial collection, *First Principles,* in 1978.

Emmett Williams, particularly in his witty poems based on authors' names; see pages 120-126 of his *Selected Shorter Poems, 1950-1970* (1975).

Finally, don't forget the two British masters of visual literature—John Furnival, whose large screens of worded images remain among the unrivaled masterpieces of the art, and Tom Phillips, whose visual novel *The Humument* I consider among the greatest avant-garde fictions of our time. "Where can I find *The Humument*?" I hear you asking. You can't, except in black and white excerpt (which loses its rich color), in my anthologies *Imaged Words & Worded Images* (1970), *Future's Fictions* (1971) and *Breakthrough Fictioneers* (1973). Actually, two pages from *The Humument* were reproduced in color in the retrospective catalogue *Tom Phillips. Works. Texts to 1974.* (1975), and approximately 75 images were reproduced, black-white, in an undersized format as *Trailer* (1971), meaning, I guess, the movie-house notion of a short teaser promoting a longer film which, in this case, has not yet come, several years later.

You might say that *The Humument* is too spectacular a novel to be published in its entirety on either side of the Atlantic. After all, if *Finnegans Wake* were written today, I doubt if it would be published either, small presses being unable to afford its gargantuan size, and the larger presses rejecting it as defiantly unprofitable. There aren't any T. S. Eliots residing, you know, in the commercial publishing houses nowadays.

I've been trying for several years to find sufficient support to do an anthology of *Scenarios,* or mostly visual scripts for performance, and a comparable collection of *New Poetries*; but neither proposal has yet, alas, found any backers.

Text-Sound Art in North America

(1977)

I want my own stuff, my own rhythm, and vowels and consonants too, matching the rhythm and all my own. If this pulsation is seven yards long, I want words for it that are seven yards long. [Hugo Ball, "Dada Manifesto," 1916]

The three most revolutionary sound mechanisms of the Electric Revolution were the telephone, the phonograph and the radio. With the telephone and the radio, sound was no longer tied to its original point in space; with the phonograph it was released from its original point in time. [Murray Schafer, *The Tuning of The World*, 1977]

Intermedia differ from mixed media in that they represent a fusion conceptually of the elements; for instance, opera is a mixed medium since the spectator can readily perceive the separation of the musical from the visual aspects of the work, and these two from the literary aspect. In an intermedial work, such as a piece of action music, where the composition is a musical metaphor, where there may or may not be a musical notation, and where the performed result involves sound plus a theatrical effect, it is pointless to try to describe the work according to its resolvable older media of music + theater, as in mixed media, and far closer to the spirit of the piece to identify it as "action music," an intermedium. Note also, however, that with familiarity each intermedium becomes a new medium, and that new intermedia can therefore be said to exist between the old ones. [Dick Higgins, *Some Poetry Intermedia*, 1976]

Concrete sound poetry today is both a return to the primitive and a succession of steps into the technological era.
[Bob Cobbing, "Concrete Sound Poetry 1950-1970," 1970]

I

The art is text-sound, as distinct from text-print and text-seen, which is to say that texts must be sounded and thus heard to be "read," in contrast to those that must be printed and thus be seen. The art is text-sound, rather than sound-text, to acknowledge the initial presence of a text, which is subject to aural enhancements more typical of music. To be precise, it is by nonmelodic auditory structures that language or verbal sounds are poetically charged with meanings or resonances they would not otherwise have. The most appropriate generic term for the initial materials would be "vocables," which my dictionary defines as "a word regarded as a unit of sounds or letters rather than as a unit of meaning." As text-sound is an intermedium located between language arts and musical arts, its creators include artists who initially established themselves as "writers," "poets," "composers," and even "painters"; in their text-sound works, they are, of course, functioning as text-sound artists. Many do visual poetry as well, out of a commitment to exploring possibilities in literary intermedia.

The term text-sound characterizes language whose principal means of coherence is sound, rather than syntax or semantics—where the sounds made by comprehensible words create their own coherence apart from denotative meanings. A simple example would be this "tongue-twister" familiar from childhood:

> If a Hottentot taught a Hottentot tot to talk 'ere the tot
> could totter, ought the Hottentot to be taught to say ought
> or naught or what ought to be taught 'er?

The subject of this ditty is clearly neither Hottentots nor pedagogy but the related sounds of "ot" and "ought," and what holds this series of words together is not the idea or the syntax but those two repeated sounds. It is those sounds that one primarily remembers after hearing this sound-sentence read aloud. As in other text-sound art, this language is customarily recited in a voice that speaks, rather than sings. Thus, the vocal pitches are nonspecific.

The first exclusionary distinction then is that words which have intentional pitches, or melodies, are not text-sound art but song. To put it differently, text-sound art may include recognizable words or phonetic fragments; but once musical pitches are introduced, or musical instruments are added (and once words are tailored to a preexisting melody or rhythm), the results are music and are experienced as such. Secondly, text-sound art differs from "oral poetry," which is syntactically standard language written to be read aloud. These exclusions give the art a purist definition, I admit; but without these distinctions, there is no sure way of separating text-sound art, the true intermedium, from music on one side or poetry on the other. Without this distinction, there would be nothing to write about. (In general, I prefer purist definitions that are elastically understood.)

The firmest straddles I know are the records made by a changing group of New York blacks calling themselves "The Last Poets," whose lead voice chants incendiary lyrics to the accompaniment of pitched background voices and a rapid hand drum, which seems to influence verbal rhythm (rather than vice versa, to repeat a crucial distinction); and *Philomel* (1963), by Milton Babbitt and John

Hollander, where the text is syntactically fragmented and aurally multiplied in ways typical of sound poetry; but the sounds in most of the work are specifically pitched.

"Text-sound" is preferable to "sound poetry," another term for this art, because I can think of work whose form and texture is closer to *fiction* or even *essays* (as traditionally defined), than to poetry.

As word-imagery must be seen to be "read," so must text-sound art be heard sound-word by word-sound. Secondhand experiences, whether by reading the original text or even a report of aural presentations (this essay!), are simply insufficient. Even when put into print, text-sound art is addressed to the ear.

One issue separating work within the art would be whether the sounds are primarily recognizable words or phonetic units. Pieces with audible words usually have something to do with the meaning of these words. Poems without recognizable words are really closer to our experience of an unfamiliar (i.e., "foreign") language. An example is this passage from Armand Schwerner's *The Tablets* (1971):

> hraldar gronen Jesu Kriste sacrifise þranódon
> þögn gardú etaión nok þök
> panaknómen proþörpe pintrpnöte ak Pinitu
>
> vituð ér enn eð hvat?
> festr mun stilna/ok freki rinna

Such words need not be "translated," because the acoustic experience of them is theoretically as comprehensible to one culture as to another.

Morse Code is not text-sound art either, even though it communicates comprehensible words to those who know its language; it is a linguistic code whose rhythm cannot be varied if communication is to be secure.

In my opinion, the better work in text-sound art emphasizes identifiable words, rather than phonemes; but it would be foolish to establish blanket rules about the viability of this or that material.

One could also distinguish pieces which are performed live from those which can exist only on electronic recording tape; those which are multivoiced (and thus usually canonical in form) from those which are univoiced; those which are texts composed exclusively of words from those which add scoring instructions; and those which involve improvisation from those which can be repeated with perceptible precision.

Though superficially playful, text-sound art embodies serious thinking about the possibilities of vocal expression and communication; it represents not a substitute for language but an expansion of our verbal powers.

One major factor separating present work from past is the text-sound artists' increasing consciousness of the art's singularity and its particular traditions.

References

Babbitt, Milton, and Hollander, John. *Philomel* (1963). Cambridge, Mass.: Acoustic Research—DGG, n.d. Record.

Ball, Hugo. *Flight Out of Time*. New York: Viking Press, 1974.

Cobbing, Bob. "Concrete Sound Poetry 1950-70." In *Concrete Poetry*. Amsterdam: Stedilijk Museum, 1970.

Higgins, Dick. "Some Poetry Intermedia," *A Dialectic of Centuries*. New York: Printed Editions, 1978.

Hollander, John. "Philomel." In *Possibilities of Poetry*, edited by Richard Kostelanetz. New York: Delta, 1970.

Houédard, Dom Sylvester. "Introduction," *Kroklok*, I/1 (1971).

Morawski, Stefan. "What Is a Work of Art," *Inquiries into the Fundamentals of Aesthetics.* Cambridge, Mass.: M.I.T. Press, 1974.

Russolo, Luigi. "The Art of Noise." In *Futurist Performance,* edited by Michael Kirby. New York: E. P. Dutton, 1971.

Schwerner, Armand. *The Tablets, I-XV.* New York: Grossman, 1971.

——. *The Tablets, I-XVIII.* Dusseldorf: S Press, 1975. Record.

Valery, Paul. "Pure Poetry: Notes for a Lecture." In *The Art of Poetry.* New York: Bollingen, 1958.

Though text-sound art is, in its consciousness of its singular self, a distinctly new phenomenon, it has roots in the various arts it encompasses. On one hand, it extends back to primitive chanting which, one suspects, was probably developed for worship ceremonies. One extension of this tradition is nonmelodic religious declamation in which the same words are repeated over and over again, such as Hebrew prayers which are spoken so rapidly that an observer hears not distinct words but repeated sounds. (Harris Lenowitz calls them "speed mantras.") Modern text-sound art also reflects such folk arts as the U.S. tobacco auctioneer's spiel, the evangelical practice of "speaking in tongues" and *Ketjak: The Ramayana Monkey Chant,* in which several score Indonesian men rapidly chant in and out of the syllable "tjak." (This last, which is available on a Nonesuch record, is a masterpiece of the text-sound art.) To Charles Morrow, a contemporary practitioner, these folk text-sound arts exemplify "special languages for special communication." However, one critical difference between these precursors and contemporary practitioners is that the former do not consider themselves "artists."

In the history of modern music, text-sound art draws upon an eccentric vocal tradition, epitomized by Arnold Schoenberg's *Sprechgesang,* in which the singing voice touches a note but does not sustain the pitch in the course of enunciating the word. In practice, this technique minimizes the importance of musical tone (and, thus, of melody) and, by contrast, emphasizes the audible word. One measure of this shift in emphasis is the sense that language in *Sprechstimme* is usually easier to understand than that in music. This technique also appears in Chinese and Korean opera, which may have influenced Schoenberg, and in German cabaret singing, which probably did. Successors to the latter include Ernst Toch's *Geographical Fugue* (1930), which is composed of place names which are declaimed by a "speaking chorus" in overlapping rhythms; and the patter-song, in which words are spoken while instruments play melody in the background (e.g., in *My Fair Lady,* "I've grown accustomed to her face. . . . ").

In visual arts, text-sound work draws upon the development of abstraction, or nonrepresentational art, and the initial figures in adapting this esthetic idea to language were Wassily Kandinsky and Kurt Schwitters. The writer Hugo Ball, himself a prominent practitioner, said in a 1917 lecture that Kandinsky, in his book *Der gelbe Klang* (1912), "was the first to discover and apply the most abstract expression of sound in language, consisting of harmonized vowels and consonants." Schwitters, himself a Dadaist like Ball, created an imaginary, nonrepresentational, aurally coherent language for his ambitious *Ursonate* (1922-32), which opens:

Fümms bö wö tää zää Uu,
　　　　　pögiff,
　　　　　　　kwii Ee.

Oooooooooooooooooooooooooooooooo

　　　　dll rrrrrr beeeee bö
　　　　dll rrrrrr beeeee bö fümms bö,
　　　　　rrrrrr beeeee bö fümms bö wö
　　　　　　beeeee bë fümms bö wö tää,
　　　　　　　bö fümms bö wö tää zää,
　　　　　　　　fümms bö wö tää zää Uu:

And he was probably the first to appropriate a musical structure for a totally verbal work. Moholy-Nagy, another sometime visual artist who was also the first perceptive historian of text-sound art, describes Schwitters's masterwork, whose title Moholy translates as "primordial sonata," as "a poem of thirty-five minutes duration, containing four movements, a prelude, and a cadenza in the fourth movement. The words do not exist, rather they might exist in any language; they have no logical only an emotional context; they affect the ear with their phonetic vibrations like music." In recent years, both Eberhard Blum, a German flutist connected with SUNY-Buffalo, and Peter Froehlich of the English Theatre at the University of Ottawa have performed this poem brilliantly, each of them surpassing Schwitters's own partial recording, which is available on a record anthology, *Phonetische Poesie*. Neither Blum's rendition nor Froehlich's is yet, alas, publicly available.

Within the conscious traditions of modern poetry, text-sound art has a much richer history. Contemporary work initially reflects the neologisms that Lewis Carroll incorporated into syntactically conventional sentences, as in the *Jabberwocky* (1855), the invented words implicitly minimizing meaning and emphasizing sound:

> 'Twas brillig, and the slithy toves
>   Did gyre and gimble in the wabe:
> All mimsy were the borogoves,
>   And the mome raths outgrabe.

Historical precursors in continental literature include the German poet Paul Scheerbart, whose most notable (and untypical) poem opens, "Kikakoku!//Ekoralaps!" (1897) or the German poet Christian Morgenstern, whose "Das Grosse Lalula" (1905) opens:

> Kroklokwafzi? Sememmi!
> Seiokrontro—prafriplo:
> Bifzi, bafzi; hulalemi:

quasti basti bo . . .
Lalu lalu lalu lalu la:

In "Zang-Tumb-Tu-Tumb" (1912), Filippo Tommaso Marinetti, himself initially a poet, invented onomatopoeia to portray the sounds of weapons and soldiers: "flic flak zing zing sciaaack hilarious whinnies iiiiiii . . . pattering tinkling 3 Bulgarian battalions marching croooccraaac. . . . " Hugo Ball's most famous poem (1915) was meant to realize a universal language, opening:

gadji beri bimba
glandridi lauli lonni cadori
gadjama bim beri glassala
glandridi glassala tuffm i zimbrabim
blassa galassasa tuffm i zimbrabim. . . .

This work exemplifies the phonetic poetry of such pioneer Dadaists as Raoul Hausmann and Richard Hulsenbeck.

In Russian literature just before the Revolution, Alexei Kruchenyk created a fictitious language, which he called *zaum* (a contraction of a longer phrase, *zaumnyj jazyk,* which can best be translated as "transrational"). Kruchenyk's most audacious manifesto declared, "The word is broader than its meaning." His colleague in Russian futurism, Velemir Klebnikov, by contrast, favored recognizable words for his nonsyntactic poems, rationalizing that "the sound of the word is deeply related to its meaning." In the 1920s, the Frenchman Pierre Albert-Birot added footnotes to specify how his neologisms should be pronounced. He is also credited with this profound adage: "If anything can be said in prose, then poetry should be saved for saying nothing."

In American poetry, the most prominent precursors

are Vachel Lindsay, a troubador eccentric, whose most famous poem, "The Congo" (1914), emphasizes heavy alliteration and such refrains as "Boomlay, boomlay, boomlay, boom"; and E. E. Cummings, whose twenty-fourth poem in *ViVa* (1931) includes:

> sorrydaze bog triperight
> election who so thumb o'clock
> asters miggle dim a ram
> flat hombre sin bangaroom
>
> slim guesser goose pin yessir wheel
> no sendwisp ben jiffyclaus
> bug fainarain wee celibate
> amaranth clutch owch

In American prose, the preeminent precursor is, of course, Gertrude Stein, who wove prose tapestries based upon repetition, rather than syntax and semantics: "In saying what she said she said all she said and she said that she did say what she said when she was saying what she said, and she said that she said what she said in saying what she said and she was saying what she said when she said what she said." ("Two: Gertrude Stein and Her Brother," written 1910-12). One successor to Stein, in post-World War II American literature, was Jack Kerouac, not in his most famous books, to be sure, but in short prose pieces like "Old Angel Midnight," which initially appeared in the opening issue of *Big Table* (1959).

> Spat—he mat and tried & trickered on the step and oo-stepped and peppered it a bit with long mouth sizzle reaching for the thirsts of Azmec Parterial alk-lips to mox & bramajambi babac up the Moon Citlapol—settle la tettle la pottle, la lune—Some kind of—Bong!—the church of St. All's blasts the Ide afternoon & all holy worshippers go confess to Father Everybody with Good Friday ears—Friday afternoon in the universe—

What unifies this collection of semantically unrelated words is, of course, the repetition of sounds, not only in adjacent words but over the paragraph; but one quality distinguishing Kerouac from Stein is that, at least to my ears, the former sounds more literary.

In English literature, the principal progenitor of contemporary text-sound work is, of course, James Joyce's polylingual, neologistic masterpiece, *Finnegans Wake* (1939), which is, incidentally, like Stein's work, closer in form and tone to "prose" than "poetry."

References

Bory, Jean-François, ed. *Raoul Hausmann*. Paris: L'Herne, 1972.

Cummings, E. E. *ViVa*. New York: Liveright, 1931.

Hausmann, Raoul. *Phonemes*. Dusseldorf: S Press, 1970. Record.

Joyce, James. *Finnegans Wake*. London: Faber, 1939.

——. "Anna Livia Plurabelle," *Finnegans Wake*. New York: Folkways, 1951. Record.

Kandinsky, Wassily. Excerpts from "Klange." In *Anthologie der Abseitigen/Poètes a l'Écart*, edited by Carola Giedion-Welcker. Zurich: Verlag der Arche, 1965.

Kerouac, Jack. "Old Angel Midnight," *Big Table*, I/1 (1959).

Ketjak: The Ramayana Monkey Chant. New York: Nonesuch, n.d. Record.

Marinetti, Filippo Tommaso. "Zang-Tumb-Tu-Tumb," as quoted by Luigi Russolo, "The Art of Noise." In *Futurist Performance*, edited by Michael Kirby. New York: E. P. Dutton, 1971.

Markov, Vladimir. *Russian Futurism*. Berkeley: University of California Press, 1968.

Moholy-Nagy, L. *Vision in Motion*. Chicago: Paul Theobald, 1946.

Morgenstern, Christian. "Das Grosse Lalula," *Kroklok*, I/1 (1971).

Pansori. New York: Nonesuch, 1972. Record.

Phonetische Poesie. [With Hausmann, Klebnikov, Kruchenyk, Schwitters]. Neuweid: Luchterhand, n.d.

Scheerbart, Paul. "Kikakoku!" *Kroklok,* I/1 (1971).

Schwitters, Kurt. "Ursonate," *Das Literarische Werk.* Cologne: Dumont Schauberg, 1973.

Stein, Gertrude. "Two: Gertrude Stein and Her Brother," *Two: Gertrude Stein and Her Brother.* New Haven: Yale University Press, 1951.

III

One post-World War II development that had a radical effect on text-sound art was the common availability of both the sound amplifier and the tape recorder, and these two technologies together did more than anything else to separate "contemporary" endeavors from earlier "modern" work. That is, after 1955, a verbal artist, now equipped with sound-tuning equipment, could change the volume and texture of his microphone-assisted voice; he could eliminate his high frequencies or his lows, or accentuate them, as well as adding reverberation. By varying his distance from the microphone or his angle of vocal attack, he could drastically change the timbre of his voice. With recording technology, the language artist could add present sound to past sound—overdub, as it is called—thereby making a duet, if not a chorus, of himself. He could mix sounds made in the studio with those from the street; or he could change the pitch of his voice, either up or down, by respectively increasing or decreasing the speed of his tape. More important, he could also affix on tape a definitive audio interpretation of his own text, and indeed it would sound exactly the same every time it was played at the appropriate mechanical speed. By expanding the range of audio experience, these new technologies also implicitly suggested ways of nontechnological innovation. As Bob Cobbing judged, "Where the tape recorder leads, the human voice can follow."

Several Europeans now about fifty years in age established themselves in the 1950s, each developing a characteristic style. Henri Chopin, a Frenchman presently living in England, records his own vocal phonetic sounds which are then subjected to several elementary tape manipulations, such as overdubbing and speed-changing, usually producing an abrasive aural experience that reminds me less of other text-sound art than of John Cage's fifties music for the pianist David Tudor. Since Henri Chopin starts not with a verbal text but with a limited range of specified vocables, and then electronically manipulates these initially vocal sounds in ways that disguise their human origins, his work is perceived as *music,* rather than as text-sound art—more precisely, as a "musique concrete" that uses only natural sounds. If only to acknowledge its author's professional origins in poetry, perhaps this might better be classified as "sound-text" or, as Chopin himself calls it, "poesie sonore" (poetic sound), as distinct from sound poetry.

François Dufrêne, a Parisian, is best known for his "cri-rhythms," which is his term for his art of extreme, hysterical human sounds; "rhythmic cries" would be the best English translation. As Bob Cobbing describes them, these pieces "employ the utmost variety of utterances, extended cries, shrieks, ululations, purrs, yarrs, yaups and cluckings; the apparently uncontrollable controlled into a spontaneously shaped performance." A piece like *Crirhythme pour Bob Cobbing* (1970)—the best of the several I have heard—sounds so extraordinary on first hearing that one can scarcely believe a single human being is producing such aural experience, even with the aid of microphones; and one dimension of hearing Dufrêne is wonderment at how he does it. (I am told that his live performances are indeed extraordinary.) However, on record, his pieces became less awesome with each rehearing; and he curiously suffers from sounding too much like Chopin, even though they produce their works in contrary ways. Perhaps Dufrêne's text-less art is really a species of vocal *theater,* to introduce yet another categorical distinction.

Bernard Heidsieck, also a Parisian, works, by contrast,

with recognizable words, either spoken emphatically by himself, or collected on the street and off the radio. These words are edited into rapidly paced, rhythmically convulsive aural collages which not only join language with nonverbal noises but also combine linguistic materials not normally found together. His term for this work is "poesie action"; and several examples strike my Frenchless ears as mixing a newscaster or other loudspeaker voice with a more intimate narrator (apparently Heidsieck himself) against a background of miscellaneous noises. Though his works appear to satirize or editorialize about current events, their syntax is essentially collage, which I regard as the great early twentieth century invention that, though once extremely fertile and also conducive to audiotape, has by now become hackneyed. Nonetheless, Heidsieck's pieces are more charming than, say, Chopin's or Dufrêne's, as well as considerably richer in audio-linguistic texture. Of those I have heard, my favorite is *Carrefour de la Chaussee d'Antin* (1973).

Another member of the Parisian scene, Brion Gysin (b. 1916, England), favors linguistic permutations, as with *I Am That I Am.* All the possible combinations of these five words are then subjected to speeding, slowing and/or superimposition. The verbal text for this work appears in *Brion Gysin Let the Mice In* (1973), and the audio version, made at the BBC in 1959, is reproduced on the initial *Dial-A-Poem* record (1972). An intimidating audiovisual rendition of both the text and tape is included in my Camera Three-CBS television program, *Poetry To See & Poetry To Hear* (1974) that is presently available from the New York State Education Department. I consider *I Am That I Am* one of the indisputable classics of text-sound art.

Among the other notable contemporary European

text-sound artists are the Englishman Bob Cobbing; the Scotsman Edwin Morgan; the Belgian Paul de Vree; the Czech Ladislav Novak; the Frenchmen Gil J. Wolman and Jean-Louis Brau; the Austrian Ernst Jandl; several Swedes associated with Stockholm's Fylkingen group (including Bengt Emil Johnson, Sten Hanson, and Bengt af Klintberg); and the Germans Hans G. Helms and Ferdinand Kriwet. The latter (born in 1942, and thus younger than the others) has edited American news broadcasts of both the 1969 moonshot and the 1972 American political campaigns into first-rate English-language audio collages; and Helms wrote *Fa:m'Aniesgwow* (1958), a pioneering book-record which resembles *Finnegans Wake* in realizing linguistic coherence without observing consistently the vocabulary of any particular language. More specifically, through attentiveness to the sound of language, Helms creates the illusion of a modern tongue:

Mike walked in on the : attense of ChJazzus as they sittith softily sipping sweet okaykes H-flowered, purrhushing 'eir goofhearty offan-on-beats, holding moisturize'-palmy sticks clad in clamp dresses of tissue d'arab, drinks in actionem fellandi promoting protolingamations e state of nascendi; completimented go!scene of hifibrow'n'. . . .

The most interesting of the other Europeans, in my experience, is Jandl, a Viennese high school teacher of English, who works exclusively in unaided live performance (the pre-World War II way), declaiming published phonetic texts, mostly in German but sometimes in English, which are usually inventive in form and witty in language. In New York in the spring of 1972, he did an exceptional performance of a long poem, "Teufelsfalle," which also appears in his book *Der Kunstliche Baum* (1970). "Beastiarim," the last piece on his record, *Laut und Luise* (1968), is a vocal tour de force. However, in part because of his antitechnological bias, Jandl's work seems to terminate a style, rather than suggest future developments.

References

Chopin, Henri. *Audiopoems*. London: Tangent Records, 1971. Record.

——. *Le Voyage Labiovelaire* and *Le Cri*. Dusseldorf: S Press, 1972. Audiotape.

——. "Poesie Sonore," *Kontexts* 8 (Spring, 1976).

Dufrêne, François. "Le Lettrisme est toujours pendant," *Opus International* 40-41 (January, 1973).

Gysin, Brion. "I Am That I Am." On *Dial-A-Poem*. New York: Giorno Poetry Systems, 1972. Record.

——. "I Am That I Am." In *Poetry To See & Poetry To Hear*, edited by Richard Kostelanetz. Albany, N. Y.: State Education Dept., 1974. Videotape.

——./ *Let the Mice In*. West Glover, Vt.: Something Else, 1973.

Heidsieck, Bernard. *Poeme-Partition J* (1961) *& Carrefour de la Chaussee d'Antin* (1972). Dusseldorf: S Press, 1973. Audiotape.

——. *Partition V*. Paris: Le Soleil Noir, 1973. Record and book.

——. *Trois Biopsies + Un Passe-Partout*. Paris: Multi-Techniques, n.d.

——. *Poesie Action Poesie Sonore, 1955-75*. Paris: Atelier Exposition Annick Le Moine, 1976. Record.

Helms, Hans G. *Fa:m' Ahniesgwow*. Cologne: Dumont Schauberg, 1959. Book with record.

Jandl, Ernst. *Laut und Luise*. Berlin: Wagenbach, 1968. Record.

——. *Der Künstliche Baum*. Berlin: Luchterhand, 1970.

Johnson, Bengt Emil, et al. "Fylkingen," *Source* 8 (July, 1970).

Kriwet, Ferdinand. *Hortext-Takes*. Dusseldorf: Art Scene, 1970. Record.

———. *Campaign Radio Text IX*. Dusseldorf: Private audio-tape, 1972.

L'Autonomatopek 1. [With Cobbing-Lockwood, Chopin, Dufrêne]. Paris: Opus Disque, 1973. Record.

Mottram, Eric. "A Prosthetics of Poetry: The Art of Bob Cobbing," *Second Aeon*, 16/17 (n.d.).

O Huigin, Sean. "Eighth International Sound Poetry Festival," *Open Letter*, III/3 (Fall, 1975).

IV

Perhaps the key issue dividing North American text-sound artists from their European counterparts is the use of electronic machinery, for American text-sound art at its best is either more technological or less technological than European. In the first respect, the text-sound artist uses either multi-tracking, sound-looping or microscopic tape-editing to achieve audiotape effects that technically surpass European work. The principal figures here are Steve Reich, Charles Amirkhanian, Glenn Gould, Charles Dodge, Jerome Rothenberg-Charles Morrow, John Giorno, and myself. The other strain of American text-sound artists consists of those who have largely avoided electronic machinery, except of course to make permanent records of their work: John Cage, Jackson Mac Low, Norman Henry Pritchard, W. Bleim Kern, Bill Bissett, Emmett Williams, Charles Stein, Michael McClure, and a Canadian group calling themselves the Four Horsemen.

Steve Reich studied music composition with Luciano Berio and Darius Milhaud before using language to explore the compositional idea of modular variation. Essentially, a limited phrase, or module, whether musical or verbal, is repeated in a gradually changing way; and with multi-tracking, a phrase that is played at one speed can interact with the same phrase played at another speed, sometimes producing a pulsing sound. Reich's earliest verbal work, *It's Gonna Rain,* was composed in San Francisco in January, 1965. As the artist remarks on the record jacket, "The voice belongs to a young black Pentecostal preacher who called himself Brother Walter. I recorded him along with the pigeons one Sunday afternoon in Union Square in downtown San Francisco.

Later at home I started playing with tape loops of his voice and, by accident, discovered the process of letting two identical loops go gradually in and out of phase with each other." That is, the two loops containing the same material begin in unison on two machines; but because of mechanical imprecision, they gradually move completely out of phase with each other, the same words creating in relation to each other their own serendipitous rhythms and melodies. The first part of this piece realizes an incantatory intensity without equal in audio language art, as the phrase "It's gonna rain" is repeated into a chorus of itself. At one point, for instance, one hears the entire phrase against the background of a pulsing "rain"; at later points, "it's a" becomes the choral bass for the aural assemblage. All this repetition of a few words, needless to say, intensifies the invocatory meanings. At times, *It's Gonna Rain* sounds like the Indonesian monkey chant, except that Reich has used electronics to do the aural work of a hundred men; as machine-assisted art, his work exists only on audiotape or record.

The second part of this piece is less dense than the first, and the words are less comprehensible, especially as the language disintegrates into an obscure belching sound. Reich's other recorded text-sound piece, *Come Out* (1966), is based on a single phrase spoken by a black teenager who had suffered a police beating, "come out to show them," which initially referred to his having to open up his fresh bruise "and let some of the bruise blood come out to show them." As Reich describes his compositional technique, "The phrase 'come out to show them' was recorded on both channels, first in unison and then with channel two slowly beginning to move ahead. As the phrase begins to shift, a gradually increasing reverberation is heard which slowly passed into a sort of canon or round. Eventually the two voices divide into four and then into eight." The piece suffers from the same hysteria as *It's Gonna Rain*; and perhaps because the original aural material is more explicitly articulated here (and the piece was premiered at a political rally), the overkill is yet more blunt. Again, however, the language disintegrates into a puzzling, sweeping sound that goes on too long. It is the first work, rather than this, which is Reich's text-sound masterpiece.

The earlier works of the San Francisco text-sound artist, Charles Amirkhanian, reflect Reich's influence. A musician who took his B.A. in literature, Amirkhanian seeped himself in both contemporary composition and high-quality tape recording as "Sound Sensitivity Information Director" (i.e., music director) at KPFA, the Pacifica foundation radio station in Berkeley. In 1971, he produced *If In Is,* which he characterizes as "an eleven-minute tape based on strong rhythmic patterns created through the repetition of three words ("inini," "bull-pup," "banjo") arranged in phrases on separate tape loops and played simultaneously on multiple tape machines." When the same words aurally coincide, a pulsing sound is produced, much as in Reich's modular art; and this pulse becomes a ground bass for continually varying aural-verbal relationships.

A similar compositional technique informs *Just* (1972), included on the record anthology *10 + 2: 12 American Text Sound Pieces* (1975), which Amirkhanian organized and produced. This starts with Amirkhanian repeating "rainbow chug bandit," which scarcely sounds like promising material. However, a second male voice (which also belongs to Amirkhanian) then says "rainbow chug bandit bong" at a faster speed. Then a third voice enters with "chug chug chug chug bandit bong," and the piece has already begun to pulse. Becoming yet more complex, it then becomes simpler, ending after four and a half minutes with repetitions of "bandit

bandit." In this, as in other post-1971 pieces of his, Amirkhanian has a sure sense of pace; his works are never too long for their material. As a conscious and respectful text-sound artist, Amirkhanian has also created individual works that reveal the influence of the people to whom they are explicitly dedicated—*Mugic* (for François Dufrêne, 1973) and *Muchrooms* (for John Cage, 1974).

In 1973 Amirkhanian developed a more characteristic way of text-sound working. Essentially, he takes recorded material and then cuts apart the tape in various ways, so that sentences or even words are broken in the middle, or the beginning of one sentence is spliced or overlayed in the middle of its predecessor, or key words are repeated in varying proximities to each other, or a single voice is multiplied into a duet or chorus of itself. On the *10 + 2* anthology is *Heavy Aspirations* (1973), which is based on the musicologist Nicholas Slonimsky's lecture on "The Revolution in Twentieth Century Music." From a tape of the whole, Amirkhanian extracted Slonimsky's characteristic phrases and speech patterns. These are aurally repeated, as the tape moves between straight transcription and doctored sound, abruptly shifting from one kind of material to another, and from one rhythm to another. Amirkhanian even dwells on Slonimsky's reference to *Just* and "text-sound" art (which he defines as "words alone"). Though *Heavy Aspirations* is as mocking in detail as its title suggests, the whole is endearing (and appropriate as a seventy-ninth birthday present for its subject). Another tighter, better effort in this style is the autobiographical *Roussier (not Rouffier)* (1973), which ingeniously takes apart the simple phrase, "Charles Amirkhanian, a composer of Armenian extraction" against a background of his earlier text-sound pieces for four full minutes. It must be heard to be believed.

Both looping and overlaying come together in *Seatbelt, Seatbelt* (1973), which I take to be Amirkhanian's single greatest piece. It opens with a male voice regularly repeating the paired words of the title, and then varying the rhythm, as his voice is divided over two tracks and his sibilants become more emphatic. Then one voice repeats "seat" while another says "belt," each proceeding at his own rhythm. Then two different voices say just "seatbelt" at different speeds, as more voices enter, saying, in normal speaking voices, either "seat," "belt," or "seatbelt." Perhaps all five acknowledged performers are speaking now. Suddenly, the chorus shifts to "chung chung quack quack bone" in unison, and then to "cryptic cryptic quack quack" before dividing into two groups, one pair saying the first sequence, the second pair the second sequence. Arrangements like this continue for nearly fifteen minutes. At one point, all the voices say "quack" in different tempi, their rhythms sometimes coinciding; and the piece runs out with two voices saying "quack quack" at the same pace as the initial "seatbelt seatbelt." This work is dense and witty and ingenious; it is utterly nonrepresentational of anything except itself and, of course, the innovative powers of human imagination.

The Canadian pianist Glenn Gould created a minor masterpiece of text-sound tape editing in the course of something else—a radio documentary on people who live in Canada's northernmost territories. Commissioned by the Canadian Broadcasting Company and entitled *The Idea of North* (1967), this program opens with a woman saying, "I was fascinated by the country as such. I flew north from Churchill [Northern Manitoba]...." Forty-five seconds later, a male voice enters, saying something different—less appreciative, more cynical about the Canadian north—while the first voice continues undistracted. Thirty seconds later, a second male voice enters this ongoing fugue, taking another viewpoint, but like the others articulating themes that are elaborated later in the documentary. The voices change in relative volume, so that one or another predominates at various times, as in a musical fugue; and then they appear to blend evenly into each other, so that one hears not individual expository lines but, for example, repetition of the key word "north." And then all three voices slowly fade out, ending this tour de force. Gould produced a second text-sound fugue for a later radio documentary, *The Latecomers* (1969), which deals with life in Newfoundland; but perhaps because the voices enter too quickly on each other, and there is no key word to connect their talking together, this later example of "contrapuntal radio," as Gould calls it, sounds comparatively jumbled and pointless.

Charles Dodge has developed a singular text-sound art which others value highly, but I find immature. His forte is computer-assisted speech synthesis. The most useful description of his extraordinary compositional procedure appears, curiously, not on the single record of his own text-sound works, *Synthesized Speech Music* (1976), but in the notes to the Amirkhanian anthology:

> The computer speech analysis/synthesis technique involves recording a voice speaking the message to be synthesized, digitizing (through an analogue-to-digital converter) the speech, mathematically analyzing the speech to determine its frequency content with time, and synthesizing the voice (speaking the same passage) from the results of the analysis. On synthesis, any of the components of the analysis (e.g., pitch, speech rate, loudness, formats) may be altered independently of the others. Thus, using synthetic speech (unlike manipulation of tape recording) one may change the speed of vocal articulation without changing the pitch contour of the voice (and vice versa).

This procedure requires so much awesome technical competence that it is perhaps gratuitous to note that little of value comes from it. It is true that Dodge can create various voices, both male and female—a testament to his virtuosity—but they sound more like each other than anyone (or anything) else. In the background are non-vocal (or nonpseudovocal) pitched sounds that have the obvious aural defect of resembling the "vocal" sounds, the work as a whole at times suggesting that Dodge is creating an alternative universe with a single all-pervasive Dodgian aural style. Then, the voices resound on pitch some of the time, moving Dodge's art into song; but these singing voices lack the charm, which is likewise synthetic, of, say, Walter Carlos's Moog-generated chorus on *The Well-Tempered Synthesizer* (1970). Dodge draws his language from some trendy poems by Mark Strand; but since most of these words are aurally obliterated, one cannot follow the language without a copy of Strand in hand. (Does Strand think these "settings" enhance his poetry? Or advance his reputation?) Since there is no perceptible relation between the language and the audio technique, the latter seems as arbitrary as Dodge's freely atonal pitches; and if there is a complementary system, nothing in the commentary suggests a key. Technological invention is so valuable in contemporary art that I am reluctant to dismiss Dodge's work completely; but since the technique itself *is* suggestive, I hope he knows how far he has to go.

A far more successful electronic text-sound adaptation of a poetic text is Charles Morrow's *Sound Work* (1968), which is based on "The Beadle's Testimony" in Jerome Rothenberg's *Poland/1931* (1974). Morrow, as "sound designer" (his own term), reorganized the one-page text so that all its words were grouped with each other—all "thes," all "jewels," all "walls," and so forth were collected together. He invited Rothenberg to record these separate lists. Morrow then took the isolated words and spliced them back into the proper order of the original poem, producing, in effect, a tape of Rothenberg reading "The Beadle's Testimony" in a stunning, emphatic style that would be impossible in live performance and probably inconceivable without the example of audiotape. Both Rothenberg and Morrow have recently done Amerindian chanting which, to repeat my initial distinctions, is not text-sound art but theatrical song.

My own work arose from an invitation to be guest artist at WXXI-FM in Rochester, New York; and though I had not worked in a sound studio before, I brought along some of my more experimental verbal texts. The medium, I discovered, lends itself to my truncated (or minimal) fictions, in part because radio is a much faster medium than live performances. For that reason, the same one-word paragraphs of, say, "Milestones in a Life" or "Plateaux," which seem terribly rushed in live performance, find a more appropriate temporal format on audiotape. For "Excelsior," which is a dialogue between two people who speak in one-word paragraphs, I used stereo distribution of my voice to enhance the aural experience in ways that would be impossible in live performance; and now instead of reading these prose narratives for audiences that request them, I would sooner play my WXXI tapes.

With my own more elaborate experimental texts, the medium offered unforeseen possibilities. *Recyclings,* for instance, is a nonsyntactic prose piece that was composed in 1974 from earlier essays of mine. Essentially, I took my own prose and subjected it to a reworking procedure that kept the language but destroyed the syntax. Each earlier essay of mine was reduced to a single page of new, recycled text. The first 64 pages (of 192) were published as a book which, I discovered, can be read vertically and diagonally just as feasibly as it can be read horizontally. To reproduce this visual experience aurally, I hit upon the technique of reading each page of *Recyclings* horizontally, then adding new voices that read the same text a few seconds behind. The result is a nonsynchronous canon where words relate to each other in several directions simultaneously. (*Recyclings* also exists on videotape, where the imagery is visually isolated pairs of my lips.) A second nonsyntactic text of mine, "The Declaration of Independence," likewise employs an eight-track recording machine to create an amateur Presbyterian chorus of myself (amplified differently on each track), this time reading the same text in ragged unison Since the text is that of the historic Declaration of Independence read backwards word by word, the ironies multiply as one hears familiar locutions reversed.

After tentative beginnings with a record on which he did not speak at all, *Raspberry & Pornographic Poem* (1967), John Giorno has become a consummate performer of his own texts. His technique, which has developed considerably in the past decade, consists of chopping apart a prose sentence, so that its words are repeated in different linear arrangements, with different line-breaks, and then duplicated in adjacent columns:

```
                       There is
      There is         nothing
      nothing          there
        there          There is nothing
There is nothing       there
        there          There is nothing there
There is nothing there
```

Giorno turned to electronic technology for a single capability, echoing, so that he need not say the left-hand column: It could be electronically reproduced as a faint replica of his initial voice, thereby increasing the potential for after-sound analogous to the "after-image" of the visual arts. The principal development in his text-sound artistry, as represented by his contributions to his own *Dial-A-Poem* anthologies, has primarily been a complication in the echoing. In his sides of the two-record set *John Giorno/William Burroughs* (1975), Giorno developed a double echo that could be varied in quality, becoming more reverberant (and reechoed) at times and more distorted at other times. Even though each generation of echo is more decayed than its predecessor, this technique makes the aural texture of his reading considerably denser. That is, the double echo increases not only Giorno's self-replication, which appears to interest him, but also the audiographic impact of his statements. Obsessive echoing has so completely become Giorno's single audio trademark that no one else can use it without having their work confused with his. (Rothenberg-Morrow tried at least once, in a private tape I have. Sure enough, it sounds like Giorno.) All this technique notwithstanding, Giorno's work is built not upon isolated words but upon whole phrases; it depends for coherence not upon sound but syntax, semantics and prose narrative—all the traditional baggage—to evoke his macabre vision. Indeed, his recent collaboration with Burroughs becomes an implicit acknowledgment of the literary origins of Giorno's sensibility. To be precise, this is not text-sound art at all, but inventively amplified poetry (which is thus more acceptable to some "poetry" circles); and that recognition perhaps explains why genuine text-sound work is so sparsely repesented in Giorno's *Dial-A-Poem* anthologies.

Other Americans making electronic text-sound art include Alvin Lucier, whose *I Am Sitting in a Room* (1970) begins with him reading a 100-word prose statement which is recorded on tape. The recorded version is then played in the same space in which the original statement was made and rerecorded on tape one generation away from the initial live statement. This procedure of broadcasting and rerecording is continued through several generations, as feedback progressively obliterates the text that paradoxically becomes less audible as it becomes, thanks to repetition, more familiar. Francis Schwartz's *Score-Painting for Julio Cortazar* (1974) is a bilingual visualization of an allusive visual text that overdubs the author's voice, saying various things at various speeds, about his subject.

References

Amirkhanian, Charles. *Roussier (not Rouffier), Seatbelt Seatbelt, If In Is, Mugic, Muchrooms.* Berkeley: Private audiotape, 1974.

Cook, Geoffrey. "Sound Poetry and Poetry Sounds," *Ear*, III/2 (March, 1977).

Dodge, Charles. *Synthesized Speech Music (1973-75).* New York: CRI, 1976. Record.

Giorno, John. *Raspberry & Pornographic Poem.* New York: Intravenus Mind, 1967. Record.

——, co-author. *John Giorno/William Burroughs.* New York: D'Arc, 1975. Record.

——. *The Dial-A-Poem Poets.* New York: Giorno Poetry Systems, 1972. Record.

——. *Disconnected.* New York: Giorno Poetry Systems, 1974. Record.

——, ed. *Biting off the Tongue of a Corpse.* New York: Giorno Poetry Systems, 1975. Record.

Gould, Glenn. *The Idea of North.* Toronto: CBC Learning Systems, 1971. Record.

——. *The Latecomers.* Toronto: CBC Learning Systems, 1971. Record.

——. "Radio as Music," *The Canada Music Book* (Spring-Summer, 1971).

Kostelanetz, Richard. *Experimental Prose.* New York: Assembling, 1976. Audiotape.

——. *Three Prose Pieces.* Syracuse, N.Y.: Synapse, 1975. Videotape.

——. "Audio Art," *Ear,* III/2 (March, 1977).

——. "Making Music of the Sound of Words," *New York Times,* 24 July 1977.

Lucier, Alvin. "I Am Sitting in a Room," *Source,* IV/1 (Jan., 1970).

Morrow, Charles and Rothenberg, Jerome. *Sound Work.* New York: Private audiotape, n.d.

Reich, Steve. *It's Gonna Rain.* New York: Columbia Records, 1969. Record.

——. *Come Out.* New York: CBS-Odyssey, 1967. Record.

——. *Writings about Music.* Halifax: Nova Scotia College of Art & Design, 1974.

Schwartz, Francis. *Score-Painting for Julio Cortazar.* San Juan, P.R.: Privately produced, 1974. Audiotape.

V

John Cage, one of the key figures in nonelectronic American text-sound art, has curiously also been a pioneer in electronic music, with tape compositions dating back to his *Williams Mix* of the early fifties; but his text-sound works have consisted largely of his live, formal, unemphatic readings of his own mostly nonsyntactic texts. Whereas several earlier Cage pieces incorporated spoken language, such as the funny narrative anecdotes of *Indeterminacy* (1958), or the aleatory words that happened to be on the twelve radios in *Imaginary Land-scape* IV (1952), Cage began in the seventies to make works composed exclusively of language; and these turned out to be as structurally nonclimactic and non-hierarchic as his musical work. *Mureau* (1970), the first in this series, is based upon Henry David Thoreau's remarks about music, which Cage then reassembles, via *I Ching* processes, into a mix of syllables, words, and phrases. The result is a verbal pastiche in which one can perceive references to music and nature (and thus to Thoreau's characteristic vocabulary). *Mureau,* whose title indicatively combines the first part of "music" with the second part of "Thoreau," has been commercially recorded on a cassette tape published by S Press in Germany; and this tape is best heard with a copy of the text (available in Cage's book *M.* [1973]) in front of one's eyes:

> sparrowsitA gROsbeak betrays itself by that peculiar squeak-ariEFFECT OF SLIGHTEst thinkling measures soundness ingpleasa we hear! Does it not rather hear us? sWhen he hears the telegraph, he thinksthose. . . .

Though the original text is more typographically various than customary typesetting can reproduce, these visual variations have no apparent aural effect. *Mureau* resembles *Finnegans Wake* in sounding somewhat familiar, in both syntax and vocabulary, to English-hearing ears. The composer-critic Tom Johnson finds "a mellifluous kind of music, with pleasant rhythms, clear formal structures, and fragments of lovely sound and nature imagery." I have personally heard Cage read this text aloud against a background tape of a previous reading, thus increasing the aural complexity (and the sense of arbitrary structure); but it is unfortunate that none of these second-generation performances have yet been publicly released.

Cage has since progressed, as he always does, to a yet more severe language mix that he calls *Empty Words.* This might best be characterized as a progressive reduction of material from Thoreau. Cage's own typically technical description is useful here: "Part II: A mix of words, syllables, and letters obtained by subjecting the *Journal* of Henry David Thoreau to a series of *I Ching* chance operations. Pt. I includes phrases. Pt. III omits words. IV omits sentences, phrases, words and syllables; includes only letters and silences." Thus, part II, which partially appeared in the second issue of *Interstate* (1974), has distinct stanzas like this opener:

s or past another
thise and on ghth wouldhad
andibullfrogswasina - perhaps blackbus
each f nsqlike globe?

The live performance of Part IV that I heard Cage do in New York in the spring of 1975 could be characterized as the most extreme presentation of its kind. Whereas most text-sound art is much faster than spoken language, this was much, much slower. Indeed, the smallest phonetic fragments—simply the sounds for the alphabet's letters—were separated by multisecond silences. Musically, the piece seems an extreme extension of Anton Webern or Morton Feldman. More precisely, it is a kind of *inferential art* whose impact depends upon the audience's contextual awareness of the work's origins and purposes.

Though initially known as a poet, Jackson Mac Low studied music composition with John Cage in the late fifties and even composed the accompanying music to the 1960 Living Theater production of his own play, *The Marrying Maiden*. Much of Mac Low's live text-sound art reflects Cage's esthetic influence, particularly in allowing his performers spontaneous choices within predefined constraints. Most of his live pieces are "simultaneities," which is his term for performances that involve more than one voice. In the subset of pieces he calls "Matched Asymmetries" (since 1960), several performers are given a multipart text and asked to read the verbal material at a pace and volume of their own choice, each of them reading the available parts in a preassigned order different from the others. Ideally, the performers should generate individual rhythms and articulations, as well as interacting inventively with each other. An example of this subset is the "Young Turtle Asymmetries," where the aural experience is primarily that of five voices repeating the same words and elongated letter-sounds at different timbres and times. The verbal material is drawn, incidentally, from a popular science magazine and then subjected to an aleatory process that Mac Low calls "through acrostic chance generation." In another subset of scores that he calls "Numbered Asymmetries," each of the performers has a completely different text, and the auditory experience is more unrelievedly chaotic.

A third kind of Mac Low score is the "Vocabulary," which is a noncentered, diffuse visual field containing words composed exclusively from the particular letters in a subject's name (e.g., "Sharon Belle Mattlin," "Peter Innisfree Moore"). To declaim these scores, Mac Low customarily recruits a motley chorus, whose members are instructed to say spontaneously whatever words from the score they wish, at whatever volume and whatever durations, with whatever pauses. A fourth related strain is the "Gatha," which is a collection of related words densely written on graph paper, one letter to a square, in a single direction (i.e., vertical, horizontal, or diagonal). Performers are instructed to read the letters in a geometrical path, which may be horizontal, vertical, or diagonal, thus producing letter-sounds, phonemes, syllables, words and neologisms. Again, the aural experience is that of occasional repetition amid general cacaphony. A fifth kind of live piece is the "Word Event," in which the performers improvise on a single, multisyllabic word, like "environmentally." They are instructed to take this word apart, uttering letters or phonemes and then words drawn from the letters of the initial word (e.g., ellen, ten, leer, tee, toe, nelly). From such limited material, Mac Low and his collaborators have been known to spin pieces lasting over one-half hour. He sometimes performs a simultaneity against a background tape of a previous performance (or two or three).

Of the dozen-plus live performances of Mac Low's text-sound works that I have heard over the years, none struck me as particularly better than the others. Both the "Gatha" and "Vocabulary" are more accessible if the audience can see the score (either in hand or on a projection screen). The concepts are more interesting than the realizations, which invariably go on too long. Mac Low's very best text-sound pieces, in my judgment, are not the live ones to which he devotes more of his attention, but his fewer, primarily electronic works.

Most of these were realized in 1973-74, when Mac Low

had access to the New York University Composers' Workshop. For *Threnody for Sylvia Plath* (1973), he took tapes of Paul Blackburn, Diane Wakoski, Sonia Sanchez, Gregory Corso and Tom Weatherly reading their own poems at Allendale, Michigan, in 1971. Using a battery of tape machines, he fed selections from these tapes simultaneously into a single second-generation monotape. Sections from this initial Mac Low tape were then fed nonsynchronously onto both tracks of a stereotape (the third generation). Thus, while passages from the live reading were repeated, they related to each other in continuously different ways. Here too, the aural experience is that of repetition within chaos, and the most memorable sections mix Diane Wakoski and Sonia Sanchez in an inadvertent duet.

In "Counterpoint for Candy Cohen" (1973), Mac Low explores tape-technique possibilities even further. A single statement of two-dozen words, spoken by a concert announcer named Candy Cohen, is repeated with irregular pauses to make an initial tape which is then transferred continuously, one channel at a time, onto a four-track tape, which thus has four separate channels of nonsynchronous repetition of the initial verbal material. (All the close echoing at this generation is reminiscent of Giorno.) Then, this tape is itself transferred continuously onto each track of a two-track machine, which then has 8 different tracks of the same repeated announcement. Then, this tape is transferred onto each track of the initial four-track machine which thus produces a tape with 32 tracks of sound. This fourth generation is two-tracked into 64 tracks, which is then four-tracked into 256 tracks. As the final piece incorporates all stages in the incremental process, what we hear is the progressive complication of the initial material (two-dozen words and a pause) through several distinct generations into a verbally incomprehensible, but rhythmically pulsing chorus. The experience is extraordinary, and it is perhaps the culmination of Mac Low's interest in nonsynchronous repetition.

The major device of Norman Henry Pritchard's pioneering text-sound art is repetition of the same phrase, so that something other than the original phrase results. In the only conveniently available recorded example, "Gyre's Galax" (1967), the phrase "above beneath" is rapidly repeated with varying pauses between each line. (The reader repeating these words rapidly aloud to himself will get a faint sense of the effect.) The same device informs "Visitary," which appears in Pritchard's principal collection, *The Matrix Poems: 1960-70* (1970). One part of this poem reads as follows:

Dewinged wings
Dewinged wings
wings dewinged
Dewinged wings
wings dewinged
wings dewinged
dewinged wings
wings dewinged
dewinged wings
dewinged wings

Lamentably, Pritchard ceased active publishing around 1971, and his work has not been included in any of the surveys, recordings, or exhibitions of language art.

In one of Pritchard's classes at New York's New School was a yet younger poet, W. Bliem Kern, who adapted the idea of the rapidly repeated phrase to his own purposes, reiterating, for example, "belief in the illusion of," until it sounds like something else. A visual poet as well as a text-sound artist, he tends to do aural renditions of his visual texts, such as the "Crickets" section of his longer poem, "On a Once Quite Evening." Here Kern reproduces in sound the intensity and space of words and letters on the printed page:

I consider this the finest piece in his first collection, *Meditationsmeditationsmeditations* (1973), in which a cassette tape is boxed with Kern's book.

His printed texts range from "straight" poetry, which is undistinguished, to visual texts of words and letters to poems that mix familiar words with unfamiliar, the former becoming semantic touchstones for the latter, as in "magweba":

psom enu how ek anu
time was psom
enu how ek anu time was
psom enu how ek anu
time was

And yet other poems are entirely in a fictitious language that Kern calls "Ooloo." ("Don't try to figure anything out," he once told an interviewer. "There is nothing to figure out.") Whereas most text-sound work is temporally static, Kern's pieces often have an underlying narrative progression. This becomes more pronounced in his book's longest poem, "Dream To Live," which narrates in words, phrases, and phonemes the end of a love affair. The piece is movingly read, through various kinds of material; and I would classify the piece as "fiction" more than a poem and, as a text-sound fiction, an exemplification of its kind.

Kern's texts are written to be performed; whereas most text-sound artists want to create autonomous linguistic structures, Kern's avowed purpose is the communication of personal feeling. "In writing," he declared in a 1973 manifesto lamentably not included in his book, "I am exploring the oral world of nonlinear phenomena, the inner speech, the dialogues with myself as a child before I learned the signs and symbols of our language. I am basically dealing with feelings and translating the verbal into the visual. In performing I am also concerned with feelings and translating the visual into the verbal."

Bill Bissett is a Canadian poet who taped his visually idiosyncratic texts for a record that accompanies his book, *Awake in th Red Desert!* (1968). His principal technique is emphatically repeating a single phrase, like that of the title, which audibly remains as it is, rather than, as in Pritchard and Kern, becoming something else. Too many pieces on this record have musical instruments that are unnecessary, if not detrimental, for the record is as widely uneven and as critically challenging as Bissett's motley books. One of the most suggestive texts in the book is "o a b a," which closes:

sheisa sheisa sheayisa heisasheisa saheis sasheisaheisa sheisa
cumisa cumisa th heart isa cumisa isa cumisa cumisa heisa
   shes
sumisa cumming is sheisa cumisa heisa cumisa cumisa heisa
   she
isa th heart is a cumisa is a earisa hear-tis a earisa eerisacum
   is

However, in his record, Bissett imposes a rhythm on the words, rather than letting them suggest their own rhythm; and the result sounds inept and unconsidered. In another work, the marvelous phrase "supremely massage" is variously repeated as a ground bass, while a lead voice reads an erotic prose text. Perhaps the most wholly successful audio poem is the simplest, which opens:

it be it so be so
it so be so it so
be so it so be so

and closes:

be so it so be so
it so be so is so

And this, unlike other Bissett, is as perfect on the record as it is in the book.

Emmett Williams is, like Bissett, a various and inventive experimentalist; but unlike Bissett, he works sparingly, producing only a few works in each direction he pursues. The best text-sound piece is "Duet," which appears both in his *Selected Shorter Poems* (1975) and on the initial *Dial-A-Poem* record (1972). It opens, with every second line in boldface type:

art of my dark
arrow of my marrow
butter of my abutter
bode of my abode
cope of my scope
curry of my scurry
den of my eden
do of my ado

Becoming a sequence of internal rhymes, so sweetly archaic, that ends:

ye of my aye
y of my my
zip zap zoff of my o zip of zap of zoff
zim zam zoom of my o zim o zam o zoom

Giorno's third anthology record, *Biting off the Tongue of a Corpse* (1975), closes with a gem by Charles Stein, "A Seed Poem," which opens:

rage judge raga
mad judge rage

A mad judge rages
a raga rides

a raga judges
a rug
a jug
a mug
  mud

a mage judge rides a rud rug

a mad judge rides as a mud mage rages

which evokes several internal rhymes within a few words and is, needless to say, delightfully comic.

Another older poet who publishes texts that he also declaims is Michael McClure; the works collected in *Ghost Tantras* (1969) tend to mix syntactically conventional phrases with guttural sounds. This is the first, in its entirety:

GOOOOOOR! GOOOOOOOOOO!
GOOOOOOOOOR!
GRAHHH! GRAHH! GRAHH!
Grah gooooor! Ghahh! Graaarr! Greeeeeer! Grayowhr!
Greeeeee
GRAHHRR! RAHHR! GRAGHHRR! RAHR!
RAHR! RAHHR! GRAHHHR! GAHHR! HRAHR!
BE NOT SUGAR BUT BE LOVE
looking for sugar!
GAHHHHHHHHHHH!
ROWRR!
GROOOOOOOOOOOOOH!

Compared to more recent works, these sound pathetically dumb when read to oneself; perhaps McClure's live declamations are more stunning.

The Four Horsemen consist of four Canadians of independent literary reputation who came together in early 1970 to jam, much as freelance jazzmen do. Bp Nichol, perhaps the most prominent, has published works in several styles, both avant-garde and "trad," as he calls it. Steve McCaffery is a younger writer, London-born, who also collaborates with Nichol in a criticism-combine called The Toronto Research Group. Paul Dutton and Rafael Barreto-Rivera I know only from the record; the latter speaks English with an audible Spanish accent. Their initial text-sound works were collected on a record called *Canadada*, which is undated. (I think it came in my mail around late 1972.) The best piece here is a fugue, entitled "Allegro 108," which opens, "Ben den hen ken len men pen ken fen men yet," with one voice chanting alone on a single note. Then a second voice enters, at first chanting nonsynchronously but then in unison with the initial voice, as a third voice enters, chanting alone on a single note. Then a second voice enters, chanting at first nonsynchronously but then in unison with the initial voice, as a third voice enters, chanting separately at first, as before, but then in unison, as the fourth voice enters. The piece develops a steady emphatic rhythm, as the voices are clearly accustomed to working with each other; and I take "Allegro 108" to be the most persuasive example of the possibilities of leaderless text-sound collaboration.

Other pieces on the record are less spectacular. One, entitled "Coffee Break," repeats the word "sugar." There is, in my judgment, a better rendition of this on the videotape *Poetry To See & Poetry To Hear*. Other Four Horsemen works have too much declarative prose, which sounds amateur in this context, but becomes yet more embarrassing when phonemes are chanted in the background. "In the Middle of a Blue Balloon" incorporates either radio broadcasts or a prerecorded tape, but it does not progress beyond funny noises. Another piece with the charming title of "I Dreamed I Saw Hugo Ball" offers nothing more than an ineffective repetition of itself. "Michael Drayton" incorporates a bass recorder and harmonica, but Barreto-Rivera's insert note confesses, "We became disillusioned with the use of instruments." He continues, "The return of poetry to its origin, the human voice, and away from the printed page has always been of importance in our work. There is a sense in which composing and performing poetry, the excitement generated by each act separately, is magnified for us when these are in conjunction. Voice as direct physical experience is then much more satisfying than voice as energy propelling sounds from an instrument."

There are several other North Americans who call their work "sound poetry" or something similar but are, in my analysis, finally creating something else. Peter Harleman, who produces the record-periodical *Out Loud,* favors syntactically conventional poetry, which is read and sometimes chanted in a continuously emphatic way, electronically amplified to a modest degree. One prominent feature of his work is a concern with personal projection, epitomized by rock-star accents, and in Volume IX of *Out Loud* (1975) he has moved into melodic singing against an accompaniment of clanging bells, all heavily reverberated. Early *Out Loud*s were made with Klyd and Linda Watkins, as well as Tony Cowan, who performed in roughly the same way; some records include needlessly brief excerpts from Bernard Heidsieck, whose superior work makes Harleman seem amateur.

The records of Toby Lurie, *Word Music* (1971) and *Mirror Image* (n.d.), are similarly full of prosy statements which make sentimental appeals to an audience of expected well-wishers; so that the work is less poetry, even, than audiodrama or melodrama, with sound effects and plots that sometimes exploit text-sound devices on behalf of other ends. (An exception is "Innocence," which I found in one of his books. Here a single word is scored, in musical notation, for several pitchless variations.) The term audio theater also defines a mysterious record out of Philadelphia, entitled *Voice Print,* the cover of which has only a photo of a man with dark glasses covering his face with a gloved hand. At the top it reads: Photographs by X⑫, 1974, T. Hatten Middle Earth Books, Inc. The principal vocal device here is whispering, which would be fine for a minute or two, but becomes excessive on both sides of a long-playing record; and the instruments in the background make undistinguished tonal sounds. The biggest bummer of the lot is Kenneth Gaburo's *Lingua II: Maledetto* (1967-68), which opens with a quiet hissing noise. I checked my record player to make sure all was well, and then discovered on the album jacket a boxed footnote, set apart from the composer's garrulous self-description. The footnote revealed that the opening "consists entirely of phoneme (s) and lasts 3 minutes." However, once Gaburo's group of garrulous gabbers got going, one wished for a return to the quiet hiss.

Other North Americans doing interesting live text-sound work include Armand Schwerner, whose great long poem, *The Tablets* (1967 to the present), incorporates a multitude of techniques, both traditional and advanced, typically including both word-imagery and text-sound; Ernest Robson, who has developed a sophisticated method for notating vocal techniques in his syntactically conventional texts; Geoffrey Cook, whose "Jabberwocky" is a modest gem; Beth Anderson, whose "If I Were a Poet" sensitively exploits repetition of choice phrases; Henry Rasof, who prefers a nonsyllabic poetry closer to the European example; A. F. Caldiero, a powerful performer of vocables both pitched and unpitched; Lawrence Weiner, a well-known conceptual artist who has done records of gerunds in two languages; Dick Higgins, whose "Glasslass" exploits the sibilants that others try to avoid; and Larry Wendt, who creates long, ambitious pieces that I find less interesting than the remarkable prose explanations accompanying them.

Of course, text-sound is an open art. There are many roads to be explored, many virgins to be seduced, many alternatives to be rethought, many combinations to be discovered. I suspect as well that there are many more North Americans working independently, unaware not only of what their colleagues are doing, but also of how their own works might be "distributed." In a situation like this, a newcomer could become (and be considered) a major artist quite rapidly. Also, whereas sophisticated Europeans tend to regard text-sound as a familiar form, with an established canon of prominent practitioners, it is open terrain in America; and this perhaps accounts for why American work already seems more varied than European work does.

References

Bissett, Bill. *Awake in th Red Desert: A Recorded Book.* Vancouver: Talonbooks, 1968.

Cage, John. *Mureau.* Hattingen, Germany: S Press, 1972. Audiotape.

——. "Mureau." On *Biting off the Tongue of a Corpse,* edited by John Giorno. New York: Giorno Poetry Systems, 1975. Record.

——. "Empty Words I." In *An Active Anthology,* by John Cage. Fremont, Mich.: Sumac, 1974.

——. "Empty Words II," *Interstate* 2 (1974).

——. "Empty Words III," *Big Deal* 3 (1975).

The Four Horsemen. *Canadada.* Toronto: Griffin House, n.d. Record.

Gaburo, Kenneth. *Lingua II: Maledetto* (1967-68). New York: CRI, 1974.

Higgins, Dick. "Glasslass," *Modular Poems.* West Glover, Vt.: Unpublished Editions, 1974.

Kern, W. Bliem. *Meditationsmeditationsmeditations.* New York: New Rivers, 1973. Book with audiotape.

——. "Sound Poetry," *Poetry Australia* 59 (June, 1976).

Kostelanetz, Richard. "The New Poetries." In *The End of Intelligent Writing,* by Richard Kostelanetz. New York: Sheed & Ward, 1974.

Lurie, Toby. *Word Music.* New York: CMS, 1971. Record.

——. *Mirror Images.* New York: Accent, 1975. Record.

———. *New Forms New Spaces*. San Francisco: Journeys into Language, 1971.

Mac Low, Jackson. *The Black Tarantula Crossword Gathas*. Dusseldorf, 1975. Audiotape.

———. Contributions to *An Anthology*, edited by LaMonte Young. 2d ed. Munich: Heinar Friedrich, 1969.

———. "Thirty-Fifth Light Poem: For the Central Regions of the Sun," *Black Box* 2 (1972). Audiotape.

———. "Chance, Silence & Language," *Alcheringa* 4 (Autumn, 1972).

———. *Stanzas for Iris Lezak*. West Glover, Vt.: Something Else, 1974.

McClure, Michael. *Ghost Tantras*. San Francisco: Four Seasons, 1969.

Nichol, bp. *bp*. Toronto: Coach House, 1967. Book with record.

———. *Motherlove*. Toronto: Allied, n.d.

Pritchard, Norman Henry II. *The Matrix Poems: 1960-70*. Garden City: Doubleday, 1970.

———. "Gyre's Galax." On *New Jazz Poets*, edited by Walter Lowenfels. New York: Broadside, 1967. Record.

Robson, Ernest. *Transwhichics*. Chester Springs, Pa.: Dufour, 1970.

———. *Poetry as Performance Art on and off the Page*. Chester Springs, Pa.: Dufour, 1976.

———, and Robson, Marion. *I Only Work Here*. Chester Springs, Pa.: Dufour, 1974.

Scobie, Stephen. "I Dreamed I Saw Hugo Ball," *Boundary 2*, III/1 (Fall, 1974).

Voice Print. Philadelphia: Middle Earth Books, 1974. Record.

Weiner, Lawrence. *7*. Paris: Yvon Lambert, n.d. Record.

———. *Having Been Done at/Having Been Done to*. Rome: Sperone-Fischer, 1973. Record.

———. *Nothing to Lose/Niets aan Verloren*. Eindhoven: Van Abbemuseum, 1976. Record.

Williams, Emmett. "Duet," *Selected Shorter Poems*. New York: New Directions, 1974.

VI

Every art generates its own critical literature just as it generates its own critical attitude in the artist during the actual moments of creativity—& this is true of both directions along which each art tends to be polarised ie the representative and nonrepresentative—the one gap in this sort of writing has been the area devoted to abstract or concrete poetry—& here over the last 20 years or so a considerable amount of attention has been directed toward the work of visual poets & has been able to operate on the impressive bulk of visual poems now available—little attention however has been similarly directed to the work of the sound poets & one reason for this has been the lack of any comprehensive anthology of soundpoems. [Dom Sylvester Houédard, introduction to *Kroklok*, 1971]

Text-sound art, it is clear, is interesting and consequential. It is a distinct artistic category, with a small army of practitioners; but the greatest threat to its survival—not to speak of its development—is, simply, its unavailability. If the reader of this essay wanted to hear Amirkhanian's *Seatbelt, Seatbelt*, for example, the only way he could satisfy his or her curiosity (or challenge my critical judgment) would be to write Amirkhanian himself, asking the artist for a copy; and if Amirkhanian wrote back that he was reluctant to go through the rigamarole of getting the master from a safe storing place, and then lining up two machines for a dubbing (and that he wanted, say, fifty dollars for the tape copy), no one could blame him. Copying audiotapes is neither as easy nor as cheap as copying manuscripts. One reason why the work of Tony Gnazzo is not discussed in this essay is that Gnazzo wrote that he was, not unreasonably, tired of making copies, even for likely supporters such as myself.

What is needed at the beginning, of course, are selective

anthologies, not only to make everyone aware of what is being done, but also to prompt current practitioners to move onto something else. For another thing, anthologies might force artists to make individual pieces more various; too much work so far is based upon a single audio idea, which is introduced at the beginning and then sustained to the piece's conclusion. The first native anthology entirely devoted to this text-sound art was Charles Amirkhanian's *10 + 2: 12 American Text Sound Pieces* (1975). This record includes two of Amirkhanian's better works, *Just* (1972) and *Heavy Aspirations* (1973); a lesser John Giorno piece, read not by himself but by a salaciously intriguing, but less talented, teenage girl; an excerpt from *62 Mesostics re Merce Cunningham* (1970), read not by Cage but by a San Francisco composer named Jack Briece; a Clark Coolidge piece that even the program notes acknowledge as "atypical" of his work; a Beth Anderson piece that is a prose monologue, rapidly spoken in a flat manner, against a background of abstract sounds—a structure roughly identical to the Robert Ashley piece that precedes it on the record; a Liam O'Gallagher piece that is silly and cannot be listened to more than once. In other words, the anthology is botched; and since the Amirkhanian pieces are by far the best things on the record, my initial suspicion was that, as the producer, perhaps he rigged it to make everyone else look inferior.

That's it; there are no more anthologies of North American work. Some text-sound art has appeared in the periodical *Black Box* and on the Giorno Poetry Systems records, but no one subscribing to either of these publications can expect a steady stream of text-sound gems. In Europe, the government-funded radio stations take responsibility for the creation and programming of text-sound work; but in the United States, no public radio station, aside from WXXI-FM in Rochester, has supported the art, while literature directors of National Public Radio have never been interested. I have myself written to the larger record companies, proposing to edit and introduce a text-sound record; but none of them have accepted my offer. One possible route for American work would involve public funding, but here the new, intermediumistic art becomes a round peg, unable to fit the square holes of funding agencies. Since the current program director of National Endowment for the Arts's literature department cannot accept visual poetry as "literature," there is no reason to believe he will be any more accepting of sound poetry; and music departments are often reluctant to accept text-sound art and artists as "music composition."

Until records and various printed materials become readily available, North American text-sound will remain a private art that will have public existence only in second-hand forms, such as this essay; and that unavailability becomes, to be frank, an example of de facto censorship that is no longer tolerable.

E. E. Cummings

1980

> Nothing is quite as easy as using words like somebody else.
> We all of us do exactly this nearly all the time—and when
> we do it we are not poets. [E. E. Cummings, in a letter]

To identify E. E. Cummings (1894-1962) as a major
modern poet is scarcely exceptional; to say that no other
major American poet of his generation remains so neglected and misunderstood would strike most readers as
more surprising and debatable. Richard S. Kennedy's
Dreams in the Mirror (1980) is only the second extended
biography of Cummings, while T. S. Eliot, Ezra Pound,
and William Carlos Williams, by comparison, have all
had several volumes devoted to their lives. Similarly,
native criticism of Cummings's poetry has been comparatively sparse, and it is not uncommon, even today, to
find aggressively conservative literary historians, such as
Daniel Hoffman in his recent *Harvard Guide to Contemporary American Writing* (1979), scarcely acknowledging
Cummings's presence. Other critics emphasize his more
conventional lyric poems, while completely neglecting
his more unusual works. Even such recent anthologists
of American poetry as Richard Ellmann (in his 1976
The New Oxford Book of American Verse) and Nancy

Sullivan (in her 1978 *The Treasury of American Poetry*) typically include *only* his lyrics. However, at a time when the reputations of both Eliot and Pound appear to be receding, it is time to reconsider Cummings and to concentrate upon his more inventive poetry.

Unlike Eliot or Pound, Cummings was for all of his life a full-time artist, who should be valued only for his contributions to the arts he practiced—and not for anything else. His social philosophy was essentially no more than a visceral libertarianism that was more agreeable than profound—invariably relevant to situations immediately at hand, but scarcely substantial enough to support a general position. His criticisms of technology and, at times, of urban life were more successfully elaborated by others. His esthetics were largely knee-jerk anti-high cult (as in the comments about theater quoted ahead). Fortunately, he had neither economic ideas nor a philosophy of history. Critics emphasizing, say, Cummings's esthetics or social philosophy are invariably trying to bolster their own points, rather than examining his artistic value. The principal theme of his poetry is the creation and thus the experience of unusual English language. Thus, what survives is not ideas but poems that radically enlarge our sense of linguistic possibilities.

As the epigraph to this essay suggests, Cummings observed a clear distinction between prose and poetry. The former was common language; the latter, exceptional language. Thus, contrary to current fashion, he enthusiastically used poetry's traditional devices, such as meter, alliteration, resonant line breaks and even rhyme. As late as 1957, in the wake of America's inaction in the 1956 Hungarian revolution, he produced a poem, "Thanksgiving (1956)," that closed with this biting satirical ditty:

> So rah-rah-rah democracy
> let's all be thankful as hell

and bury the statue of liberty
(because it begins to smell)

However, what distinguished Cummings from the rhyming tribes was his sense that traditional devices hardly sufficed; he discovered new ones which would function to enhance language poetically. He was from his first book to his last an incomparably inventive poet.

One of his fundamental motives was breaking apart the traditionally geometric format of poetry. Instead of always using rectangular blocks of type with flush-left margins, Cummings often placed his poems on the page in a great variety of alternative shapes:

```
    ---                    ------              --------------------
   -----                   ------              --------------------
  --------                                     ----------------
  --------              --      -----             -----
 ---------------        -----                     -----
 --------------                                   ---
 -----------------              --                ---
 ---------------        -----                     -----
----------------------  --------------------      -----
------------------      ------- --------
------------------        ----    ----            -----
 --------------                                   ---
  -----------           -----                     ----
   -------                                        ----
   -------                    -----                --
    ----                                           --
    ----                                            -
```

among others. The point of all these experiments was not just the creation of attractive designs but sensitively varying the reader's perception of printed language. He knew what could be gained by enlarging or reducing or even eliminating the horizontal spacing between consecutive words. He saw that the vertically rectangular page of a book was itself a poetic field that could be filled in various ways and that a distinctive image on the page could enhance a poem.

A second Cummings device was the use of one part of speech to function in place of another. Thus, verbs appear as nouns.

> my father moved through dooms of love
> though sames of am through haves of give

As Malcolm Cowley carefully observed in *New Republic* (Jan. 27, 1932), nouns also "become verbs ('but if a look should april me') or they become adverbs by adding '-ly,' or adjectives in the superlative by adding '-est' (thus, instead of writing 'most like a girl,' Cummings has 'girlest'). Adjectives, adverbs, and conjunctions, too, become participles by adding '-ing' ('onlying,' 'softlying,' 'whying'); participles become adverbs by adding '-ly' ('kneelingly')."

Phonetic spellings could be poetically used not only for wit—"the hoe tell days are teased" for a classy Manhattan residence known as the Hotel des Artists or "Gay-Pay-Oo" for the Soviet secret police (G.P.U.)—but also for the representation of spoken dialect:

> oil tel duh woil doi sez
> dooyuh unners tanmih eesez pullih nizmus tash, oi

On more accessible levels, Cummings doubled words for emphasis, much as Malayans do—"slowlyslowly"; and he used prefixes such as "un-," "im-" or "not-" and then suffixes such as "ing" and "ingly" to modify their root word in various subtle ways. A favorite epithet, "unalive," is not synonymous with dead.

He recognized that individual words could be expressively taken apart:

r-p-o-p-h-e-s-s-a-g-r
             who
     a)s w(e loo)k
     upnowgath
              PPEGORHRASS
                          eringint(o-
     aThe):l
             eA
                !p:
S   a
                    (r
     rIvInG   .gRrEaPsPhOs)
                                   to
     rea(be)rran(com)gi(e)ngly
     ,grasshopper;

rendering not only a distinct visual image (especially on
a vertically rectangular page) but visually enhancing the
connotations of the key word. Incidentally, Cummings
may have been the first American writer to discover a
truth initially familiar to architects—less could be more.
    He who had taken words apart could also combine
them sensitively, gaining resonance by omitting spaces—
creating in English a reasonable ersatz German with such
conjunctions as "bookofpoems," "curselaughgroping,"
"driftwhirlfully," and "truebeautifully." Even in punctuation marks he found expressive possibilities. No one
before or since has used hyphens and semi-colons so
resonantly. The single word "taps" is considerably different when it is punctuated, as Cummings does, "t, a, p, s."
In the middle of a poem about acrobats,

                    hes shes

          &meet&
                swoop

the ampersands add poetry that would otherwise be lost. In a comparative sense, some of his discoveries are incredibly, perhaps dubiously simple, but the point is that no poet before him dared be so simple. Compared to his more pretentious contemporaries, he had a casual sense of poetry that some of us find attractive.

No doubt aware of Apollinaire's forays into representational visual poetry, such as the shape of raining in "Il Pleut," Cummings knew he had to create something else. What he discovered was that properties within typeset language, such as capitalization, could contribute to poetic communication. "SpRiN,k,LiNG" has ideographic connotations that "sprinkling" lacks. In *ViVa* is a poem, numbered XXXVIII, which visually-verbally represents an electrical storm in its opening lines:

```
N(o)w
        the
how
    dis(appeared cleverly)world

iS Slapped:with;liGhtninG
!

at
which(shal)lpounceupcrackw(ill)jumps

of
   THuNdeRB
        loSSo!M iN
```

Anyone who has heard Cummings's recordings of his work can understand how the unusual typography prompts spoken rhythms quite different from those engendered by conventional poetic scoring.

The placement of words in space could also introduce kinetic qualities that would be impossible in conventional poetic design. The theme of his "grasshopper"

poem, quoted before, is a certain kind of animal movement; the point of the following passage from number
XII in "Portraits" is a representation of a change in
pace:

                                                    pho
              nographisrunn
              ingd o   w,   n   phonograph
                                      stopS.

In the foreward to *Is 5* (1926), one of his few statements on his purposes, Cummings spoke specifically of
the creation of "that precision which creates movement."

The opening poem in *1 x 1* (1944) presages the current
interest in poetic abstraction, its words and phrases cohering in terms not of syntax or semantics but of diction,
meter, and other qualities indigenous to poetry:

                    nonsun blob a
                    cold to
                    skylessness
                    sticking fire

                    my are your
                    are birds our all
                    and one gone
                    away the they

                    leaf of ghosts some
                    few creep there
                    here or on
                    unearth

He also wrote pure sound poetry, in which sounds
become the principal element of coherence and enhancement. In *ViVa* is a poem, prefaced "from the
cognoscenti," which opens:

> bingbongwhom chewchoo
> laugh dingle nails personally
> bung loamhome picpac
> obviously scratches tomorrowlobs

and continues in a similar style to a single line which is set below and to the left of the six four-line rectangles: "of radarw leschin," which suggests that only a radical change in language can realize a *revolution*. Though Cummings was an exact contemporary of Vladimir Mayakovsky (1893-1930), they never met and probably had no effect upon each other; nonetheless, Cummings illustrates Mayakovsky's dictum: "Neologisms are obligatory in writing poetry."

At his Harvard commencement in 1915, Cummings gave a stunningly prophetic lecture on "The New Art" that featured a sensitive appreciation of Gertrude Stein, and it was perhaps from her that he learned about the advantages of an intentionally limited vocabulary. In *No Thanks* is an extraordinary poem beginning "brIght" which contains only eleven discrete words, all six letters or less in length; they are successfully broken apart and nonsyntactically recombined to form fifteen lines of forty-four words—all three-letter words appearing thrice, all four-letter words four times, etc. With this rigorous structure, as well as others, Cummings presaged several formal innovations that have since become major developments in contemporary avant-garde poetry. He also showed that one could spend a lifetime earnestly practicing more than one art, in spite of discrepancies in recognition. The fact that Cummings discovered these present possibilities several decades ago adds to his current stature.

One reason why our understanding of Cummings has been so deficient is that his work has never been fully available. A *Collected Poems* appeared in 1938, but it was scarcely a complete representation of Cummings's work to then. A *Complete Poems, 1923-54* appeared in 1954; but since it included nothing written after 1950, its title was subsequently changed to *Poems, 1923-54* and amended a decade later to *Complete Poems, 1923-62.* However, totally unpublished poems have since turned up, so, it is obvious by now, nearly two decades after his death, that a definitively complete edition is due.

Prior to issuing a promised Collected Poems, Liveright-Norton has recently published several volumes of "transcript editions" of Cummings's original manuscripts. Thus, their new edition of *Tulips and Chimneys* (1976) includes not only the poems published in the first edition with that title (1923), it also includes those poems that the original publisher cut from the manuscript and that Cummings then put into later volumes, *XLI Poems* (1925) and *&* (1925). In 1979, Liveright issued typescript editions of *ViVa, No Thanks* (1935), and *Xaipe* (1950), and the texts here likewise differ from those in the previously published books, mostly in correcting minor errors.

These "typescript editions" are not facsimiles of Cummings's original manuscripts but something else—retypings of definitive versions of the manuscripts, with the unit spacings of the typewriter (one letter-one space). Why these poems should be retype*written,* rather than retype*set,* is not explained in any of these volumes. The unstated assumption, let me suggest, must be that since the variable letterspacing of all typography distorts the typewriter's layout, it would be appropriate to duplicate their original typewritten appearance. To put it differently, if a poem was originally composed on a typewriter, any typesetting represents necessarily a typographical translation that is ultimately different from the original.

In my opinion, this retyping is scarcely necessary. Since Cummings worked closely with a sympathetic type-setter, a Greenwich Village neighbor named S. A. Jacobs, and since Cummings was also notoriously insistent about examining and correcting typesetter's proofs, there is every reason to believe that the original published editions exemplify his wishes about the definitive typography of his poems. Indeed, the 1970 paperback reprinting of, say, *ViVa* strikes me as visually more successful than the more recent typescript edition of the same book. As an aside, let me wonder if Cummings ever wanted his poems lowered on their pages, rather than scrupulously observing the traditional custom of placing every poem at the top of the page; many of his shorter poems, especially, would look better with more white space on top and less on bottom.

Richard S. Kennedy's biography, the second stone in the Cummings revival, perhaps epitomizes the second generation of all biographies of contemporary writers. The first generation, exemplified by Charles Norman's thrice-revised *The Magic Maker* (1958, 1964, 1972), is invariably written by an admiring friend, while its subject is still alive, often with the subject's collaboration and approval. The first-generation biography is filled with long quotations not only from the author's fugative works but from interviews and even informal conversations, as well as, sometimes, notes and journals that the subject selectively makes available. First-generation biographies are invariably fresh and enthusiastic and yet discrete and courteous.

The second-generation literary biography appears after its subject's death. The author is usually an academic who had no contact with his subject and thus needed to spend at least a decade interviewing everyone who knew the subject and examining all the manuscripts and papers on deposit at university libraries. The second-generation biographer quotes less from the subject's published writings and more from the unpublished, and he is generally more detailed and less discrete. Kennedy, for instance, discusses at length an episode that Charles Norman avoids—Cummings's persistent attempt to adopt legally the daughter he fathered by Elaine Orr, while she was still married to Scofield Thayer, and then the adult daughter's belated reaction to new information about her real paternity. In part because second-generation biographers have spent so much time picking fruit, their books are often tediously paced, incorrigibly digressive and ineffectively long.

Kennedy's *Dreams in the Mirror* is better than most of its kind, perhaps because its subject is more interesting; but it is probably not the last Cummings biography. One dimension Kennedy neglects is Cummings's professional economy and thus his patrons, perhaps because the principal collector of his paintings is still alive—James Silbey Watson, Jr., a Harvard classmate who cofounded *The Dial* (1920-29) and later became a University of Rochester medical school professor who personally funded the university art gallery that gave Cummings his major exhibitions. Watson's colleague, Dr. Harold Segal, became Cummings's principal physician, and it was at their Rochester hospital, Strong Memorial, that the poet had his major surgery. Since no other American writer of note had, to my knowledge, such a loyal, if occasional, patron for a lifetime, one would like to know more about this singular relationship.

Neither Kennedy nor Charles Norman addresses the question which has long troubled me—what Cummings himself felt about the differences between his accessible lyrics and his more inventive work? In the *Selected Poems, 1923-58* that he personally prepared for the

British publisher Faber & Faber, he included only the former and thus made it different from *100 Selected Poems* (1959) he had prepared for a U.S. publisher, Grove Press, around the same time. However, Faber was T. S. Eliot's firm and the British poetry audience had previously been utterly unappreciative of Cummings's work. We know that discrepancies in critical appraisals of one's various works can upset an insecure artist—the sorts who trust critics more than they trust themselves—but my own suspicion is that outside opinion had little effect, fortunately, on Cummings's artistic production.

From the beginning of his career to the end, he simply continued writing his inventive poetry with the same confidence and enthusiasm that he pursued in his visual art (which was even more scorned and neglected). As both a classicist and a romanticist, who typically mixed his elaborate education with anti-intellectual attitudes, Cummings was accustomed to incorporating disparities. However, when it came time to make a self-selection—for example, in compiling a British edition, or in reading his work aloud to a large audience—Cummings bowed to prevalent opinion and gave his audiences that part of his work which he expected they would like best. In my opinion, Cummings's reputation would be better served today with a *Selected Poems* that would rescue him from the lyric-lovers and instead gather together the radical poems he could not select from himself.

Acknowledging the distinction between poetry and prose did not keep Cummings from writing a fair amount of the latter. Much of his prose includes poetic devices and even poetic passages, but it nonetheless remains fundamentally prose. The most familiar is his memoir of imprisonment in World War I, *The Enormous Room,* which was also recently reissued in a "typescript" edition that corrects earlier publishers' errors and tamperings (and is retypeset, rather than retypewritten). A more interesting book, in my judgment, is his *Eimi* (pronounced "aMe," meaning "am"), a spectacularly written 1933 memoir of his disillusioning 1931 trip to Soviet Russia. His political courage complemented his literary guts.

Cummings also wrote numerous stylistically marvelous essays, mostly about art, often under pseudonyms. In *The Dial* (April, 1926), for instance, Cummings criticized several current theatrical performances and exhibitions before concluding with praise for Minsky's National Winter Garden: "A singularly fundamental institution, whose Scratch is a noble clown, whose first wink is worth the struttings of a hundred thousand Barrymores, who are the unmitigated bunk: since the direction of all spectacle lives in Aristophanes and the 'theater' has a great future behind it, said 'future' being The Circus." Some of these fugative pieces were collected by George J. Firmage in *E. E. Cummings: A Miscellany* (1958, 1965); but since this prose is marvelous and that book has long been out of print, a new edition is in order.

Cummings was also a serious visual artist who worked as hard at his paintings and drawings as he did at his writing, the former being done by day and the latter at night. More than 2,000 paintings exist; the Houghton Library at Harvard reportedly has over 10,000 sheets of drawings. It is hard for most of us to know whether any of this work is good, let alone how it looks. Some were reproduced in *CIOPW* (1931), a limited 9½-by-12½ inch clothbound whose title is an acronym for the media in which Cummings worked: *c*harcoal, *i*nk, *o*il, *p*encil, and *w*atercolor. However, this scarce book has never been reissued, and he did three decades more of visual work. The absence of at least a *Selected Drawings and Paintings* raises questions about Cummings's other art: Was he a Wyndham Lewis, who excelled at both visual and verbal arts? Or was he a Henry David Thoreau, whose drawings were merely curious? With insufficient evidence at hand, who dares decide?

Cummings was scarcely the only American poet to contribute significant inventions to the machinery of the art. It was Walt Whitman, the godfather of us all, who discovered that the extended line could produce a radically different poetry; it was Vachel Lindsay who discovered the poetic value of onomatopoeic sounds. Among Cummings's inventive contemporaries were Eugene Jolas (1894-1952), a needlessly neglected figure, who pioneered both a trilingual poetry and a nonsyntactic sound poetry; and Abraham Lincoln Gillespie (1898-1950), whose experiments, still uncollected, defy familiar definition. Cummings exceeds them in the variousness and abundance of his inventions.

Contemporary inventive poets include John Ashbery (in poems he wrote around 1960; *not* in his more recent work), Jack Kerouac (especially in his *Mexico City Blues* of 1959), Jackson Mac Low, Norman Henry Pritchard II, Courtenay P. Graham, Bliem Kern, John Cage, and Clark Coolidge, among others. Indeed, their works suggest, to me at least, that the principal mark of American poetry— the dominant characteristic that distinguishes it as a whole from other poetries—is a series of inventions in the materials of poetry. If that is true, then Cummings is the central modern figure.

Even though Cummings insisted upon living entirely off his writing and readings and art (and compromised only once, when he became the Charles Eliot Norton Professor of Poetry for a year at Harvard), he received remarkably few awards and fewer fellowships. The literary powermen of his time tended to regard him as an inconsequential eccentric—an agreeable lyric poet whose disagreeable "gimmicky" experiments undermined his reputation. They inevitably preferred his aphorisms to his inventions, though aphorisms do not a major poet make. Some could never excuse Cummings from failing to write the kind of pretentious long poem they had come to identify with modern masterhood, for he was to his end a sprinter more comfortable with short poems and small paintings. Academics could never forgive him for failing to pass through the distinct states that they equate with "development"; but what was really more extraordinary, the more you think about it, was how much of his mature poetic style was fully present in his very first book. For much of his life, Cummings lacked a regular publisher, and two of his collections were initially self-published. (One, in 1935, was pointedly entitled *No Thanks* and audaciously dedicated to the fourteen publishers who previously refused it!)

Let me suggest the opposite of the conventional view. If you favor the lyric verse ("my father moved . . . ," etc.) while excluding the radical poetry, Cummings is indeed a minor figure. However, there is another, better Cummings—the most inventive American poet of his time, the truest successor to Whitman and in poetry the peer of Charles Ives and Frank Lloyd Wright. If you focus upon Cummings's more extraordinary poems—those that distinguish him from everyone else, before or since—you are more likely to recognize him, as I do, as the major American poet of the middle-twentieth century.

Polyartist's Poetry

(1979)

John Cage is one of those few contemporaries who do indubitably major work in more than one art. Initially recognized for his innovative music compositions, he has worked with creditable success in nonliterary ("mixed-means") theatre, in visual art and in poetry, creating in each domain works that are radically different from what others are doing and yet, in their esthetic principles, characteristically Cagean. Instead of rejecting one art before pursuing another, he continues to work seriously and adventurously in several arts at once. Rather than being "a composer" who also writes, or "a poet" who also makes graphic art, he is by now something else—a master of several arts, a slave to none. The epithet I coined and prefer to use is "polyartist."

His new book, *Empty Words* (1979), contains expository essays on "The Future of Music" and "How the Piano Came To Be Prepared," and these are of interest to followers of Cage's musical thinking. Another section, ostensibly about both the choreographer Merce Cunningham and food, illustrates Cage's genius for storytelling. However, most of this new book contains language constructions that must be called "poetry," partly because they are not prose, but mostly because they cannot be persuasively classified as anything else. Since these *poems* are radically unlike everything else in American writing today, it is scarcely surprising that they are rarely discussed by "poetry critics" and never mentioned in the current surveys of American literature.

Notwithstanding his advocacy of "chance" and artistic freedom, Cage is an artistic formalist, who invents alternative ways of *structuring* language. One device is the mesostic. Whereas the familiar acrostic has a word running down the left-hand margin of several lines, the mesostic has a recognizable word running down the middle. In Cagean practice, this vertical word is usually the name of a friend—Merce Cunningham, Jasper Johns, Norman O. Brown. Within this mesostic constraint, Cage makes concise statements:

<pre>
        not Just
          gArdener
      morelS
        coPrini
      morEls
        copRini.
        not Just hunter:
    cutting dOwn
       ailantHus
        cuttiNg down
    ailanthuS.
</pre>

The title piece of *Empty Words* is a four-part poem drawn from Henry David Thoreau's remarks about music and sound. What Cage did here is copy relevant passages out of Thoreau's books and then subject them to *I Ching*-aided chance processes that, in effect, scrambled and combined them, producing a nonsyntactic pastiche of Thoreau's language:

                    speaksix round and longer than
                the shelloppressed and
            now ten feet high heroTheclosely isor
                    have looked wellthat and spruces
                the and a darker line below it

This stanza comes from the first page of the first part, which contains phrases, words, syllables, and letters (characters) from Thoreau. The second part of "Empty Words" contains just his words, syllables, and letters; the third part just syllables and letters; and the fourth part just letters.

"Empty Words" is less about Thoreau than about sound, or the sound of language about sound, compressed and recombined; reading it is not about assuaging our powers of literary understanding but about challenging and expanding them. This is rigorously Platonic poetry that takes initially spiritual literature and recomposes it into a yet more ethereal realm. In my opinion, "Empty Words" is better heard than read; for not only has Cage performed selections from it dozens of times around the world, but his reading of the entire work will soon appear as a fourteen-record set.

Scarcely contented with past poetic inventions, Cage has recently developed a series of conceptually ambitious schemes for extracting language from James Joyce's multilingual masterpiece, *Finnegans Wake*. In the initial scheme, Cage works from the beginning of Joyce's book to its end, taking out words that contain letters that fit into a mesostic structure based upon the name "James Joyce." Since the first "J" in *Finnegans Wake* appears in the word "nathandjoe," Cage takes out that word and then, by a decision of taste, decides to take as well the words to the left of it (ignoring those to the right). For the "A" of "James," he selects only the article (and implicitly decides against both sets of words adjacent to it). The next "M" appears in the word "malt"; the next "E" in "jhem"; and the next "S" in "Shen." Thus, Cage's opening stanza reads:

wroth with twone nathandJoe

A

Malt

jhEm

Shen

It is a measure of Cage's originality that nobody ever made poetry like this before—the method is, like so much of his work, at once sensible and nutty. To my mind, *Writing through Finnegans Wake* is interesting in part because it is so audaciously innovative; it succeeds in part because it recycles James Joyce. Hearing Cage read it aloud, with sensitive precision, is a special pleasure.

Empty Words contains only the second of Cage's workings with the *Wake*; the first, longer Joyce piece appeared initially as a special issue of the *James Joyce Quarterly* and has since been reissued as a book, *Writing through Finnegans Wake* (1978). Both Cage *Wake* pieces appear together in a third book, a large-format signed and limited edition titled *Writings through Finnegans Wake* (1978) (note the plural). Reproducing Cage's manuscript in its original size, this sumptuously produced volume is superior to the reduced versions, even though its price is amenable, alas, primarily to libraries and collectors of Cage's visual art. (On the other hand, at the rate that book prices are currently escalating, two hundred dollars may seem less unreasonable a few years from now.)

Cage describes "Empty Words" as progressing, over its four parts, from literature to music, and it seems to me that both this work and its Joycean successor finally realize an identity between the two traditional arts.

"Text-sound" is the epithet I use to define language works that cohere primarily in terms of sound, rather than syntax or semantics; and Cage, as a literary musician, is clearly a master of that domain. On the other hand, since both "Empty Words" and "Writings through Finnegans Wake" are language-based, they fit snugly into the great American tradition of poetry that realizes an eccentric innovation in the machinery of the art—a radical change not in meaning or in sensibility but in the materials indigenous to poetry: language, line, syntax, and meter. (In this sense, Cage's principal poetic precursors are Whitman, Cummings, and Gertrude Stein.) Considered in this way, Cage is not a literary curiosity but an exemplary American poet.

Jerome Rothenberg

(1978)

Jerome Rothenberg is indisputably a master anthologist, who compiles collections not to exploit established tastes—that is the business of textbook-makers—but, first, to resurrect neglected literature and, then, to show how initially miscellaneous examples form a coherent cultural entity. He has produced seven anthologies, two of which are coedited, and each of them contains, in addition to Rothenberg's selections, his own considered commentaries on the material.

His first, *Technicians of the Sacred* (1968), has a subtitle, "A Range of Poetries from Africa, America, Asia, & Oceania," that is actually incomplete. In addition to poetries from so-called primitive peoples, the book also contains imaginative works by contemporaries, both American and European, whose works resemble in crucial respects this primitive poetry. Intellectually, *Technicians* echoes that strain of art criticism that shows how modern abstraction resembles primitive art. From its polemical introduction to its elaborate commentaries, *Technicians* is not just a radical reinterpretation of the nature of poetry; it also attempts to define for present-day English-language poetry a "tradition" that differs considerably from that of British verse.

To define this expanded view of the cultural past, over a decade ago, Rothenberg coined a term, *ethnopoetics,* that has since been widely accepted. More recently, he wrote me of a desire "to create a broadly human poetics, to explore poetic process (*poesis*) by expanding the range of instances at hand; to challenge the literary-civilized framework by articulating a larger-than-literary/primitive/visionary tradition that shows up again in contemporary experiments with language & structure—in other words, a polemical approach to the past that reflects the present."

As a fellow anthologist, I am perhaps in the best position to envy the influence that *Technicians* has had—not only in total sales, but in the numbers of readers (and writers) who treasure it among the most important books they have ever read. Indeed, there is good reason to consider it perhaps the single most influential literary anthology of the past decade. Its successor in Rothenberg's own history is *Shaking the Pumpkin* (1972), which is devoted exclusively, as its subtitle says, to "Traditional Poetry of the Indian North Americas."

Revolution of the Word (1974), subtitled "A New Gathering of American Avant-Garde Poetry 1914-1945," collects not the staples of the textbooks but other, more eccentric kinds of poetry from this period—visual poems, minimal poems, hysterical prose poetry and even sound poems, by such neglected American writers as Charles Henri Ford, Bob Brown, Harry Crosby, Eugene Jolas, Kenneth Patchen, and Abraham Lincoln Gillespie. This is the native between-the-wars poetry that the "New Critics" and their post-World War II academic epigones neglected, and seeing it gathered together should be a revelation to any student of American literature. Rothenberg's brilliant introduction complements the selections both in revealing a hidden history and in providing a rationale for current experimental poetries. Its companion, *America a Prophecy* (1973), is a less concise and less coherent anthology—the victim of an unfortunate collaboration.

The implicit purpose of Rothenberg's newest major anthology, *A Big Jewish Book* (1978), is a reinterpretation of our sense of "Jewish literature." In contrast to those who would emphasize fiction about the social and psychological condition of Jewish people, Rothenberg resurrects a more prophetic, more formally inventive, and more mystical literature, concerned less with psychology and society (and thus less with self-pity and/or nostalgia) than with the individual's relation to nature and the unknown. Moreover, instead of just a German-Russian-American Jewish literature of the nineteenth and twentieth centuries, *A Big Jewish Book* contains earlier writings, both Sephardic and Ashkenazic, from all over the Diaspora. Among its surprising inclusions are the visual poems of Abraham Abulafia (thirteenth century), sound poems from the first and second centuries, "Sayings of the Lord" by the eighteenth century false messiah Jacob Frank, and Judeo-Arabic poetry, in addition, typically, to such contemporaries as Armand Schwerner, Jackson Mac Low, Allen Ginsberg, Rochelle Owens, Louis Zukofsky and Charles Reznikoff.

The product of prodigious, premeditated research, often in original sources (with translating assistance from Harris Lenowitz and Charles Doria), *A Big Jewish Book* aims to expand our sense of Jewish literature both geographically and chronologically, which is to say both stylistically and linguistically as well; and it resembles Gershom Scholem's legendary scholarship in Jewish mysticism in resurrecting cultural materials previously regarded as disreputable, if they were acknowledged at all. Another way to understand how different *A Big Jewish Book* is would be to compare it with Saul Bellow's anthology of *Great Jewish Short Stories* (1963) or Irving Howe and Eliezer Greenberg's three treasuries of Yiddish literature (1954, 1969, 1972), and in that contrast is also epitomized the difference between Saul Bellow's or Philip Roth's fiction on one hand and the poetry of, say, Allen Ginsberg or Rothenberg himself on the other.

He has produced eighteen separate books of his own poetry, with nearly as many publishers (mostly alternative, rather than commercial); but once gathered together, it can be seen that, their stylistic variety notwithstanding, these books have certain common characteristics. The key concept is that his poems tend to be derived from the kinds of literature that went into his anthologies. That is, although Rothenberg has been an advocate of oral poetry and of writings and writers previously regarded as nonliterary, he is, in his own practice, a poet very much inspired by his readings. Out of both the materials he collected in *Technicians of the Sacred* and the experience of living near an Amerindian reservation (a move also inspired by his readings) comes not only *A Seneca Journal* (1978), but also the marvelous audiotapes of Amerindian "Horse Songs" whose "total translations" rank, in my judgment, among his most extraordinary creations.

Out of the interest in experimental literature comes the work initially collected in *Poems 1964-1967* (1968) and then subsequently reprinted and extended in *Poems for the Game of Silence* (1971), which collects Rothenberg's poetry of the sixties and, in its paperback edition (1975), remains the most convenient introduction to his own writing. Out of his research into the Jewish past came both a book-length poem of "ancestral explorations," *Poland/1931* (1974) and *The Notebooks* (1977), in addition to an engaging collection of cards of Hebrew translations done with Harris Lenowitz, *Gematria 27* (1977).

The opening of "Cokboy," a long poem included in *Poland/1931,* brings both the Amerindian and Jewish traditions together:

> saddlesore I came
> a jew among
> the indians
> vot em I doink in dis strange place
> mit deez pipple mit strange eyes
> could be it's trouble
> could be could be
>
> ***
>
> vot em I doink here
> how vass I lost tzu get here
> am a hundred men
> a hundred fifty different shadows

And the poem itself tells of a Jew dreaming himself a cowboy ("a cokboy") and then a cocksman among the Indians.

Born December 11, 1931, Jerome Dennis Rothenberg grew up in the Bronx, speaking Yiddish before English. He attended public schools and then City College, graduating with a B.A. in 1952. After a year at the University of Michigan, where he took his M.A., he served in the U.S. Army in Germany for two years. Returning to New York, he worked on his writing while his wife Diane taught school. In 1961, he landed a job as a part-time lecturer in English at the Mannes College of Music, where he taught until 1970. Meanwhile, from his home in Washington Heights, he became an active contributor to the New York poetry scene, making many loyal professional friends, performing his work in public as frequently as anyone, discussing literature and things over food and drinks into the wee hours, editing and publishing the magazines *Poems from the Floating World* (1959-62), *Some/Thing* (1966-69) and *Alcheringa* (1970-76), founding the Hawk's Well Press (1958-65) to publish books of his own poetry along with the works of others—contributing to a local literary community distinct from the academic poets on one hand and the New York school on the other. Always industrious, he also produced many translations from the German, including the anthology *New Young German Poets* (1959) and the "American Playing Version [Broadway]" of Rolf Hochhuth's controversial play, *The Deputy* (1965).

In his quiet and yet persistent way, Rothenberg has had a professional career as avant-garde as, say, Allen Ginsberg's. He produced a poetry so different from the post-Eliot and post-post-Eliot establishments that his professional elders thought it unacceptable. I can remember a prominent literary editor telling me over lunch, as late as 1965, that "Jerry has never written a wholly successful poem." Rather than beat his head against closed doors, Rothenberg created his own channels of cultural communication—his own magazines, his own small press, his own anthologies—that eventually won the support of his contemporaries and juniors, in addition to lecture invitations and guest professorships. Thanks to the bulk and force of his professional presence, he is by now a major force on the American literary scene—not only as a poet but as a collector of literature that will surely inform the creation of subsequent poetry.

Dick Higgins

(1977)

Though Dick Higgins's work may be conventionally categorized as "writing," "theater," "music," "film," and "book publishing," it is best to regard him as not a specialized practitioner of one or another of these arts, but as a true polyartist—a master of several arts, subservient to none. Indeed, he is as various as Moholy-Nagy or van Doesburg, to cite two exemplary precursors; and some of his works contribute to two arts at once. In less than twenty years, he has produced a wealth of work, both large and small, permanent and ephemeral, resonant and trivial—uneven, to be sure; no two people familiar with his art agree on which are best and which worst. All this diversity notwithstanding, Higgins reveals five fundamental ways of dealing with the materials of each art he explores, as shown in the following table. These procedures are collage, representation, permutation, aleatory, and expressionism. In nearly all works, one or another procedure (or two) is dominant. Collage, briefly, is the juxtaposition of dissimilars; representation is the accurate portrayal of extrinsic reality; permutation is the systematic manipulation of limited materials; aleatory is chance; and expressionism reflects personality or personal experience.

	Collage	Representation	Permutation	Aleatory	Expressionism
Visual Arts	7.7.73 (1973)	Some Poetry Intermedia (1976)	7.7.73	Graphis (1957 to present)	A Thousand Symphonies (1967)
Writing	Foew&ombwhnw (1969)	Postface (1962)	Modular Poems (1975)	A Book about Love & War & Death (1965, 1969, 1972)	Amigo (1972)
Theater	St Joan at Beaurevoir (1959)	Act (1969)	The Freedom Riders (1962)	Stacked Deck (1958)	Death and the Nickle Cigar (1973)
Music	In Memoriam (1961)		To Everything its Season (1958) Glasslass (a text-sound piece, 1970)	Graphic scores	"Danger Music No. 17 (May, 1962)
Film	Men & Women & Bells (1969)	Flaming City (1962)	Hank and Mary Without Apologies (1969)	Men & Women & Bells	Flaming City
Publishing	Emmett Williams's An Anthology of Concrete Poetry (1967)	Henry Cowell's New Musical Resources (1930, 1969)	Gertrude Stein's The Making of Americans (1926, 1965)	John Cage's Notations (1968) Merce Cunningham's Changes (1969)	Geoff Hendricks's Ring Piece (1973) (1973)

To give substance to this table, it might help to describe a few of these pieces. *7.7.73* (1973) is a series of 899 unique prints of various visual imagery, both abstract and representational, mostly on paper (but also on other materials), with forms repeated from one print to the next; its organizing principles are collage and aleatory. *Amigo* (1972) is a book-length poetic memoir of Higgins's love for a young man. "Danger Music #17 (May, 1962)" reads in its entirety: "Scream! Scream! Scream! Scream! Scream! Scream!" *Postface* (1962) is a percipient and prophetic critical essay about advanced arts in the early sixties. *St. Joan at Beaurevoir* (1959) is a complicated long scenario that includes such incongruities as Dr. Johnson and St. Joan appearing on the same stage. *Men & Women & Bells* (1959) is a short film that incorporates footage made by both his father and his grandfather. I remember it as the best of his films. *Foew&ombwhnw* (1969)—pronounced "F,O,E,W," for short—is a book with four vertical columns across every two-page horizontal spread; one column continuously reprinting critical essays, a second column with poetry, a third with theatrical scenarios (including *St. Joan at Beaurevoir*), a fourth with drawings. Though the experience of reading *Foew* is that of collage, the book as a whole is, of course, a representation of a multifaceted man.

Emmett Williams

(1975)

Emmett Williams's name is better known than his poetry, and one reason for this discrepancy is that he edited *An Anthology of Concrete Poetry* (1967), which has outsold its competitors (including an anthology of mine), while most of his poetry remains unpublished, particularly in his native country. Unlike other American writers of his generation, Williams became closely involved, back in the fifties, with the European intermedia avant-garde, epitomized by the "Darmstadt Circle," in which he figured prominently. By the sixties, he was an initiator of Fluxus, an international post-Dada, mixed-means movement which won considerable attention at the time (but has so far escaped most historians of contemporary art and literature). Thus, his writing reflects, to an unusual degree, the experimental tradition in the nonliterary arts. He echoed not Dylan Thomas but Kurt Schwitters, for instance, in his early "performance poems," to use the term that refers to poetry whose most appropriate form is not the printed page but live performance.

It was Williams's good fortune to learn, back in the fifties, that English-language poetry could be composed in radically alternative ways—different not only from the academic poetry of that time but also from the declamatory expressionisms of, say, Allen Ginsberg. Instead, Williams pioneered the art of "concrete poetry," in which the poet eschews conventional syntax (and related devices) to organize language in other ways. Rather than "free form" (whatever that might be), Williams favored such severe constraints as repetition, permutation and linguistic minimalism. His masterpiece, the book-length *Sweethearts* (1967), consists of one word (the title) whose eleven letters are visually distributed over 150 or so sequentially expressive pages, the work as a whole relating the evolution of a man-woman relationship. Like Williams's other work, *Sweethearts* is extremely witty; and like much else in experimental writing, it must be seen (and read) for its magic to be believed.

John Cage

(1979)

Language has been the base of much of John Cage's work for the past decade—language that is meant to be read and spoken without specific pitches (that would, by contrast, make the words song). These works are not essays, or even antiessays, like his earlier "Lecture on Nothing" (1959). As literary creations, these new works are generically closer to poetry than to essays or to fiction in that they represent compressions of language, rather than extensions into narrative (fiction) or definitions of extrinsic reality (essays). Cage's first departure in this poetic direction was the essayistic "Diaries," produced in the late sixties, which are, in essence, a formally rigorous and typographically various shorthand for miscellaneous remarks. Three of these "Diaries" appeared in *A Year from Monday* (1967), and in the course of reviewing this book, I suggested that Cage's work with words had not been as radical as his work with sound: "In all the essays, not only is the type laid out in horizontal lines, but Cage also usually composes in sentences,

---

In this conversation with Richard Kostelanetz, John Cage's comments are in boldface type.

which, though clipped short, similarly impose unnecessary restraints. Indeed, even though he must know that precisely in syntax and linearity is the inherent conservatism of language as an expressive medium, Cage still strives for aphorisms, which are, after all, linear *bon mots*. It seems apparent to me that, if only to follow his predilections (something he is wont to do), Cage might inevitably need to reject sentences entirely and experiment with expressively designed words, or visual poems, which would draw upon those talents for visual composition and penmanship that are already evident in his exquisitely crafted musical manuscripts." Rather than dispute me, Cage remembered my criticisms (and repeatedly reminded me that he had) and moved ahead, not only making a sequence of cleverly structured visual poems in memory of Marcel Duchamp, *Not Wanting To Say Anything About Marcel* (1969) and then *Sixty-Two Mesostics re Merce Cunningham* (1971), a series of vertically organized words that exploit the unique possibilities of rub-off lettering, but then developing, in *Mureau* (1971), a nonsyntactic prose that was based not, like the "Diaries," upon his own experience and his own language, but upon words drawn from Henry David Thoreau's *Journal*.   Having agreed to write a text about electronic music, and having noticed that HDT—that's Thoreau—listened to sound as electronic composers listen to it, not just to musical sounds but to noises and ambient sound generally, it occurred to me that making a chance-determined mix of his remarks in the Journal about sound, silence, and music would make a text relevant to electronic music. Therefore, I gave it the title Mu(music)reau(Thoreau).   What was your method?

I went through the index of the Dover edition of the Journal, and I noticed every occurrence in the index of anything that could be remotely thought to be connected with music, and then I listed all of those appearances; then I subjected it all to chance operations in terms of sentences, phrases, words, syllables and letters. I made a permutation of those five possibilities, so that it could be each of the five alone, or in any groups of two, or any groups of three, or any groups of four, or finally all five. In gathering the original material for *Mureau,* you took phrases out of Thoreau and sentences out of Thoreau and words out of Thoreau. **First I listed all the things having to do with sound.** Listed in what form? Sentences? Words? Page references? **Page references, just as they appear in the index.** Then I asked, what it was of all those permuted possibilities I was looking for, whether I was looking for all five together or a group of four of them, or a group of three or a group of two or one. And when I knew what I was doing, my next question was for how many events was I doing it? And the answer could be anywhere from one to sixty-four. Let's say I got twenty-three. Then if I knew that I was looking for twenty-three events which were any of these five, then I ask of this five which is the first one. Which is the second? Which is the third? So I knew finally what I was doing. And then when I knew what I was doing, I did it. By what kind of process did you deduce a syllable? **I used the syllables as they appear in the dictionary—the breakings of the words.** You took the words as they existed in Thoreau and simply broke them apart and made them part of the syllable collection. **If I was looking for syllables.** So you have a syllable collection, along with a word collection, along with a letter collection. **My letters become quite interesting. Letters are either vowels or consonants. But it was the diphthong that taught me to think of letters as possibly being in combination. AE, for instance, is a diphthong. Therefore, I thought if vow-**

els can join together to make diphthongs, why can't they join in larger groups and why can't consonants join one another? And I decided they could. Then, if I landed, by chance, on the letter T in the word "letters," the T is connected with another T. My next question would be: Do I take just the T I landed on, or do I take the one adjacent to it also? And if it were B and J in the word "subject," and I landed on the B I would accept the J if chance said I should. By what process did you land on the *B*? Well, by counting the letters in the line, and then relating that number to the number sixty-four and the I Ching, giving me the number that would give me the B. I think you've skipped a step of your process. Let's say there are one hundred and twenty-eight letters on the line; you consult the *I Ching* and get, say, the number four. That would mean you'd use the numbers eight and nine? I'm making a very simple example—one hundred and twenty-eight letters. Let's make it really simple—sixty-four. And we get the number fifty-three, so it would be the fifty-third letter. The letter, say, is a B and it's adjacent to a J and preceded by a vowel. So we ignore the vowel, since we're dealing with consonants— And the word, in this case, is "subject." And I ask whether I use just the B or the B and the J. You make it then an either/or question. If I throw one to thirty-two, it would be the B alone, with the J being thirty-three to sixty-four. But say there were five consonants. Here are four: N, G, C, H—the NG from the word "I Ching" and the CH from the word "chance." Then my question is, since I've landed on the G, do I take the N in front of it and the C and H after it? Or what do I do? My first possibility would be to take the G alone. My second would be to take the NG, because it's in the same word. The next would be to take NGC, and the fourth would be to take NGCH. Is that

right?   There are more possibilities.   **What are they?**
Well, if you landed on the *G*, why not take just the
G and the *C* that follows it?   **Because the N came before and belongs in the same word. That's how I worked
anyway. I did leave out the GC; you're quite right. Or
the GH too. I took the G as being primary—**   If you
took the *G* as being primary, therefore the *G* is necessarily connected to the *N* because both come from the
word "Ching," but as not necessarily connected to the
letters of the second word.   **Well, you're quite right.
Now I think that that's a very good question. What you
suggested could bring about a change in the way I work,
because I realize I've omitted certain possibilities. I didn't
mean to. What would you do? You would have the G,
the NG, the GC, the NGC, and the NGCH; would you
accept that as the limit? That's five. Then one to twelve
will be the first, thirteen to twenty-five the second,
twenty-six to thirty-seven the third, and thirty-eight
to fifty-one the fourth, and fifty-two to sixty-four the
fifth.**   And that's how you divide the sixty-four options
of the *I Ching* when there are five alternatives.   **That's
how that works.**   One reason why your poetry is so
distinctive is that no one else writes poetry in this way—
no one. Then how did you decide to begin work, in the
case of *Mureau*?   **I wanted to make a text that would
have four parts, and it was written for a magazine in
Minneapolis called** Synthesis. **And they were written to be
columns.**   Written to be columns?   **I was a columnist
for the magazine. I don't think of these texts as lectures.
They were conceived as columns, initially, and if you'll
notice, the columns have different widths. I did that
on purpose.**   In *Empty Words* you went back—   **I was
continuing** Mureau, **but extending it beyond Thoreau's
remarks about sound and music to the whole of the Journal. To begin with, I omitted sentences, and I thought**

of Empty Words as a transition from literature to music. We would agree, then, that *Mureau* is a literary work basically. It's meant to be printed in a magazine or book. Yes. In the first notebooks of Empty Words, each part is called a lecture. So *Empty Words* was initially conceived as a performance piece. It was something to be read aloud, and therefore I made it a length that some people would consider excessive; I made a length of two hours and a half for each lecture. How did you determine that? Most people consider this excessive, and they don't want me to give it as a lecture. I think that's because the average lecture, say in a college, should be forty minutes. Why did you make your own lectures nearly four times as long? I don't know whether I can answer that question. I had been very impressed by an experience I had in Japan, in 1964, of going to a Buddhist service in a town called Naga— Nagasaki? No, the one where all the temples are. It's in the same valley as Kyoto. Anyway, we went to an evening lecture there that went on for hours and hours, and we had been warned that it was going to be tiresome. I was with Merce Cunningham and the Dance Company. It was very cold, and we were not protected by any warmth. They had told us it would be uncomfortable and long, but we were told also that we didn't have the right to leave once we had decided that we wanted to stay. So we all suffered through it, and it went on and on and. . . . How long? Three hours? No, more than that. It was like six, something like that. And then a few days later, or maybe it was on another trip to Japan, I was in a Zen temple in Kyoto. When I was invited to go to an early morning Buddhist service, I did. I noticed that after a lengthy service they opened the doors of the temple, and you heard the sounds coming in from the outside. So, putting these two things together, the long night business and then the dawn of the opening of the doors, I thought of the opening of the doors occurring at dawn, and making four lectures and the fourth would begin at dawn with the opening of the doors to the outer world so that the sounds would come in—because you see it was a transition from literature to music, and my notion of music has always been ambient sound anyway, silence. Actually, your idea is that our experience of music *includes* ambient sound. Well, yes, and this was Thoreau's notion of music too, you see. Music is continual, he said; it's only listening which is intermittent. Really? I can read to you from the Journal long passages written when he was twenty-one years old, if you please, or twenty-two at the most, on the subject of silence. He said silence was a sphere, and sounds were bubbles on its surface. Incredible! Isn't that beautiful? When did you discover this passage? In writing Mureau, because I listed every one of his remarks about sound or silence. So your idea of *Empty Words* was a lecture heard for ten hours— And you'd have half hour intermissions between the parts. So you'd first have to find out when dawn was coming, the way fishermen do, and then you'd figure back and you'd finally know when the lecture was to begin. So, with three half hours intermissions, you'd therefore have to begin eleven and a half hours before dawn. That's right. I then thought, probably because of Margaret Mead, that those intermissions should include food, that people eating together is an important thing and that is basic to Margaret Mead's notion of ritual. So that's how the record of *Empty Words* should ideally be heard as well? Yes, during that length of time, if one does listen to it over that length of time, there should be periods when one stops listening and has something to eat. Let me go back to the origins of the work? Why does it have the title *Empty Words*?   It comes from a description of the Chinese language that was given to me by William McNaughton, who has made marvelous translations of both Japanese and Chinese texts. The Chinese language, he said, has "full words" and "empty words." Full words are words that are nouns or verbs or adjectives or adverbs. We don't know in Chinese which of these a full word is. The word is so full that it could be any of them. For instance, the word "red" is an adjective. It could be—I'm hypothesizing now—it could be the same as the verb to blush, to turn red. It could be the same as ruby or cherry, if those were names for red.   It is a full word because it has several semantic possibilities.   It can mean any one of those things.   An empty word, by contrast, is—   A connective or a pronoun—a word that refers to something else.   Or it has no meaning by itself. For example, if I say to you "it," that would be an empty word. But if I said "microphone," that would be a full word.   Yes. I'm not being at all scholarly about my use of the term "empty words." I'm suggesting something more in line with what I've already told you, namely the transition from language to music, and I would like with my title to suggest the emptiness of meaning that is characteristic of musical sounds.   That is to say they exist by themselves.   Yes. That when words are seen from a musical point of view, they are all empty.   They're empty semantically?   How do you mean?   "Semantic" refers to meaning. They are also empty syntactically.   I would rather say that they're empty of intention. And now we come back to the emptiness of full words. Because we don't know if the full word intends to be an adjective or a verb or a noun, it's the reader who brings the intention into it.   Which is to say, when you say the word "red" in Chinese, you can—   You can go in any one of four or five directions.

And the person who lets it go there is the receiver.   No, but when you say the word "red," you may mean nothing more than the word "red"; but when I hear the word "red," I think of red apples, red cherries, red beans, and so forth.   I think this is going even farther than I meant to go. I would like to go back to the difference between red and blush and cherry—because that's very basic—that's more basic than a red apple or a red cherry. It's whether it's a noun or a verb or an adjective. In other words, we don't know at all what it is.   It doesn't know what it is. *We* give it a syntactical context.   And it could be any one of these things. It is without intention. And I think haiku poetry is somewhat without intention. I think it may be that the author, if not without intention in writing a haiku poem, has a plurality of intentions, more than one.   How so?   In writing a haiku poem, which as you know is just five, seven, five syllables, there are so few ideas present. An example is: "Matsotake ya / Shiranu ko no ha no / Hebaritsuku," which is mushroom / ignorance, leaf of tree / adhesiveness. That's all there is in the poem. And it's by Basho.   A master.   What does it mean? R. H. Blythe translates it: "The leaf of some unknown tree sticking on the mushroom."   He inserts a lot of syntactical connection which is not present in the original.   He has to; he is obliged to. Now we don't know what Basho meant. It could be, "Mushroom does not know that leaf is sticking to it."   There are all kinds of connectives the translator or reader can put between Basho's words.   Many.   Those words are very full words.   Yes, but you see, what I'm saying now is that, full as they are, they are somehow in Basho, too, devoid of intention.   I can't believe that, not with full words like those—   But then if he was intending something, why wasn't he more explicit?   (Pause.) You're right. So, therefore, you had this notion of *Empty Words* in your mind at the beginning. You also had the notion of developing a piece that would be away from something that was just read on the page to something that would be performed, as it approaches music.   The approach to music is made by steadily eliminating one of the aspects of language, so that as we start Lecture One of Empty Words, we have no sentences. Though they did exist in Mureau, now they're gone. In the second one, the phrases are gone, and in the third part the words are gone, except those that have only one syllable. And in the last one, everything is gone but letters and silences.   So you've had a further reduction within the piece. But let me go back a step. Were the same compositional methods used in manipulating the material from Thoreau in *Mureau* as were used in *Empty Words?*   Yes.   Then why is *Mureau* generally written continuously, like prose?   Because it was a column.   And as we can see *Empty Words* was written with lots of white space between the various parts.   Mureau was a column to be printed in a magazine, and Empty Words is a lecture. In fact, the whole thing is, through chance operations, put in the form of stanzas.   *Poetic* stanzas or *musical* stanzas?

Well, just stanzas. That is to say that one part of it is separated from another part.   Okay, parts; let's say parts.   And the parts were determined by the appearance of a period following whatever word, syllable, or letters that was chance-obtained.   When you found a period in Thoreau, that punctuation mark ended your stanza, and forced you to go on, vertically to another part.   This made a situation that brought about too many parts. Let's see if I can give you a—   You're showing me notebooks which have Roman numerals—

The Roman numerals are volumes of Thoreau's Journal.   Page numbers, and then occasionally English words.   Right. Now I'm trying to find an example of too many periods close together. Well, here's one. There's a period. "Hauling off, period." And before it is "teenth, period."   As part of, say, "nineteenth," you had just a syllable there.   And "hauling off."   Which you took as a phrase.   And each was followed by a period. And I did not want there to be so many parts that every time a period came that would be a stanza. So when they are adjacent like that, I asked the question, which one of them disappears.   By a decision of taste, you decided that one should disappear.   Yes.

Then you used the *I Ching* to decide which one would disappear.   Now when they were that close I had another device to see whether one of them disappeared and in this case they didn't necessarily disappear. It was just more difficult for them to disappear. So that sometimes two words can make a complete stanza, as in this case: "comes hawk."   Which are two words vertically aligned. Where do those words come from?   One comes from the eleventh volume, and the other from the sixth volume. But they were both . . . let's see what they . . . they were both words.   Now I'm lost. Go back again.   Here I have the notation "W 32."   That means you had to choose a word. And "32" means—   There are thirty-two words to be found. One, two, three, four, five, six, seven, eight, nine, ten, eleven, twelve—   Thirty-two words in that section.   And now we have phrases, words, and syllables, and there are fifty-four of them.   So then you found fifty-four, and once you found fifty-four—   Then I found word, syllable, word, syllable, syllable, word, phrase, phrase, phrase, phrase, word, phrase, word, phrase—   It's an interesting way to work, and it follows the title—it's emptyheaded.   I understand that. But it's still dealing with a very pregnant, resonant, and, to you, very relevant, text in Thoreau's *Journal.* So there was an exercise of choice in selecting it, rather than another book, and that choice would influence an awful lot. **I know, as you know too, that were the same kind of thing done with** Finnegans Wake, **the result would be entirely different.** Or if it were an urban writer, it would be different. If it were done with a— **Or with a different language. Or with a combination of languages. It was certainly suggested by** Finnegans Wake **that one should do that.** Since *Finnegans Wake* is a combination of languages—that is its principal linguistic characteristic— any work derived from it would reflect that fact. Let me go back to the question of the four major sections, or "Lectures" as you call them. When did one of them end? **When there were 4,000 events at least.** In other words, there had to be 4,000 separate extractions from Thoreau. **In the case of the First Lecture, there are 4,060, and the reason for that excessive number is this: when I got to the 3,997th event—** You threw a sixty-four. **Right. I threw a sixty-four, and it took me up to 4,060.** What are those halfmoon marks in your notebook—halfmoon marks that we use to connect letters to each other over space, as when we make a superfluous space in typing. You have these all over the text; what are they about? **It was the last thing I did before I finished the text. I went through and found out which things were to be read as connected to each other, so that this "R" from "hear" instead of being separate from the 'Th" of "the" in the following word goes together with it, so it's "RTH", instead of "R,TH."** The letters are printed together in the text, and pronounced together when you speak them. So these were derived from an either/or situation with the *I Ching.* So, half the bits—should we call them "bits" or is "events" your word?—are connected, and half of them aren't. How did you decide, in typing out this work, to go onto another line? How did you decide that the space should not be a space between words, so to speak, but a space between lines? **I set up a certain number of characters for each line, a maximum, and I did not permit the breaking of a word, and I used commas as ends of lines.** So, whenever there was a comma in the original text, that indicates the end of a line. **Or any other kind of punctuation.** Including a period—a period that you ruled would end a stanza. So, it's simply a matter of when the words or bits fill up the available line, then you go onto the next line. **I hope I can show you that.** We're looking now at *Empty Words,* Part One, as it appears in the book. **"notAt evening comma," so that was the end of the line.** A comma in the original ended the line in your text, but that comma is not reproduced here in the book. **That's right.** "Right can see," and there's a hyphen. And those three words are separated. **"Suited to the morning hour."** And those five words are separated from the following stanza. Now, in the opening line, the first two words "not" and "at" are run together, into "notAt," because by the *I Ching* process that was thrown they had to run together. You kept the capitalization of "A" in "at," which was in the original Thoreau. **Yes. Then the indentation here is obtained by subtracting the number of characters in the line from the maximum number, which is probably something like forty-two or forty-three.** If you have forty-three characters in a line, what do you subtract? **Subtract the number of characters in the first line from the maximum. And then subjecting that number to chance operations to discover where the indentation was.** I'm lost; I'm sorry. **There are one, two, three, four, five, six, seven, eight, nine, ten, eleven, twelve, thirteen characters in "notAt evening." I subtract** that from forty-three, and I get thirty. And now relate thirty to the number sixty-four to find out how many spaces in from the edge I should indent the line. Say, I got the number two. I'm working with thirty characters here. The I Ching works with the number sixty-four. So looking at the table that relates thirty to sixty-four, taking my next I Ching number, I find out, if I get the number one, for instance, I got something very small. I have to begin the line one space in from the left. But the next line, instead of being right underneath the first line, is indented toward the middle.   In the second line again, by the same procedure, you counted the number of characters, subtracted that from forty-three, put that number through the *I Ching* with its sixty-four options, and thereby determined where your second line begins.   Now, when there was no comma, because it looks like there wasn't one here, then I went as far as I could in the line, up to the maximum, without breaking the line and without breaking the word. If there were only one or two, then I left just an either/or about the indentation, and it looks like it—   Started flush left, until you go to one of those punctuation marks that would prompt you to go onto another line.   That's right.   So you did the first 4,060 lines, and thereby finished Part One of *Empty Words*. In Part Two, you continued with your method but you removed the possibility of phrases.   That's right.   And continued to do the same thing.   Right.   And in *Empty Words,* Three, you removed the possibility of words, so you had just syllables and letters, and then in Four, just letters.   I had one further idea, but I guess that it doesn't apply to the record. That was to sit in profile for the first one. Then face the audience for the second one. To sit in profile again but on the other side for the third. And then with my back to the audience for the fourth.

And it was actually at Naropa that I sat with my back to the audience, and they became infuriated. Each of the four works comes with a preface—actually each section has a preface that incorporates the prefaces of its predecessor, until there is a four-part preface to the last one. What are they meant to do? All the information, all the answers to all the questions, such as those you now are asking me, are given as conscientiously as I can in these introductions. I tried to imagine what it is anyone would want to know and then I give them that information in the introduction, but not in any logical sequence. How were these prefaces written? The first thing I did was find out how many words I had at my disposal for the first remark or for the first answer. one, two, three, plus two plus two plus two, eleven. I had eleven words. Now I thought, well, what shall I say. And it occurred to me to say at the beginning how it was that I came to be in connection with Thoreau. That seemed to be a reasonable beginning. And it reads: "Wendell Berry: Passages outloud from Thoreau's *Journal* (Port Royal, Kentucky, 1967)." That's eleven words. It was at that time and in that place that Wendell Berry picked up a copy of the Journal—we had just had dinner together; I was in his home. He read passages out loud to me. And the moment he did that was the next remark, which has thirty-four words: "Realized I was starved for Thoreau (just as in 1954 when I moved from New York City to Stony Point, I had realized I was starved for nature; took to walking in the woods)." I thought I should have said after that, but I didn't have room, that I took to reading Thoreau just as I had taken to walking in the woods; but I thought that once I'd said it in that way—that since I realized I was starved for Thoreau, I think you'd realized I started reading the Journal. And then, "Agreed to write work for voices

(Song books)" and so forth. The third line of the first preface seems like a very long statement, but then you have a very short statement about "Syntax: arrangement of the army," which is a reference to Norman O. Brown's sensitive remark that conventional syntax, in its lining up of words, represents the militarization of language. **These are answers to possible questions about** Empty Words. Admittedly in skeletal form. You also explain here how you use the *I Ching* in this piece. **And do you know what?** I was able—you see, time passes and I get involved in different projects and I had forgotten—and I had for years been reading Part Three. Every time anyone asked me to give a lecture I would read that. And I forgot how I had read Part One. Or Part Two. And when I tried to do it for the record, I found I couldn't. I didn't know how. So I thought, how will I find out. Then I realized that I'd answered all these questions in the introduction. **Really?** Yes. So I got out the Introduction to Part Three and it says there, "Searching (outloud) for a way to read. Changing frequency. Going up and then going down; going to extremes. Establish (I, II) stanza's time. That brings about a variety of tempi (short stanzas become slow; long become fast)." **I counted the number of stanzas and divided the total length, two hours and one-half, by the number of stanzas and thus determined that most of the stanzas in Part One would be forty seconds long. Some, the longer ones, would be a little longer.** In your own score for your readings, what you've done is timed when you should begin each stanza, and beside you as you read is a stopwatch. You have other marks suggesting where words should be divided into syllables. **This could be "thee berries" instead of being "the-e berries." This could be "flo-were" or "flowere" or "flow-er-e" instead of "flower-e."** We're now talking about the seventh line of Part One.   There are many possibilities, but these marks indicate to me what I am to do. I left them out of the printed text in order to remove my intentions from it, so that one could read it in a variety of ways rather than one way.   Let's say you have a stanza, like the twenty-third, which has twelve lines. If you have only forty seconds, you'd have to speak quite quickly to get through that.   **Right. A stanza that long has to be read very fast. See it has forty-four seconds actually. In order to make the thing come out evenly with two hours and one-half, I made a complicated but symmetrical arrangement, and I gave a few more seconds to the longer stanzas so that reading them became more practical. Not a great many, but like four seconds. I was delighted to learn how to read this and to learn this from my introduction.**   That is why those introductions are so important, not only to readers but to you.   There was a criticism of this text by our dear friend Jackson Mac Low in that interesting critical magazine called L=A=N=G=U=A=G=E. **Jackson said that though he enjoyed hearing Empty Words, he had no interest in reading it. He found that he never picked it up to read. The only reason he doesn't pick up the text is that he doesn't know how to read it. If he knew how to read it, he would immediately become fascinated by it.**   Well, how should we read *Empty Words*?   **I've shown that with the recording, and I've found it out from reading the introduction, that the moment you set up the stanza time and then follow that—** Visually? **No, timed with a stopwatch.**   I'm sorry, John; do you want me to read *Empty Words* with a stopwatch?   **Yes. Then immediately you become fascinated with the whole problem of reading it.**   Let's go back a step. You mean to say—   **That's the musical problem.**   Let's go back to the very beginning of Part One, "notAt evening." You have that section marked for forty seconds and the one after that for eighty seconds on the stopwatch and then for one-hundred-twenty seconds and then the one after that for two minutes. Is it your notion that one should read each part for forty seconds?   **No. The forty seconds will include your reading of those lines. And anything else that's in those forty seconds is silence, which is to say ambient sounds.**   Therefore, I look at those first three lines, and I have forty seconds to think about them, while I glance at the stopwatch to measure myself. When I look at the next two lines, I get forty more seconds to consider them.   **No, no. You** read **them. You've been advised to do this by James Joyce in connection with** Finnegans Wake. **He says the book was not to be read silently, but should be read out loud.**   Out loud to oneself?   **Yes. Not just looked at but said out loud.**   So just as a Bach score is meant to be taken to the piano to play, *Empty Words* is meant to be taken with a stopwatch and read aloud to oneself. Or to one's friends, whoever's there. If someone asks you, as I had planned to do, what is the difference between hearing it and reading it, you would reply that there is no reading without hearing—you haven't *read* the text unless you've heard it.   **And then I saw at some other place . . . where is it? . . . look here, how beautiful this is. "Making music by reading outloud. To read. To breathe. . . . Making language saying nothing at all. What's in mind is to stay up all night reading."**   So, therefore, one can in eleven hours have the experience, the full experience, of *Empty Words* entirely by oneself.   **It's conceivable, don't you think, that if someone initiated such a search as that, and such a discipline, that he might discover another way to read it.**   I was going to ask about that. Once you've recorded it, haven't you prejudiced its sound, to most of us; and your answer would be, no, I've given you only my way to do it, but that's not necessarily going to be your way to do it. What then do I hear when I hear *you* reading it, in performance or on the record? What would I hear when I hear myself reading it?   I think that this is a question that changes with each listener. And the answer would have to change with each listener. There are people, as you know, who are color blind. So there must be people who just have no interest in sound whatsoever and who are insensitive to everything in language but "meaning."   And they would say that in *Empty Words* they had heard nothing.   And then there may be, on the other hand, people who are musically inclined who are not so oppressed by meaning.   Or the need to have meaning.   Right. There are very many ways to hear something. I think one of the things to pay attention to . . . I think I'll put it this other way: I think one should pay attention to everything when one does anything. And if one is listening one should be attentive to all the various characteristics of sound and language that there are, because we are dealing with a complex situation, a transition from language to music, or from literature to music.   Is it then comparable to the experience, which we've all had, of being in a room where everybody's talking in a language we don't know and we thus try to appreciate the music of the language itself.   There is only one line at a time in Empty Words, so I don't think the parallel to many people in the room is right.   Let's say—   Someone speaking a foreign language, except that the language is not entirely foreign. It's from Thoreau. When it gets inscrutable, because it does with letters and syllables and so on, people remark to me frequently that it sounds like old English—something else they don't understand. What's interesting are all the variety of things that happen: the sounds, the rhythm, the inflections, the this, the that—all these things. You can never tell when something's going to set your faculties working.   So, indeed, it is meant to remind you of other things as well.   It's unavoidable, don't you think, Richard? Because the human mind is more complex than a computer; the moment something comes into it, it touches bells, it rings bell, with regard to the rest of the mind. And everybody's mind is like this, even the man in the street, who's not supposed to be bright. But he is very bright. He's brighter than a computer.   Now it seems to me that *Empty Words* demands of us a kind of discipline in that, as it goes from Part One to Part Four, it does get harder and harder to listen to, as the intentional verbal or vocal content gets sparser and sparser.   This varies with people. Very frequently someone gets up and leaves during the course of the reading, but at the same performance someone will come to me after the reading and say that I could have gone on forever. As far as he was concerned, it would have been a pleasure. And this is true of Part Three which I've been reading so frequently. Part Four, well, offered problems to the audience at Naropa. And part of it came, I think, from my sitting with my back to them, for I'd no sooner begun to read than they began an uproar.   Really?   And I had to be protected physically by quite a redoubtable group of people, including Allen Ginsberg.   How large an audience was there?   Three thousand.   Three thousand people, incredible.   Three thousand people, and they went into a state of disenchantment—complete disenchantment.   How many stayed until the end?   I would say at least three quarters of the audience.   Really?   And it went on for two hours and a half.   And you had your back turned. Were you amplified in any way?   Yes. Some of the silences were twelve and thirteen minutes long. After the performance I promised them that I would go through a period of self-examination, and I counseled them to do likewise, since we had gotten along so badly together that night.   I first heard you perform Part Four at St. Marks Church in the spring of 1975. Then you spoke it; since then, I've heard that you've developed a singing style for it.

A chanting, yes. Well, it was part of this reexamination that I counseled the audience at Naropa to do. And I decided to make this text more musical than I had.

And this decision came after your Naropa reading?

It was for the recording, actually. And now that I've made it, and now that I've done it, I enjoy it, and I will in the immediate future, when I'm asked to give a lecture, do this chant.   Just for Part Four. Does it bother you when people walk out?   No. It doesn't bother me because they are the ones who are walking out. I myself am staying.   Does it bother you when people heckle, as apparently they did at Naropa?   I can't say that it doesn't bother me, but I can say this: That it does not bother me to such an extent that I stop what I'm doing. What I'm doing is so exigent, so demanding, it requires me to pay attention to everything I am doing. I don't have much time to be bothered by the people who are walking out.   How many times have you performed *Empty Words* around the United States?   Oh, gosh.   Twenty? Forty?   More. I don't know.   In the area of fifty? Sixty?   In Europe, too. You see it's a text that, since it doesn't mean anything, can be read in a foreign country. This is one of the advantages of nonsyntactical writing.   That's an advantage of music as well—   That it moves toward a whole world.   Have you ever read it to an audience that has copies of the text in front of them, as people owning the record will?   I think that will happen more, because Empty Words is my next book and the book will be included in the package with the recording.   Does it help? Is it a good idea?   I think it will help. Yes.   Do you recommend it?   It's according to whether you're the sort of person who likes to read the score while listening to the music.   On this recording, Maryanne Amacher is your collaborator. How did you conceive of her role and how would you describe what she is doing?   I've done a number of works involving environmental sound, ambient sound, and one of them was Score with Parts (1974), which I did for the St. Paul Chamber Orchestra. I used the environmental sound of dawn at Stony Point, New York, where I had written the music, and David Behrman made that recording, and he made another recording for me for the piece called Etcetera. Again it was ambient sound not at dawn, just anytime during the day. It was composed for a dance that Merce did in Paris called Un Jour ou Deux. One Day or Two. And when I was invited by the CBC to make a bicentennial piece called Lecture on the Weather, I thought also of asking David Behrman to make a recording of wind, rain, and thunder for the whole thing. Somehow he didn't receive the letter that I sent him. He was at York University in Toronto, and it went to the wrong part of the university. It just wasn't received. Finally I telephoned him, but he was then committed and couldn't do it and thought I should engage Maryanne Amacher, for, he said, she did the best recordings of ambient environmental sounds. I knew that her work was very beautiful. I had heard it, and I agreed with him immediately. So I engaged her to do that and her friend Luis Frangella, an Argentinian, to make a film of lightning with the drawings of Thoreau as the flashes of light. So that Thoreau himself became the thunder. And the speakers preferably would be people who had given up their American citizenship and were becoming Canadians, so it was a dark bicentennial piece. Like Thoreau, it criticized the government and its history. And the twelve speakers are speaking quotations from the "Essay on Civil Disobedience," the Journal, and Walden, according to chance operations. Which are coherent quotations, or fragments, as in *Mureau* or *Empty Words*? They're coherent, but they're so superimposed that you can't understand anything. It's the same experience you would have if you had twelve radios going at once. Or if you had tuned between stations and could hear several going at once. That's not the same experience at all, because you're dealing with a fixed and highly charged body of material. That's true; you're right. It would be closest to my own *Recyclings* which is, as you know, dedicated to you. In *Recyclings* nonsyntactic reworkings of earlier essays of mine are read simultaneously by myself multiplied, thanks to audiotape, into a nonsynchronous chorus of several voices. There's always my language, and that's what *Recyclings* is ultimately about. It turned out that Luis Frangella had never made a film before in his life. I had assumed that he was a filmmaker. He accepted to make a film, even though he had never made one, and the film he made is absolutely beautiful. Let's go back to Maryanne Amacher. What is she doing for this record? She is gathering sounds at Walden Pond and will then mix them, superimposing several recordings. She's most sensitive to this kind of thing, and she uses the recordings of environmental sounds as instruments. She orchestrates them on a most intuitive level. She doesn't make a recording and then just listen to it. She makes a record and then plays it like a musical instrument. She makes it sing. What she does is hard for me to understand, because I don't work the way she does. She's a troubadour. Her music cannot be separated from her. Whereas I hope not only physically but in every other way too, if possible, to separate my music from me. That's not entirely true, but you're working at it. My theory of this position, which as you know I hold myself, is that always we try to think of methods to divorce what we are doing from self-expression, but the work we do nonetheless reflects us. **I suppose so.** Often in unobvious, highly subtle ways. **But that's not our intention. Nor was it Thoreau's intention. He said very early, at the age of twenty-one or twenty-two, that he was not interested in self-expression. Isn't that amazing.** Your subsequent literary work has—

To do with Finnegans Wake. It's quite different from Empty Words. Writing Through Finnegans Wake and Writing for the Second Time Through Finnegans Wake have been mesostics on the name of James Joyce. That's a different discipline and doesn't involve chance operations, but involves something else entirely—painstaking examination. Coupled with devices in selecting from Joyce's work to ensure that something other than the original Joyce emerges. What in past poetry have you been relating to? **When I was first aware of literature beyond high school, it was Pound and Eliot and Joyce and Stein and Cummings.** The great modernists. **And then I lost interest in literature in the thirties. I didn't become interested in the social concerns of Auden and Isherwood, and who were the others?**

That was English poetry; comparable Americans would be Kenneth Fearing and perhaps Muriel Rukeyser. **I wasn't interested in that. I wanted a poetry that would continue from these five I just mentioned. It took a long time for that to come about. There was a kind of revolt against them, wouldn't you say?** Well, not against Eliot, to be sure, but against some of the others, yes—against Cummings and Stein for sure. They were definitely neglected for a while. **And Joyce too. Joyce is only accepted by Joyce scholars, don't you** think? In Joyce, as in Stein, there are what can be called litmus tests. In Joyce, the test is *Finnegans Wake.* It was quite fashionable when I was in college, twenty years ago, to hear literature professors say that Joyce was very interesting as far as *Ulysses,* but that *Finnegans Wake* represents "an ambitious failure"—that was their term. As I've come to appreciate *Wake* for myself, I've begun to evaluate other people's tastes by whether or not they accept *Finnegans Wake.* If they acknowledge it, then they are up to date; if not, then they're back at least to the Dark Ages of early modernism. With Gertrude Stein you can do the same thing, curiously enough. The test goes like this: If someone says that Stein wrote a "marvelous" *Autobiography of Alice B. Toklas,* a "good story" called "Melanctha" and "a lot of incomprehensible crap," you know they too are in the Dark Ages. If they know *Geography and Plays, The Making of Americans,* and *Mrs. Reynolds,* then their literacy in other people's work is probably current as well. In talking about the reputations of Joyce and Stein, I think you have to keep these distinctions in mind. **Oh, how I love what they both did, but I'm crazier at the moment about Joyce.** I'm crazier about Stein myself, mostly because there is more to steal there. There are lots of things in Stein you can pick up on and make your own work out of. In Joyce, there is no way either you or I—or no way I know about at the moment—either you or I can write in seventeen languages, although we have one mutual friend who did, Hans G. Helms. Did I ever tell you this story before? One night, roughly in the fall of 1969, he was sitting in my living room, and I said, "Hans, nobody's ever written a polylinguistic work since *Finnegans Wake.*" And he replied, "I have." And I said assuredly, "No, not two languages like *A Clockwork Orange,* but many languages." He said that his book *Fa:m' Anhiesg-*

wow (1959) had fifty-something languages, as indeed it does. If there was one person in the entire world who could definitively contradict my generalization, there he was in my living room, right there. **Yes. His work is amazing, though he has not continued it.** It is too bad *Fa:m' Ahniesgwow* is so hard to find in this country, because it is very suggestive and very special. Are there any other current writers who have meant a lot to you? **In the forties I would pick up new books and see nothing interesting. It was in the fifties I became aware of Jackson Mac Low. I admit that his work was difficult for me at first, but Jackson faithfully sent me things as they appeared; he had been in my class at the New School.** **In 1956.** **And gradually I became devoted to his work and enthusiastic about it.** Jackson is a friend, whom I admire as much as you do, but it seems to me that Jackson, interesting as his methods are, missed the trick. He doesn't know that you have to cut it somewhere. That's why his pieces invariably go on too long. Even if you're involved with chance operations, the trick is that somewhere you must impose taste—you must decide that one procedure is not going to work any longer or that another device is a more inventive way of doing things. **That may occur in Jackson's work because, if he's using chance operations, he works with a rather limited reservoir of material, like a page from a particular book or something.** And then one not as interesting as Thoreau's *Journal* or *Finnegans Wake*. **And you immediately get the notion of repetition. Or if he's using the words that appear from a single person's name, as he often does, words naturally get repeated: repetition becomes the dominant characteristic of his work. I thought for a while that, since he was involved, as I am, with chance operations, I ought not to bother using chance operations with language; but then when I saw that I was interested in nonrepetition, it was as though I could enter** the same field Jackson was in without stepping on his toes. And that's why I continued to do it. Jackson's also very eclectic in his esthetics, as you know. He has expressionistic poems as well as those we've spoken about. I first encountered this among artists, the people who painted oil paintings, and who refresh themselves by painting water colors. And I think that's what it is with Jackson. In order to refresh himself from the one, he does the other. I went to a reading the other night, and he read a more recent poem—in fact, he said it was a poem written that very day. It was another Light Poem. And it was more or less off the top of his head. It was that sort of thing. But, oh, Richard, his head has a lovely top, and the least thought that enters his head is a very good thought. I doubt that. No, I think so, because it was really rather his least thoughts that were in the poem. And then there was another poet that evening whose considered thoughts were less entertaining than Jackson's offhand ones. Are there any other writers that you're— Well, we should mention you. Thank you. And I think, in general, that we can say that the act of picking up a magazine or something to do with literature now is a less pat matter than it would have been in the thirties or even the fifties, because there's far more experimentation going on, so to speak, generally, than there was in those decades. And "reading" has also become more problematic, in a fundamental sense. And I've noticed too that an audience—for instance, the audience listening to Jackson read the other night at St. Marks—was really attentive throughout and delighted with things that would have completely confused an audience of twenty years ago. Or at least twenty-eight years ago, twenty-five years ago. You're calculating for the early fifties, I can tell, which you regard as the extreme nadir of experiment in art in this country. Is 1953 your calculation? No, 1952.

Prefaces

In the summer of 1967, I put aside expository prose, which I write for a living, to try "creative work" again. I had always wanted to do poetry and fiction, but nearly everything I produced soon struck my critical eye as obvious derivatives of texts I had admired before. My radical solution to this impasse lay, that summer, in starting my activity at a wayward point. If I had previously written in sentences, a form whose demands I had more or less mastered, perhaps, I thought, it would be advantageous to avoid sentences entirely and deal, instead, with individual words in isolation—a form with few artistic precedents. Remembering a lecture I had heard in London two years before, I decided to cast these chosen words into expressive shapes, utilizing only those lines embodying the letters and familiar 8½-by-11 inch sheets of white paper. Although prose continues to provide my livelihood, I have, from time to time, had sporadic outbursts of this other kind of nonlinear writing.

Largely because I began from such a radical point, my creative activity from the start spoke no clear echoes (and even within the developing traditions of visual poetry, my pieces still exhibit, I am told, a recognizably personal style). For the first time I found myself satisfied with my imaginative work, sensing not only a break-through at least in my own relationship to standard sheets of white paper, but also perhaps a way of rejuvenating our poetically worn-out language; so I eagerly sent off copies of this new work to those periodical editors who had previously published my prose. Rejections were the unanimous result, several of my earlier benefactors asking, with varying degrees of politeness, why I was wasting my energies. Innocently believing those reactionary critics who charge that editors and their audiences are eager for everything "new," I was truly surprised (and a bit hurt) at the time, but given how different my new works were from everything else printed in their pages (and, more important, from what they expected of me), their negative response was predictably obtuse and, in the end, perhaps critically flattering. Since manuscripts on my desk only accumulate dust, I continued to mail them out and around, usually to perfunctory and uncomprehending refusals, until scattered acceptances, as often as not from anthologists, helped establish confidence for future work. A collection of the best pieces also went to book publishers, who generally showed less editorial sadism or snobbishness than pure subservience to commercial considerations; my proposed book never found a sponsor. Since I believed this eccentric work was doing something important to literature, the best solution to my frustrations lay in following a long and respectable succession of poets who published their first collections entirely at their own expense.

In the fall of 1967, the poet Paul Carroll, who was then editing *The Young American Poets* (1968), asked me for a statement of purposes; the reply I then supplied still strikes me as appropriate to most of the pieces collected here: "The discovery, or the devising, of expressive shapes for individual words or groups of words that particularly haunt me; or the infusion of words and letters into resonant and/or familiar shapes. In both these respects, the ideal result of my ingenuity would be a word-picture whose meaning and shape are so effectively complementary that the entire image would have a unified integrity and an indelible impact." In retrospect, the major inadequacy of this statement lay in my failure to distinguish simple and obvious representationalism—most conspicuously popularized by Robert Carola in *Playboy*—from more complex and unusual visual forms for words. What I discovered in "readings" before live audiences—done with slides in a carousel projector and voice-over narration—was that, while obvious shapes were easily forgotten, the less expected, or more imaginative forms had both greater immediate impact and stronger potential for "after-image," not to speak of other esthetic virtues. This superiority is particularly true of those shapes that not only enhance the legible words but do something else besides, such as referring to other realms of experience or to more general processes. I wish I had added three years ago that, despite its structural constraints (which serve to discipline the imagination, especially away from the temptations of familiar expressions), I find this new medium is capable of representing a wide range of meanings and emotions.

My rather explicit title for my first book is *Visual Language*, the fourteen horizontally stretched letters in the cover design emulating lines of traditional poetry or, more specifically, *a sonnet*; and all of the pieces collected were drawn by my own hand, a few of them shamelessly revealing that fact. As I noted in the anthology *Imaged Words & Worded Images* (1970), the word "concrete" does not classify such works, referring instead to everything produced, most of it dreadful and inscrutable, by that cabal of artists who call themselves "concretists," who are mostly European but have henchmen in America. Whether these pieces can justly be called "poetry" remains an unsettled question. "Poetry," writes the structuralist critic and linguist Roman Jakobson, "means the giving of form to the word, which is valuable in itself"; in my work language is formally enhanced by both selective isolation and visual display. Nonetheless, my pieces are sufficiently different from most "poetry" to merit perhaps another name, and "word-imagery" strikes me as probably the most generally appropriate and least pretentious term. In "writing" of this kind, I believe, lies one propitious future for literature.

The publication of *Visual Language* also caps a particular way of working, initiated in 1967 and largely culminated by 1969, for my creative endeavors in the past year have been largely in sequential forms—closer to fiction than poetry—that nonetheless eschew the prosaic form of expository sentences. By 1970, the pieces collected here seem very spare, and from this "minimalist" beginning, I would now like to work outwards, not only beyond the single page but also into visual space (such as a piece now in progress, whose most appropriate published form would be as a map). Contemporary art, I once suggested, must be either much more, or much less, than earlier art; whereas these pieces are largely much less, in the future I should like to emulate the complexity and abundance of, say, the British word-image artist John Furnival at his very best. "So far as I am individually concerned and independent of pocket," wrote Herman Melville, "it is my earnest desire to write those sorts of books which are said to fail."

1974

In visual poetry, unlike other kinds, the way that words are placed on the page is the primary means of enhancing language; pictorial shaping makes words poetic by generating semantic and symbolic connotations that would not otherwise be present. *Conversely, language in visual poetry would have considerably different meanings if presented in uniform, horizontal type; for one thing, it would lack the poetic dimensions that the pictorial increment provides. *Visual poetry is not synonymous with "concrete," although all anthologies with "concrete" in the title included some visual work. The principal characteristic of "concrete" appears to be the countersyntactical use of language, and although most pictorial poetry likewise eschews conventional linguistic syntax, that is not its primary particularity. *"Visual poetry" is a genre, or a species of *poetic* literature, as distinct from fictional literature or expository writing. The epithet is used as a critical-historical classification that, like a genus term in biology, tells us not only what the work at hand is, but also what it isn't. *Another feasible term is "verbal painting," but I for one prefer to emphasize its linguistic base. *Visual poetry is an intermedium between poetry and design, for all visual art intended for *re*print is "graphic." *One man's visual poetry is another man's "design" and a third man's "Art." *The history of modernist poetry has witnessed a succession of emancipations from some constraints, coupled with the introduction of new ones, which function to open the art to something else. *As the creative processes behind visual poetry tend to be more disciplined and self-effacing than hedonistic or expressionistic, it cuts against the dominant psycho-esthetic orientation of contemporary poetry; nonetheless, a gathering of an artist's work probably reveals idiosyncracies that in turn implicitly reflect personality. *The constraints of word-image art provided me, as a professional essayist, with a sure means of avoiding the conventions of expository writing, for I assumed from the beginning that a writer's poetry should evolve from processes different from, if not contrary to, his prose. For one thing, poetry, unlike prose, does not intend to communicate information; it is not conducive to discursiveness. *Even though my creative works differ considerably from my critical writings, both endeavors reflect similar fundamental assumptions about art in our time. *Certain things can be articulated in pictorial poetry that cannot be said in prose, and vice versa. *Visual poetry must be seen to be "understood"; even second hand descriptions are as inadequate as other forms of paraphrase. *Visual enhancement should be considered one of many possibilities for contemporary poetry; no pictorial poet pretends it is an exclusive successor to the past. *Visual poetry represents a revolt not against language *per se* but against the clichés of standard syntax. *Representationalism is one strategy available to the pictorial poet, though shapes that do nothing more than resemble the meaning of words are scarcely sufficient; exclusively mimetic interpretations of visual poetry are similarly insufficient. *Not even my simplest pictorial poems strike me as "primitive," mostly because they reflect, rather than repudiate, the history of modernism in art and literature. *I personally find dada more sympathetic than surrealism, constructivism more suggestive than cubism, and the Russian futurists more relevant than the Italians, but all of these mixed-means movements contributed to my acknowledged "tradition." *Visual poetry depends not only upon design but upon language, revealing, intrinsically, why one word was chosen, rather than another; neither word nor design is arbitrary. *Pictorial poetry exploits the advantages of nonverbal communication without relinquishing language. *The poems collected in *I Articulations* incorporate, at last count, the following certifiably poetic devices: alliteration, allegory, allusion, ambiguity, irony, metaphor, paradox, satire, puns and wit, some of which are realized not verbally but pictorially. *A pictorial poem ideally creates a field of visual-verbal activity; and though both the visual and the verbal dimensions are perceived simultaneously, their relationship is usually comprehended progressively. *Some pictorial poets try, often with the help of professional collaborators, to realize the precision of commercial design, but since my own works descend from poetry, rather than from design, some of them reveal, at times conspicuously, the presence of the poet's own hand. *One reason why I have so far avoided colors other than black and white is that the outlets I initially had in mind afforded only monotonal reproduction—books and literary magazines. *The designer Jan Tschichold once said that "typography is the arranging of words to be read," implying that the words were servants of an ulterior message; in pictorial poetry, words stand mostly as an end in themselves. *As in my initial collection, *Visual Language* (1970), my aims include the making of a visual-verbal impression comparable to the "afterimage" of painting. *I once considered studying calligraphy but decided against trying to approximate, or even approach, the uniformity of typography. *What distinguishes my own pictorial poems not only from those by others but also from my "fictions" has been, I think, the complete avoidance so far of visual materials other than letters. *My own poetry has also been more literary than painterly, in part because it alludes to books more often than pictures, but also because all my works so far were originally done with pens or a typewriter on rectangular sheets of white paper. *However, this mode of composition, like much else in my creative work, may soon change. *Visual poetry may be the first truly international movement in literature. Works of mine have been exhibited and published, untranslated, all over Europe, in Latin America, and in Japan as well. *American visual poets find that publishers abroad have been more cordial than those at home, while readers in the States seem to send more letters of appreciation.

1977

> Typographical devices, employed with great daring, have given rise to a visual lyricism almost unknown before our time. These devices are capable of being carried much further, to the point of bringing about the synthesis of the arts—music, painting and literature. All this is merely a search for new, perfectly legitimate forms of expression. [Guillaume Apollinaire, "The New Spirit and the Poets," 1917]

In visual poetry, unlike other kinds, words are enhanced by visual means, for without their pictorial dimension something poetic would be lost. Visual technique can condense verbal material, sharpen both meaning and impact, and add connotations that transcend literal definition—in sum creating *poetry,* which is an honorific term for language that draws attention to itself. More specifically, were the words of a visual poem placed differently on a page, or set in conventional linear type, some poetic meanings would be appreciably changed, if not lost.

There is no legitimate reason why the print of poetry must resemble an army of precisely aligned, evenly sized men. The concept of "poetry" implies the liberation of not only the syntax and style of language, but its typography as well. In the beginning was the Word, which did not arrive in mechanically regular sizes. Poets should write military language only for money or for preaching.

Visual poetry is not new, as current work echoes Blake,

Cummings, and Apollinaire, among others. What is new, however, is the recognition of a distinct realm of communication—a separate artistic category—that is *both* verbal and visual, in addition to consciousness of a viable poetic tradition that must, for now, be transcended.

Recent visual work also reflects another tradition, most commonly associated with Charles Olson, of "open field" poetry, where words are expressively laid out within the available space ("field") of a rectangular page. Graphic space becomes not just a structural element but a dimension of content. In poetry, unlike fiction, less words reveal, if not indicate, more art; economy is a discriminatory measure.

Visual poetry resembles so-called concrete work in their mutual rejection of conventional poetic syntax; however, visual poetry and "concrete" are actually quite different, the latter emphasizing the fragmentation of language, the former its visual enhancement. To me, the elimination of conventional syntax—the real intention of "concrete"—is merely a prelude to subsequent invention; "concrete" is an antithesis prior to the synthesis of visual poetry.

Critics might characterize this work as marrying the contemporary notion of "intermedia" with the traditions of poetry—as integrating an awareness of recent art with an earlier commitment to language. It is true that most experimental poetry today is closer to contemporary painting and contemporary music than to "modern poetry"; that is one reason why it is experimental.

Visual poetry could be very popular, flirting, as it does, with signmaking and after-image, but most work nowadays reflects avant-garde attitudes and coterie aspirations.

Were visual poetry *not* genuinely innovative, it would

not be almost always excluded from the standard poetry magazines and anthologies, excluded from the platforms of "readings," excluded from the disbursement of awards and fellowships, and omitted from the current surveys and encyclopedias of poetry. Nonetheless, the history of every modern art shows that the "nots" eventually become keystones in their respective modernist traditions.

Most poetry today seems written either to impress other poets and professors of poetry or to be read aloud to an appreciative audience; this work is not.

Visual poetry eschews nearly all traditional poetic devices and yet remains "poetry," instead of "design." The antithesis of poetry is prose; yet visual poetry is scarcely prosaic. Indeed, one measure of its poetry is precisely its avoidance of prose. The perception of poetry has always differed from the reading of prose precisely in deemphasizing both linearity and "message" to concentrate on language.

Because familiar expression is so easily forgotten, experimental poets are interested in alternative ways of perceiving and possessing (remembering) language; their concerns include revamping the reader's experience of literature. Emancipating words from the clichés of conventional syntax, the visual poet gives them a different presence. He discovers rather than defines, invents rather than succumbs, escribes rather than describes.

My own visual poems employ a variety of lettering techniques—stencils, rub-off sheets, typewriters, handwriting; for even in its choice of letters, visual poetry scarcely resembles conventional typography. The visual poet customarily does more than type his work for the printer; he delivers the final image in camera-ready form. Nothing need be typeset (and visually changed, if not damaged, in the process).

One ideal implicit in my own visual poetry is economy

of both language and line. A second is the rejection of shapes other than those forming the letters. A third is the realization of images that stick in the reader's mind. A fourth is direct communication of surface meanings, which can be observed, rather than hidden meanings, which must be deduced. One distinction to be made among my works is that some incorporate their titles, while others have a headline.

The principal resemblances between my creative work and my critical writing are common assumptions about artistic modernism and the importance of formal experiment; otherwise, my poetry descends from thoroughly different impulses and realizes different effects.

These poems originate not with the ego (or the id) but with words and a desire to visualize those elements. They exhibit not personality but personal style.

Initially committed to drawing on rectangular 8½-by-11 inch pages, I have recently begun to work with larger areas, not only in posters and silkscreened prints but in original objects and canvases. Extending my language art yet further, I have also been making audiotapes of "sound prose," videotapes of "literary video," and nonrepresentational film, hopefully, in sum, extending the range of Literature.

In visual poetry as in sound poetry, there is no substitute for experience of the work itself; secondhand descriptions are inadequate. Comprehension begins with the resolution of verbal information with visual or aural perception.

Visual poems, unlike other kinds, are nearly always remembered in the same form as they were originally expressed—as a single visualizable picture. They represent not a return to the primitive but an advance into the future.

One feels, quite often, that he is constructing a new poetry out of the ruins of the past.

Art Autobiography

(1978)

Towards the end of his career, Moholy-Nagy described the
purpose of a retrospective exhibition as that of making the
spectator 'travel' as far as he had travelled himself, and
added, 'What a long way to go!' [Frank Popper, *Art-Action
and Participation*, 1975]

The thought of doing my own visual poetry initially
came to me while bored with Antonioni's *Blow-Up* early
in July, 1967. The next day, I wrote—rather *drew*—my
first poem, "Tributes to Henry Ford," using rulers,
French curves, and stencils that I purchased at a neighborhood store; and the fact that this five-image poem
remains among my most reprinted, most familiar works
both pleases and depresses me. I had already seen some
visual poetry, initially at London's Institute for Contemporary Art two years before and again in the then-current
"concrete" issue of the *Chicago Review*. Even though
most of the work collected under that "concrete" label
did not particularly appeal to me, I thought that the
idea of casting language in an alternative visual form was
profoundly suggestive.

Much of that glorious summer of 1967, just after my
twenty-seventh birthday, was spent working with my

new art, producing many pieces that have since become more familiar—"Disintegration," "Echo," "Nympho-mania," and the "Football Forms," among others. Some of these early works are explicitly mimetic, my drawing enhancing the words in representational ways, for my aim then was the creation of a visual form so appropriate to a certain word that the whole would make an indelible impact—an afterimage that would be implanted in the viewer's mind, primarily because the shape endowed the word with an incipiently mythic resonance. Though limited by a lack of artistic training, I nonetheless felt obliged to do all the drawing myself; since my works were poetry, rather than commercial design, I decided that they should not hide the idiosyncracies of my own hand.

Toward the end of that summer, I discovered the tech-nology of photostating and then began to submit my work to periodical editors I knew, mostly because they had published essays of mine; but nearly all of them were unresponsive, some even suggesting that I was wast-ing my time with this poetry. My initial acceptance came from Paul Carroll, who was then editing his pioneering anthology, *The Young American Poets* (1968); and my appearance there served the crucial professional func-tion of certifying, in my own mind at least, my status as "a poet" as well as "a critic." To celebrate the publi-cation of his anthology, Carroll sponsored a series of "readings" in New York; and in response to his invita-tion to participate, I developed the presentational form I still use—"an illuminated demonstration," in which a carousel projector throws my visual poems up on a screen while I, their author, standing behind the audience, de-claim a nonsynchronous, voice-over narration that is filled not with specific explanations but general concepts that the audience may or may not choose to relate to what they see. A decade ago, I had only enough slides to fill a single carousel tray; now I can fill several and often project two different sets of images simultaneously.

Since a book's worth of poems existed almost from the beginning, I decided early in 1968 to dedicate the volume to my most inventive teacher at college, S. Foster Damon, and even announced the dedication that February at Foster's seventy-fifth birthday party. Copies of my initial collection were submitted to several publishers, some of whom had previously issued my books; none of them took it. By 1970 I reluctantly recognized that commercial publishers in America were not yet hospitable to visual poetry. (Several years later, none of them have yet matured that far.) It was thus inevitable that *Visual Language* should be published under the imprint of Assembling Press, which I had cofounded that summer. In printing the book, I had two ulterior motives in mind: I wanted to see this work reviewed (it wasn't) and I needed sufficient copies to distribute to anthologists and friends. Photostats were becoming an unnecessary nuisance and expense.

The publication of *Visual Language* also forced me to consider alternative ways of making nonsyntactic visual poetry. I tried to make a complete visual alphabet, parts of which are reprinted in my second collection, *I Articulations* (1974); I also compiled collections of synonyms that were then visually enhanced, such as the "Live-Kill" pair (1972). Another new development, begun in 1970, is the handwritten visual poem, such as "The East Village" (1970-71). Here I wanted to get away from the centered space and single perceptual perspective of my earlier work. Since I am scarcely able to invent a situation from scratch—or, to be more precise, since I am more inventive with materials than imaginative with situations—I chose a familiar subject: the neighborhood in which I then lived. As my theme was the variousness of the individual side streets, each of which had its own characteristic spatial qualities, its own details, and its own sounds, I did a one-page portrait in language and space for each block. I thought of hiring a professional calligrapher to redo my peculiar handwriting, but the single sample I saw reminded me too much of the rigors of linotype. And *that* was precisely what I was trying to avoid. So, once again, the best solution was letting the work reveal my own hand. I originally wanted Assembling Press to publish *The East Village* as a single book, on large 11-by-17 inch pages. However, since twelve images seemed insufficient for a book, even in such a large format, I eventually incorporated the work into the 7-by-10 inch pages of *I Articulations.* Instead, a later, longer, handwritten poem, "Portraits from Memory," appeared as an entire thirty-five page book (1975), in which each page contains a verbal-visual portrait of a woman I might have known. Here, as elsewhere in my work, the titles of individual pieces tend to be rather explicit.

I had always thought that my best visual poems should be available for a gallery exhibition in enlarged forms, not only to publish them but also to enhance their after-image capabilities. Back in 1970, I made a large photostat of "Concentric" for a two-man exhibition. In the summer of 1974, I took a silkscreening course which resulted in a few enlarged prints; but since my technical competence was limited, in the following year I commissioned the printmaker Stephen Procuniar to make *Word Prints,* a set of seven, 26-by-40 inches. By 1976, I got into photolinens, with images even larger than the prints, and had them stretched, much like paintings, over wooden bars. I still enjoy visual poetry more than the movies.

Probably from the time I began to read, I had an ambition to write fiction, but everything I drafted between my freshman year of college and early 1968 eventually struck me as an obvious echo of some text I already admired. At least seven times I began a novel that, upon close inspection, was clearly an imitation of Nathanael West's great work, *The Day of the Locust*; so this ambition subsided, along with my dreams of becoming a professional football player or a rock musician. I felt no need to recapitulate what had already been written, and did not yet know how to write what had not.

In doing poetry, I had already discovered the idea of a constraint so severe that it would prevent me from using language in familiar forms, and that primary restriction was the use of only one word that would then be visually enhanced. An imposed constraint, I discovered, serves to force the creative imagination to resist convention, if not cliché; and like meter in traditional poetry, the constraint I chose also encourages puzzle-solving and other forms of playfulness. This approach struck me as rather useful at generating original work, and perhaps the easiest measure of the difference or newness of my work is whether or not the reader feels challenged to discern sense and significance in what at first seems inscrutable.

Early in 1968, I began to think about a similar kind of severe constraint for writing fiction; after a few abortive experiments, I hit upon the hypothesis of writing a story with no more than two words to a paragraph, and for a subject I chose the conveniently familiar one of boy meets girl. This plot appears frequently in my fiction, not because I have anything particularly profound to say about heterosexual encounters, but because a familiar, transparent subject makes both myself and my readers more aware of the technical issues that really interest me. Once the two-word paragraphs of "One Night Stood" were drafted, I typed them out, indenting alternate lines, and the following winter I realized that each two-word phrase could take up the entire page of a book, thereby expanding the story into a minimal novel (that was not published until 1977). Subsequent verbal fictions are similarly skeletal: "Excelsior," with only one word to a paragraph; "Milestones in a Life," in which chronological numbers are followed by just a single word or sometimes two; and "Dialogue," which is composed of only two words, yes and no, repeated in different ways. One attractive result of these technical departures is a fluid, indefinite sense of fictional space and time.

That summer of 1969, I discovered how to make visual fiction, realizing an implication of my much-reprinted "Football Forms"—that images in sequence could tell a story, whose temporal rhythm is based upon the time a typical reader takes to turn the page. That perception informed not only my alphabet novella, *In the Beginning* (1971), but also my initial abstract fictions—those consisting only of lines, lacking words, save for their titles. That summer I also drafted the theoretical statement, "Twenty-Five Fictional Hypotheses," that even several years later is still reprinted for its radical possibilities. It suggests, among other things, that anything can be used to tell a story, not only nonsyntactic language but visual materials as well, and of course I practiced what I preached. I also noticed a crucial difference between poetry and fiction: whereas the former tends to concentrate both image and effect, fiction creates a world of related activity.

A further development in my storytelling is the work composed of sequential four-sided symmetrical line drawings that metamorphose in systemic sequence. Begun in 1974, these "constructivist fictions," as I call them, presently include not only two published collections of short fiction, *Constructs* (1974) and *Constructs Two* (1978), but two more unpublished collections, in addition to two full-length novels, *Symmetries* (1979) and *Intermix* (unpublished). A variation of this constructivist theme is *And So Forth* (1979), a visual fiction in which the geometric images, by contrast, are *not* perfect symmetries, and their order is *not* fixed.

In the summer of 1970, I drafted another verbal fiction, entitled *Openings & Closings,* which remains, in one crucial respect, the most conventional imaginative piece I have ever written—it contains full sentences! Nonetheless, it resembles my other verbal fictions in observing a truncating constraint; whereas the earlier stories had one or two words to a paragraph, here I decided to suggest, within single sentences, either a story that might follow or one that could have gone before. The isolated sentences were literally either the openings (of hypothetically subsequent stories) or the closings (of hypothetically previous stories). These could be considered incomplete stories, it is true; yet it was my aim to make a single sentence be artistically sufficient (and let readers imagine the rest). As there is no internal connection between any particular opening or any closing, I thought from the beginning that the stories should best be set in two different styles of type—italics for the openings, roman for the closings—with plenty of white space between them, but not until 1975 was *Openings & Closings* published. Invited, in 1976, to exhibit the work in a gallery, I typed the sentences out on individual cards—one card to a sentence—again using italics for the openings and roman for the closings. These cards were then scattered, in no particular order, initially over a display board and later around a gallery's walls. I like this work for its leaps in space and the changes of its voices and tones, from item to adjacent item, but I doubt if I could ever again do a fiction that was so dependent on conventional expository sentences.

In my first numerical work, "Accounting," drafted early in 1969, I wanted to see if numbers could be used in lieu of words or letters. That numerical piece was also the first of its kind to appear in print, initially in my anthology *Future's Fictions* (1971) and then as a separate booklet (1973). The profession of accounting, like this numerical piece, documents processes of accumulation; but not until 1972, when preparing a revised version for chapbook publication, did I realize that this incremental sequence should end, like an accountant's tabulation, with a row of zeroes. That new numerical conclusion gave the narrative an ironic twist that, in my judgment, enhanced the work considerably. *Accounting* visually resembles my novella *In the Beginning,* composed around the same time, but whereas the former comes to a definite end, the final page of the latter suggests that the narrative could continue forever. That diametric difference in their sequential form indicates, of course, comparable differences in meaning.

Late in 1972, I set everything else aside to see how far I could take my growing interest in numbers—to see whether I could create a Literature composed of numbers alone. I thought at the time that I was making a book of "poems and stories," remembering my earlier distinction. However, by the following year, I realized that these works were actually becoming something else—a "numerature," perhaps; a "numerical art," to be sure. My aim in working with numbers was no longer the writing of poems and stories but the creation of a numerical field that is both visually and numerically coherent, with varying degrees of visual-numerical complexity. These works do not merely incorporate numerals within visual concerns, like, say, certain Jasper Johns paintings; my pieces are literally about the language of numbers. A principal difficulty in communicating this work, I belatedly discovered, is that audiences must be *numerate* to comprehend them, much as they must be *literate* to read modernist poetry and fiction.

My initial arrangements were numerically simple. "1024," for instance, incorporates both the parts and the factors of that variously divisible number, while "Indivisibles" is a field of visually unrelated numbers whose common property is that nothing can be divided into any of them (except, of course, themselves and one). As before, titles in my works tend to be explicit. Realizing that my aim was arithmetical patterns that could, like art (and unlike puzzles), be numerically appreciated again and again, I then tried to create numerical fields whose relationships were more multiple and less obvious. In works like the diamond-shaped "Parallel Intervals," I began, I think, to approach the levels of complexity that I admire in serial music and *Finnegans Wake,* for numbers were more conducive than words for my penchants for rigorous systems, structural complexity, and geometric order. (Simply because one number can go next to any other number, numerical syntax, unlike that of words, is also infinitely permissible.) In addition, these number pieces realize an empirical ideal that, though esthetically heretical, has long haunted me—that all the artistic activity that one identified in the work could be *verified* by another observer and yet be rich enough to be appreciated again and again. My first numerical prints were done in 1974 and the first photolinens in 1975.

In the spring of 1974, I completed *Recyclings,* the third and most successful of my initial series of experiments with continuous nonsyntactical prose. *Recyclings* was made by subjecting earlier essays of mine to selective processes that destroyed their original syntax, while retaining their characteristic language. The pages of *Recyclings* can thus be read both horizontally, like normal prose, or vertically, as the eyes, moving down and around the page, can perceive not only consistencies in diction but repeated words that usually indicate an identifiable ulterior source or subject.

Considering how to declaim this work aloud, I hit upon a structure that could aurally incorporate both the horizontal and the vertical—recruiting a chorus of readers each of whom would speak the text horizontally, one word after the other, but rather than read in unison, each new reader would start declaiming from the opening word, beginning to speak approximately one line behind his or her predecessor. Since I was not aiming for any specific vertical juxtapositions, but constant vertical relationships, each reader could go at his own pace, and in his own manner. I assumed that an audience listening carefully would hear vertical relationships—words spoken simultaneously, much like chords in music—amid the horizontal polyphonic declamation.

When invited to be a guest artist at the new radio studios of WXXI-FM, Rochester, New York, March, 1975, I realized a seven-track version in which all the declamatory voices are my own, each one amplified differently from the others. Although it was my initial intention to realize aurally certain qualities that were visually present in *Recyclings,* I found that the experience of listening to this audiotape is really quite different. This is not poetic declamation, as we customarily know it, but something closer to the performance of a musical score, probably because it mixes a language text with compositional structures more typical of music. Though "sound poetry" to some and "text-sound" to others, I prefer to classify this particular audiopiece as "sound prose," because the initial material is not poetry but prose.

My other initial audiotapes are largely straight declamations of my truncated stories, amplified and enhanced

in various, comparatively modest ways. For *Openings &
Closings*, I put the opening sentences on one side of a
stereo system, and the closing sentences on the other; in
Foreshortenings, a later verbal fiction, a voice clearly
identifiable as mine swaps single-sentence lines with a
chorus of my voice, both sides repeating the same reper-
toire of eighty-four simple sentences in increasingly different ways. (The principal reason why my own voice
takes both sides of this and other audio conversations is
that most of my tapes were done late at night, with only
an engineer and myself in the studio. And someone else
had to watch the voice levels on the recording machines!)

Since 1976, I have favored familiar religious and political texts, such as the Declaration of Independence or
the Lord's Prayer, electronically modified in ways that
make them aurally incomprehensible to most ears, were
not the texts already familiar. Indeed, religious materials
strike me as especially suitable for electronic enhancement, which generally increases the suggestion of sacred-
ness. Sometime after completing the initial recording of
"Praying to the Lord," where a single voice speaking a
familiar text is electronically multiplied into a vibrantly
cacophonous chorus, I came across R. Murray Schafer's
observation, in *The Tuning of the World* (1977), "It was
not until the Renaissance that God became portraiture.
Previously He had been conceived as sound or vibration."
In the back of my mind, when I began this piece, was
the experience, the previous summer, of seeing the valley
to the west of Mount Sinai, and then imagining the presence of thousands of noisy Israelites waiting for Moses
to return. Vibration, I now thought, could also be inter-
preted as the sound of the multitudes venerating God.
Schafer's remark also reminds me of Marshall McLuhan's
observation that electronic media of communication
recreate the sensory experience of preprint peoples.

The main distinguishing characteristics of my audiotapes so far have been the use of inventive, uncommon language structures, whether truncated lines or nonsyntactic prose, and then the realization of aural experiences that would be unfeasible, if not impossible, in live performance. It makes no sense for me or anyone else to do in one medium something that could be done better in another.

Late in 1975, I was invited to be guest artist at the Synapse Studio of Syracuse University. Here I worked not with a single engineer-producer, as at WXXI-FM, but with an institutional staff of young instructors, graduate assistants, and undergraduates. With their help, I realized video versions of earlier texts. To do "Excelsior," a truncated story in which two people make love in one-word paragraphs, I created a circular visual image for each character. As voices change, the screen flashes rapidly from one moving image to the other. In "Plateaux," with its single-word paragraphs, each relating a different stage (or plateau) in the development of a love affair, we used video feedback to create a kaleidoscopic moiré pattern that changes slowly in no particular direction, complementing visually the pointless, ultimately circular development of the fiction's plot. For *Openings & Closings,* I instructed the large staff, first, to alternate between color cameras for the openings, and black and white cameras for the closings, and then to make each new image (mostly of me reading) as different as possible from the one before, thus realizing visually the leaps of time and space that characterize the radically discontinuous prose text. Finally, whereas the audio *Recyclings* has nonsyntactic prose read by nonsynchronous voices (all mine), for the color video I hit upon the image of pairs of speaking lips (all mine again)—one pair of lips for the first "Recycling," two pairs for the second, etc. We went up to eight pairs of lips in the studio; however, one-inch videotape that has been passed, or superimposed, eight times has an electronically weak signal, so not only were the last two generations lost completely, but the next two (counting backwards) had to be reshot in black and white to survive on tape. Were *Recyclings* to be redone in a professional quad (two-inch tape) studio, all the images would have a much surer chance of surviving in their optimal form.

In 1977, long frustrated in my desire to work only with the sophisticated video equipment necessary for my technologically complex ideas, I began to think about working with the more limited possibilities of ½-inch or ¾-inch videotape. Most of the pieces I made in this format exploit a contrast between words that are heard and facial images that are seen, the camera's close-up eye assimilating only part of the speaking figure. I also used the character-generator to put directly on the screen visible words that would either enhance or counterpoint the language spoken on the tape. Again, it was my aim to create not documentations of live performances or dramatizations of stories—both current fashions in video art—but works based on language that could exist only on videotape, because they exploited the unique potentialities of the medium.

In 1976, I began to work with film, initially as an informal guest in a graduate animation course. With Barton Weiss, I made films composed entirely of words, which thus must be *read,* quite rapidly, in order to be "seen." The common joke is that these silent movies are "all titles, no action." What makes such entirely verbal films interesting to me are two complementary phenomena: the inordinate concentration of the viewers, who realize that they must pay constant, strict attention if they are to see everything, and then the experience of reading in unison with a crowd of strangers, in contrast to the conventional experience of reading a text of one's own choosing, at one's own speed, by oneself. The second set of films, made in collaboration with Peter Longauer, shoot the "constructivist fictions" in negative, so that four-sided symmetries of white lines appear on the black screen, in sequences that are systematically composed (complementing the systemic composition of the drawings). Of all the media in which I have worked, film requires the most laboring time and seems, in terms of what I would ultimately like to do with it, the least developed.

In the summer of 1977, I finally completed photographs worth preserving. I had been thinking about the art of photography ever since doing my documentary monograph on *Moholy-Nagy* (1970), for the example of Moholy taught me not only that I could work in several arts at once but that, if I did photography, I should create images that could exist only as photographs—that would not be "moments" from films, say, or extensions of documentary reportage. After several abortive experiments, I hit upon the idea of taking a single 8-by-10 inch photograph of myself, cutting it apart into eighty equally sized squares, and then recomposing these squares into eighty new pictures which I called *Reincarnations.* Given my recent ambiguous feelings about exact systems, the geometric rearrangements of each of the photographs is recomposed only roughly, or incompletely, systemic, while the order of the pictures is not fixed. (The analogue in my constructivist fiction is *And So Forth,* which was done around the same time.) For a second sequential piece, completed in 1979 and tentatively called *Recall,* each of the photographs is recomposed within scrupulously systemic principles, and the order of the pictures is fixed. At the time that examples of *Reincarnations* first appeared in print, I did not own a camera and never had, but one theme of this Moholyan memoir is that the lack of such prerequisites, let alone "education," should never prevent me, or anyone else, from working in any art.

The next step would take me into holography, a new technology for three-dimensional photography that surpasses the stereoscope of photographic history. I had followed the development of holography for over a decade without developing any ideas for working with it until I saw a circular (360°), cylindrical, rotating hologram. Then, it occurred to me that I could use one of my favorite artistic materials, the English language, to write syntactically circular, grammatically seamless statements. I had used this circular form before, in the "Manifestoes" that opens *Visual Language* and was subsequently reprinted as a broadside poster (1975); so I recognized that it would be more appropriate in a 360° hologram. Since the words of my earlier circular work dealt with my theories of visual poetry, it followed that my initial hologram should contain statements about holography and that it should likewise have an explicit title, *On Holography* (1978).

In their original, typed-out form, the statements looked like this:

holos = complete; gram = message;
representation in depth = hologram =
the hologram creates a world of incorporeal activity that
    exists only within
the illusion not only of depth but of equal focus to all
    distances are characteristics particular to holography
    which creates
by capturing on photo-sensitive material the amplitude, the
    wave-length and, most important, the phases of light
    reflected off an object a hologram reconstructs a three-
    dimensional image

In the hologram, the ends of these lines are attached to each other, making the statements visually circular and linguistically continuous. As these statements have different word lengths, they inevitably vary in circumference.

As the largest one is at the bottom and the shortest one on top, the five statements take a pyramidal form.

Rather than having the statements turn in unison, as a stationary pyramid, I wanted each line to revolve at a different speed. Given the nature of the circular hologram, they had to move in ratios of 1:2:3:4, with the longest statement being the base. Thus, when the longest statement runs once around the entire circumference of the cylinder, the second statement is repeated twice around the cylinder and the third statement three times around and the shortest statements are placed atop each other and they move in unison four times around the cylinder. Therefore, during the time it takes the cylinder to complete one revolution, the bottom statement can be read once in its entirety, the second statement twice, the third statement three times and the top statements four times.

However, since the circles made by these statements have different circumferences, their words *appear* to move before one's eyes at roughly the same speed. That is, at the same time that the bottom line traverses its entire thirty words, the second line moves 20 x 2 words, and the third line 12 x 3 words and the top two lines each 4 x 4 words. At first I thought this unanticipated result sabotaged the initial desire for the appearance of different linear speeds. However, I later realized that, had these speeds *not* been different, the movement of the top line's words would have been very slow—boringly slow—while that of the bottom line would have been intolerably fast. In any case, *On Holography* was indubitably holographic in that its effects could exist only within a hologram.

For its initial exhibition, at New York's Museum of Holography, I added an audiotape of five voices reading the same words on individually continuous, aurally seamless audiotape loops. These voices were then mixed down into a single cassette that went through stereo speakers beside the hologram, so that spectators could hear in five-voice unison the same words that they see in five-line unison. In more extravagant circumstances, these voices might emerge from four different speakers that would surround the hologram.

Books both authored and designed by me have been appearing since 1970, when *Visual Language* was published, and an interest in alternative forms of bookmaking goes back to critical essays I published in 1968 and 1969. Not until 1975, however, did I realize that Book Art as such was a conscious creative concern of mine, and I immediately produced a set of volumes that explore alternative book forms: the accordion books, *Modulation* and *Extrapolate*; the handwritten book, *Portraits from Memory*; a chapbook with horizontal images spread over two open pages, *Come Here*; and then the card-book, *Rain Rains Rain* (1976); a book that exists only on audiotape, *Experimental Prose* (1976); the two-front book, *Prunings/Accruings* (1977) and the two news-print books, *Numbers: Poems & Stories* (1976) and *One Night Stood* (1977). That last title, *One Night Stood,* also appeared as a small paperback book 4-by-5 inches for the existence of both editions creates the illustrative contrast of reading the same verbal text of two-word paragraphs in two radically different book forms. That is, not until one reads both books together will he or she realize how perceptibly different the two formats can be.

In my creative work so far, there has been a continuing concern with alternative materials for traditional genres, such as poetry and fiction, and then with alternative media, such as audio and video, which sometimes enhance the preexisting materials and other times function as a willful constraint. Predisposed to invention, I had intended from the beginning to make imaginative works that looked and "read" like nothing else anyone knew, and since my reasons for making art were quite different from those behind my critical essays, separate fundamental concerns insured that my professional functions were not confused. In doing things differently, I have accepted the likelihood of losses with the gains, and should people complain, as they sometimes do, that certain qualities they like in my criticism are absent from this creative work, my reply is that the latter stems from different purposes in myself and hopefully exhibits certain qualities absent from my criticism. "In contemporary art," Moholy-Nagy once wrote, "often the most valuable part is not that which presents something new, but that which is missing. In other words, the spectator's delight may be derived partly from the artist's effort to eliminate the obsolete solutions of their predecessors."

Though superficially diverse, not only in media but styles, my creative works still exhibit certain unifying qualities, such as riskiness, rigor, clarity, structural explicitness, variousness, empiricism, and conceptual audacity—qualities that might also characterize my critical writing, perhaps because they define my personal temper (and are thus as close as the work can be to being me), and my creative concern with innovative structure is also a principal theme of my criticism and my anthologies. Two goals in mind for both my art and my criticism are that they be more complex and yet more accessible, if only to prove that these aims need not be contradictory.

All my creative work can also be seen as the dialectical result of pitting my traditional education and professional experience (with expository writing) against my antithetical effort to transcend conventional forms —to write a poetry of intentionally limited language, to make a fiction exclusively of lines, to compose with numbers, to multitrack declaimed language, etc. Since much of the work involves a mixing of materials, the process of perceiving it customarily combines at least two perceptual modes—the visual with the verbal, the verbal with the aural, the visual with the linear, the numerical with the visual, etc.; for the work is usually meant to be perceived not just in one traditional way but, more likely, in a few ways. It could also be said that I have endeavored, first, to synthesize my education in literature and history with a growing interest in music and the visual arts and, second, to test my inventive proclivities against the resistances of several unfamiliar media. This background may explain such idiosyncrasies as why even my constructivist fictions, which are totally devoid of language, usually embody a strong narrative line, or why my works seem at once so intellectual and so anti-intellectual, or why I am more interested in results than in processes, or why I find myself so often talking and writing about the work, and finally why this essay is as it is.

One might also characterize my art as premeditated, impersonal, experimental, and intelligent, although eschewing such traditional symptoms of how intelligence functions in art as allusions to past literature and history. My works are particularly indebted, in different ways, to such precursors as Moholy-Nagy and Theo van Doesburg, in addition to my friends John Cage and Milton Babbitt; and I will gladly acknowledge the influence of such earlier cultural movements as constructivism, dada, and transcendentalism, in addition to the "intermedia" developments of the past two decades. Except for my video art, I have so far favored black and white as the sole colors indigenous to art, believing that all other hues belong primarily to the realm of "illustration."

Though I once said that my creative work made me "a poet," I now speak of myself as an "artist and writer," wishing there were in English a single term that combined the two. "Maker" might be more appropriate, its modesty notwithstanding. The variousness of the total work confuses not only the art public but also those critics who still expect someone to be just "a poet" or "a composer" or "a visual artist," rather than *all* of these things, and *much else* besides. On further thought, the principal problem with person-centered epithets such as "painter" and "writer" is that they become not descriptions but jails, either restricting one's creative activity, or defining one's creative adventure in terms of one's initial professional category (e.g., "artist's books"), for it should be possible for any of us to make *poems* or *photographs* or *music* as we wish, and, better yet, to have these works regarded, plainly, as "poems" or "photographs" or "music." Perhaps the sum of my artworks is ultimately about the discovery of possibilities—not only in the exploitation of media but in art and, by extension, in oneself as a creative initiator.

Another reason for *my* discarding narrow terms is to suggest, if not insure, that the work as a whole be finally judged not just as Literature or just as Art but as something among and between, for it is only with my own kind, rare though they be, that I wish my total creative self ultimately to be compared. Perhaps the most accurate term for my imaginative endeavors would be "Language Art" and the most appropriate title for a retrospective exhibition would thus be *Wordsand.*

MANIFESTOES

THE TRUTH OF FICTION IS THE POWER OF ARTIFICE IS ARTISTRY FROM ART CREATES WORLDS DUPES MADE ENTIRELY POETRY OF LIFE COPIES THE ARTISTLY BELIES ARGUMENT

Index of Proper Names

Cott, Jonathan, 25, 31—32, 99,
    108—9
Cowan, Tony, 209
Cowley, Malcom, 219
Cowper, William, 102
Coxe, Louis, 21
Crane, Hart, 30
Creative Arts Book Co., 84
Creeley, Robert, 24, 124
Crosby, Harry, 58, 237
Cummings, E. E., 17, 42, 153,
    158, 176—77, 216—30, 235,
    270, 282
Cunningham, J. V., 21—22
Cunningham, Merce, 4, 214,
    231—32, 243, 248, 252,
    268

Dada, 116, 173, 175, 245
Daiches, David, 57
Damon, S. Foster, 35, 38, 287
Darr, Ann, 11
Davie, Donald, 21
Davis, Stuart, 115—16, 153
de Kooning, Willem, 93
Dickey, James, 21, 29—30,
    38—39, 42, 123—24
Dillard, R. H. W., 67
DiPalma, Ray, 67
Dodge, Charles, 185, 190—91,
    195
Doesburg, Theo van, 3, 152,
    242, 304
Dohl, Reinhard, 155
Doria, Charles, 67, 238
Dorn, Edward, 24
Doubleday & Co, Inc., 13
Dragonfly, 13
Drake, Albert, 67
Duchamp, Marcel, 90, 248
Dufrêne, François, 180—81,

183—84, 188
Dugan, Alan, 30, 38
Duncan, Robert, 24—25
Dunn, Anne, 93
Dutton, Paul, 207

Eagleton, Thomas, 6
Eberhart, Richard, 29, 39, 84
Edwards, Jonathan, 19
Eliot, T. S., 4, 8—9, 13, 15,
    17—23, 25—29, 31, 35—37,
    39, 44, 49—50, 71, 97, 142,
    156, 159, 165, 216—17,
    227, 241, 270
Ellmann, Richard, 216
Empson, William, 17
Esquire, 13, 96
Essary, Loris, 163—64
Evans, David Allan, 64
Everson, William, 11, 26

Faber & Faber, Ltd., 227
Fahlstrom, Oyvind, 151
Farrar, Straus & Giroux, 13
Fearing, Kenneth, 270
Feldman, Morton, 199
Ferlinghetti, Lawrence, 27, 85
Fiedler, Leslie, 24, 41, 44
Field, Edward, 71—74, 76, 78
Fifties, The, 42
Finkel, Donald, 21
Finlay, Ian Hamilton, 117, 155
Fitzgerald, Robert, 11
Ford, Charles Henri, 237
Ford, Henry, 160, 285
Four Horsemen, 185, 207—8,
    211
Fox, Siv Cedering, 11, 67
Frampton, Hollis, 142
Frangella, Luis, 268—69
Frank, Jacob, 238

Morawski, Stefan, 171
Morgan, Edwin, 118, 155, 182
Morgenstern, Christian, 153,
    174, 177
Morrison, James, 6
Morrow, Charles, 172, 185,
    191–92, 194, 196
Moss, Howard, 42, 69, 78
Mother, 13
Mottram, Eric, 184
Museum of Holography (New
    York), 300
Myers, John Bernard, 94, 109

Nemerov, Howard, 18
New Republic, 219
New Yorker, 13, 40, 42
New York *Herald-Tribune*, 98
New York *Times*, 13, 84
New York *Times Book Review*,
    14, 43, 60, 94, 101
New York *Times Magazine*, 7
Nichol, bp, 140–41, 149, 207,
    212
Nims, John Frederick, 56
Norman, Charles, 225–26
Norton, Charles Eliot, 229
Novak, Ladislav, 182

O'Brien, Flann, 92
Ockerse, Tom, 140, 149
Oerke, Andrew, 62
O'Gallagher, Liam, 34, 38, 140,
    149, 161, 214
O'Hara, Frank, 31, 42, 92–93,
    123
O'Huigin, Sean, 184
Olson, Charles, 7–8, 23–25,
    28, 38, 50, 58, 123, 133,
    282
Orr, Elaine, 226

Ortiz, Simon J., 78
Ostriker, Alicia, 135, 140, 149
Owens, Rochelle, 238
Oxford University Press, 93
Oyewole, Abiodun, 141, 149

Pack, Robert, 21, 70
Panache, 13
Parisi, Joseph, 52, 55–57
Parmigianino, 88, 108
Patchen, Kenneth, 123, 237
Penmaen Press, 84
Phillips, Michael Joseph, 67,
    134, 149
Phillips, Tom, 118, 164
Phoenix Bookshop, 14
Pietri, Pedro, 127, 134, 149
Pignatari, Decio, 151, 154
Plath, Sylvia, 26, 38, 42, 87,
    123
Playboy, 276
Podhoretz, Norman, 69, 83
Poems from the Floating World,
    241
Poetry, 13, 52–56, 58–59,
    62–63, 101
Pollock, Jackson, 71, 92
Popper, Frank, 285
Porter, Bern, 140
Pound, Ezra, 8, 17–18, 22–24,
    27–28, 36, 45, 48–52, 54,
    87, 122–23, 136, 142, 156,
    216–17, 270
Price, Jonathan, 67, 118, 136
Pritchard, Norman Henry, 136,
    141, 149, 161, 185, 202,
    205, 212, 229
Procuniar, Stephen, 288
Pudim, Alafia, 141

Quasha, George, 50, 148

Rago, Henry, 55
Rahmmings, Keith, 163–65
Randolph, Leonard, 69
Ransom, John Crowe, 17, 39
Rasof, Henry, 210
Reich, Steve, 141, 185–87, 196
Reichardt, Jasia, 151
Reineck, Gay Best, 117, 140, 161
Rexroth, Kenneth, 28, 38, 58
Reznikoff, Charles, 238
Rhys, Jean, 92
Riley, Terry, 141
Rimbaud, Arthur, 27, 102
Rivers, Larry, 93
Robson, Ernst, 210, 212
Rodgers, Carolyn M., 78
Roethke, Theodore, 17, 22, 25, 38–39, 42, 44–45, 123
Rosenberg, Harold, 121, 149
Roth, Philip, 239
Rothenberg, Jerome, 58, 127, 185, 191–92, 194, 236–41
Rothko, Mark, 92
Roussel, Raymond, 95–96
Rukeyser, Muriel, 22, 270
Russolo, Luigi, 171

Saint Paul Chamber Orchestra, 268
Salmagundi, 43
Samperi, Frank, 126, 149
Sanchez, Sonia, 201
Saner, Reg, 78
Saroyan, Aram, 34, 131, 149, 158
Schafer, R. Murray, 166, 295
Scheerbart, Paul, 174, 178
Schlossberg, Edwin, 140
Schoenberg, Arnold, 172–73
Scholem, Gershom, 238

Schulman, Grace, 67
Schuyler, James, 105
Schwartz, Delmore, 20–21, 42–44
Schwartz, Francis, 195–96
Schwerner, Armand, 35, 38, 141, 149, 169, 210, 238
Schwitters, Kurt, 116, 153, 173–74, 178, 245
Scobie, Stephen, 212
Scott, Winfield Townley, 22
Segal, Harold, 226
Seidel, Frederick, 42
Serpent Power, 131
Sexton, Anne, 10, 38, 42, 44
Shahn, Ben, 117
Shakespeare, William, 8, 15
Shapiro, David, 32, 38, 67, 99, 109
Shapiro, Harvey, 7, 30–31, 38–40, 93, 123
Shapiro, Karl, 20, 28, 56
Sharits, Paul, 142
Shore, Jane, 67
Simon, John, 98
Simpson, Louis, 39, 70
Sitwell, Dame Edith, 156
Sixties, The, 42
Skinner, Knute, 78
Slonimsky, Nicholas, 188
Smith, Sidney Goodsir, 59
Smith, William Jay, 28
Snodgrass, W. D., 26, 38–39, 42
Snyder, Gary, 17, 29, 38, 61, 85
Sobiloff, Hyman J., 11
Solomon, Carl, 85
Solt, Mary Ellen, 34, 117, 140, 150–51, 155, 157–58
Some/Thing, 241
Spencer, Theodore, 91

315